AD/HD For Dummies®

Cheat Sheet

W9-CCJ-092

The Three Types of AD/HD

AD/HD consists of three basic types:

- **Predominantly inattentive type.** Having this type of AD/HD means that you have difficulty focusing but are able to sit still. Classic symptoms include:
  - Making careless mistakes
  - Not seeming to listen as someone else speaks
  - Being disorganized or forgetting things
  - Having trouble focusing on a specific task

- **Predominantly hyperactive/impulsive type.** If you have this type of AD/HD, maintaining attention is less of a problem than being able to control your body movements or behaviors. The basic symptoms include:
  - Speaking or acting out of turn
  - Not considering consequences before acting
  - Fidgeting or feeling restless when trying to sit
  - Being excessively physically or verbally active

- **Combined type.** If you have a number of symptoms from both the inattentive and hyperactive/impulsive lists, you may have the combined type of AD/HD.

To have AD/HD, your symptoms must meet certain guidelines, including:

- Existing for at least six months
- Appearing before you were 7 years old
- Having a significant impact on your life in more than one setting
- Not being attributable to a different condition (such as bipolar disorder)

Looking Beyond Basic Symptoms

Aside from the classic (or *primary*) symptoms, AD/HD can have other *(secondary)* symptoms that negatively impact your life. These include:

- Worry
- Boredom
- Loss of motivation
- Frustration
- Low self-esteem
- Sleep disturbances
- Hopelessness
- Procrastination
- Difficulty getting along with others
- Difficulty managing time or money

For Dummies: Bestselling Book Series for Beginners

AD/HD For Dummies®

Treating AD/HD

The most effective way to treat AD/HD is by using a *multimodal* approach — one that combines biological, psychological, and social strategies.

Biological

Biological treatments change the way your brain works. The change can be accomplished several ways and can be temporary or permanent, depending on the approach you take. The options we cover in this book include:

- ✔ Medication (see Chapter 8)
- ✔ Diet (see Chapter 11)
- ✔ Vitamin supplements and herbal remedies (see Chapter 11)
- ✔ Repatterning therapies, such as neurofeedback, Rhythmic Entrainment Intervention, auditory integration training, and vision therapy (see Chapter 12)
- ✔ Rebalancing therapies, such as homeopathics, acupuncture, sensory integration therapies, and manipulation therapies — osteopathy, chiropractic, and CranioSacral Therapy (see Chapter 13)

Psychological

Psychological therapies (see Chapters 9 and 10) help you deal with the feelings that come from your symptoms and understand how to change the way you think and act to improve your life. Psychological treatment strategies include:

- ✔ Counseling and psychotherapy, such as insight-oriented therapy, supportive therapy, play therapy, skills training, psychoeducational counseling, and parent training
- ✔ Behavior management, such as behavior modification, cognitive-behavioral counseling, and awareness training

Social

Everyone needs certain skills in order to function in the world, but people with AD/HD often struggle with basic life strategies. After you deal with the biological issues associated with AD/HD, you need to start developing your social skills in the following areas:

- ✔ Organization
- ✔ Relationships
- ✔ Communication
- ✔ Lifestyle choices
- ✔ Occupational skills

Part IV of this book contains details about how to develop social skills to make your home, school, and/or work life as healthy and productive as possible.

For Dummies: Bestselling Book Series for Beginners

AD/HD
FOR
DUMMIES®

by Jeff Strong and
Michael O. Flanagan, MD

WILEY

Wiley Publishing, Inc.

AD/HD For Dummies®

Published by
Wiley Publishing, Inc.
111 River St.
Hoboken, NJ 07030-5774
www.wiley.com

WILEY

About the Authors

Jeff Strong: Jeff Strong is Founder and President of the REI Institute, a music medicine research center and clinic focusing on people with developmental disabilities, including those with AD/HD. His research on the use of auditory stimulus for people with developmental disabilities has been presented at over two dozen professional scientific conferences and has been featured in numerous books and journals. He is a recognized expert on the use of sound and music for people with AD/HD, having appeared on many radio and television programs, including two documentaries. His therapy is being used by thousands of people around the world. Mr. Strong is the bestselling author of six books and is an adult with AD/HD.

Michael O. Flanagan, MD: Michael Flanagan began his training in AD/HD at birth. In spite of constant distractibility and procrastination, he managed to get a B.G. (barely graduated) in Philosophy from Yale College and an M.D. from the University of New Mexico. He later recognized why his career had such a meandering course when he started working as a physician/therapist in Bob Gurnee's Albuquerque AD/HD clinic. That was in 1992, when he figured out that he has AD/HD after having been through medical school and post-graduate training in neurobiology, neurology, and psychiatry. He is currently practicing neuropsychiatry in Albuquerque and Santa Fe, New Mexico.

Authors' Acknowledgments

From Jeff Strong: I'd like to thank all the folks at Wiley who got this book started — Joyce Pepple, Holly Grimes, and Stacy Kennedy — as well as my agent, Carol Susan Roth. I'm also grateful to my project and copy editor Joan Friedman and technical editor Michele Novotni. Special thanks go to my coauthor, Michael Flanagan, and my friend, sounding board, and fellow author Elizabeth King. Most importantly, I'd like to thank my wife, Beth, and daughter, Tovah, for their love and support during this arduous process.

From Michael Flanagan: I would like to thank all my patients over the last 20 years for living up to your name with patience and for teaching me all the things my teachers couldn't. I'm sorry I wasn't more help to you, but hopefully you got something out of our relationship. Thanks, too, to Gaynor Wild, who taught me all I could learn about biochemistry and neuroscience, as well as putting in his two cents' worth about psychodynamics and life. Thanks to Martin Pollock who gave me a chance to go to New Zealand, make some friends, and learn something more about neurology. Bob Gurnee deserves recognition for allowing me to get paid for learning about AD/HD. My wife, Valerie, should be given a medal for putting up with all my shenanigans — that goes for all my other friends, enemies, associates, accomplices, bosses, critics, and creditors, as well.

Publisher's Acknowledgments

We're proud of this book; please send us your comments through our Dummies online registration form located at www.dummies.com/register/.

Some of the people who helped bring this book to market include the following:

Acquisitions, Editorial, and Media Development

Project Editor: Joan Friedman

Acquisitions Editor: Stacy Kennedy

Assistant Editor: Holly Gastineau-Grimes

Technical Editor: Michele Novotni, PhD

Senior Permissions Editor: Carmen Krikorian

Editorial Managers: Michelle Hacker, Carmen Krikorian

Editorial Assistants: Courtney Allen, Nadine Bell

Cover Photos: © O'Brien Productions/CORBIS

Cartoons: Rich Tennant, www.the5thwave.com

Composition

Project Coordinators: Maridee Ennis, Adrienne Martinez

Layout and Graphics: Andrea Dahl, Denny Hager, Joyce Haughey, Michael Kruzil, Barry Offringa, Jacque Roth, Heather Ryan

Illustrations: Kathryn Born, M.A.

Proofreaders: Carl William Pierce, Brian H. Walls, TECHBOOKS Production Services

Indexer: TECHBOOKS Production Services

Publishing and Editorial for Consumer Dummies

Diane Graves Steele, Vice President and Publisher, Consumer Dummies

Joyce Pepple, Acquisitions Director, Consumer Dummies

Kristin A. Cocks, Product Development Director, Consumer Dummies

Michael Spring, Vice President and Publisher, Travel

Brice Gosnell, Associate Publisher, Travel

Kelly Regan, Editorial Director, Travel

Publishing for Technology Dummies

Andy Cummings, Vice President and Publisher, Dummies Technology/General User

Composition Services

Gerry Fahey, Vice President of Production Services

Debbie Stailey, Director of Composition Services

Contents at a Glance

Table of Contents

Introduction

· ·

A lot of people have attention deficit/hyperactivity disorder (AD/HD). Researchers estimate that in the United States, people with AD/HD constitute anywhere from 3 to 6 percent of the population (or more, depending on which study you read). On the low side, this totals about 8 million people. So rest assured that if you have AD/HD, or are related to someone who does, you're not alone. Almost everyone knows at least one person with AD/HD (whether they're aware of it or not).

Despite the fact that so many people have AD/HD, this is widely a misunderstood condition. Some people — including many healthcare professionals — believe that AD/HD isn't real. These people believe that AD/HD is a made-up excuse for bad behavior and bad parenting.

We want to assure you right from the start that AD/HD is a real condition that affects millions of people. For many, it makes life very difficult. AD/HD has a biological cause and can't be willed away through discipline or hard work. And the symptoms of AD/HD can't be ignored in the hopes that the person will simply grow out of them.

To reduce (and sometimes eliminate) the symptoms of AD/HD, you need to understand this condition and receive knowledgeable intervention. The purpose of this book is to help you gain a better understanding of AD/HD and discover where to look for help. Our goal is to give you the tools to effectively address AD/HD in your life, whether you, your child, your spouse, or your friend is the one with AD/HD.

About This Book

AD/HD For Dummies is unique among books on this condition in that it was written with the AD/HD person in mind. We don't go into long explanations with obscure points; we go right to the heart of the matter and give you the information you need to know with as little fuss as possible.

When we set out to write this book, obviously we wanted to offer basic information about what AD/HD is and where it comes from. But we also wanted to provide information on cutting-edge treatment approaches and simple, effective strategies to help you start getting the symptoms under control and begin living the life you want to live. As a result, this book is short on background details and jargon, and it's long on real-world advice. Both of us have many years' experience working with people with AD/HD, and we draw heavily from these experiences in the pages that follow.

Not So Foolish Assumptions

In this book, we make only one assumption about you: We assume that you want to read a book about AD/HD that doesn't dilly-dally around with poetic descriptions and lengthy anecdotes, because you have very little time and want to get the bottom line quickly. We don't waste your time with lengthy explanations, but we do want to make this book fun to read, so we include some references to people we've worked with in order to give you insights into life with AD/HD.

Now that we're clear on what we assume, we should mention the thing that we don't assume in this book: We don't assume that you are the person with AD/HD. In this light, we try to offer a view of this condition as if you, your spouse, your child, your grandchild, your friend, or your student has AD/HD. (Whew, that's a lot of perspectives in one book!)

Conventions Used in This Book

Given the enormity of perspective that we try to cover in this book, we can't very well list each of the possible relationships you may have with AD/HD in each paragraph. To keep things simple, we generally refer to *you* throughout the book as if you are the person who has AD/HD. However, in some instances we do mention a specific perspective as it relates to a particular relationship, and in those cases we write about *your child, your spouse,* and so on.

The only other convention we want to clarify up front is how we reference the condition we're writing about. In the mental health field, this condition is called *attention deficit/hyperactivity disorder,* or AD/HD. Most likely, you've also heard it called simply *attention deficit disorder,* or ADD. We're talking about the same condition; we've simply chosen to use its formal name in this book. (As you find out in Chapter 2, this condition has had many names over the years, and we expect its name to change again soon.)

How This Book Is Organized

This book is organized into five parts to help you quickly and easily find areas of interest. The sections below explain what you'll find in each part, and you can check out the Table of Contents at the beginning of the book to see more specifics about what's covered in each chapter.

Part 1: The ABCs of AD/HD

Part I introduces you to AD/HD. In Chapter 1, you get an overview of the disorder — a sort of preview of what you'll find in the rest of the book. Chapter 2 looks at the cause of AD/HD from several different perspectives and examines the role of biology in creating your symptoms. Chapter 3 explains the symptoms of AD/HD — both the core symptoms and the secondary symptoms that can emerge from the core symptoms.

Part 11: Diagnosing AD/HD

Part II examines how AD/HD is diagnosed and who can best make a diagnosis. Chapter 4 introduces you to the many types of professionals who can diagnose or treat AD/HD and offers advice on choosing the best professional for you or your child. Chapter 5 walks you through the evaluation process by examining the criteria for AD/HD and presenting the many types of assessment procedures you may have to go through to determine whether you have AD/HD. Chapter 6 explores conditions that look like AD/HD but aren't and provides the guidelines that professionals may use in order to make a diagnosis.

Part 111: Treating AD/HD

Part III explores the many types of treatment for AD/HD. Chapter 7 introduces you to the basic types of treatment options and helps you develop a plan to make the best choices for you or your loved one. Chapter 8 is all about medication and explains the different types of medications available for people with AD/HD, as well as how to work with your doctor to find the best one for you. Chapter 9 examines counseling, coaching, and training, and shows you how they can help you or your loved one. Chapter 10 explores one of the oldest approaches to dealing with the symptoms of AD/HD: behavior modification. Chapter 11 gets you up to speed on the many ways that nutrition, supplements, and herbs can help with the symptoms of AD/HD. Chapter 12 digs into *repatterning therapies* — treatment approaches that are designed to help you change the way your brain works over the long-term. And finally, Chapter 13 looks into *rebalancing therapies* — therapies that strive to rebalance your nervous system.

Part IV: Living with AD/HD

Part IV is all about effectively living with AD/HD. Chapter 14 starts you off with tips and suggestions for making life at home as low-stress and rewarding as possible. Chapter 15 explores schooling by offering tips on dealing with bureaucracy, developing positive relationships with your child's teachers, and ensuring that your child gets the help he needs to do his work well. Chapter 16 helps you make the most of your job by offering you tools to handle the demands of work, as well as suggestions to help you find the best type of work for you. In Chapter 17, we examine the often-overlooked positive attributes of AD/HD and help you explore ways to enhance them in your life.

Part V: The Part of Tens

The Part of Tens is a staple of every *For Dummies* book. This part contains three chapters that are sure to help your life with AD/HD. Chapter 18 contains ten helpful suggestions for getting and keeping your life organized. This chapter explores everything from tried-and-true organization approaches to the newest high-tech tools to keep you plugged into the pulse of your day. Chapter 19 presents ideas to help you develop and maintain family harmony, including ways to take care of yourself and to learn better communication skills. Chapter 20 finishes this section with ten types of resources that can help you find out more about AD/HD and get the support you need.

After Part V, we've included an appendix that contains treatment tracking forms. These forms are great tools to use if you want to assess the positive and negative outcomes of treatments you choose to try — especially treatments that have a biological impact, such as medications.

Icons Used in This Book

As with all *For Dummies* books, we use a few icons to help you along your way.

Certain techniques are very important and bear repeating. This icon gives you those gentle nudges to keep you on track.

This icon sits next to paragraphs that define tough terms, get a little scientific, or otherwise offer information that may be a little more difficult to digest.

This icon highlights expert advice and ideas that can help you to better deal with AD/HD in your life.

This icon alerts you to instances when you need to take special care not to hurt yourself or someone else.

Where to Go from Here

This book is set up so that you can either read it cover to cover and progressively build on your knowledge or jump around and read only those parts that interest you at the time. For instance, if you don't know anything about AD/HD and want to get up to speed on the basics, start with Chapter 1. On the other hand, if your child is having trouble in school and you want to find some ways to deal with his challenges, you can head straight for Chapter 15. If you want to find out about the latest alternative treatment methods for AD/HD, check out Chapter 11, 12, or 13 first.

Regardless of where you start in this book, if you run across a term or idea that is covered in more detail somewhere else, we offer a cross reference so you can locate the background information you need.

Part I
The ABCs of AD/HD

The 5th Wave   By Rich Tennant

"The saving grace of living with someone who has AD/HD is that any arguments you have over it never last very long."

In this part . . .

Quite simply, this part of the book introduces you to the basics of AD/HD, including the theories about what causes it and the symptoms that most people with AD/HD experience. If you, your child, or another loved one has just been diagnosed with AD/HD, the chapters in this part offer a good overview of what you're dealing with.

Chapter 1

AD/HD Basics

*I*n 1980, a new term entered our vocabulary: *Attention deficit disorder.* It described a condition that has been recognized since the latter part of the nineteenth century but called a variety of other names. This term — which later morphed into *attention deficit/hyperactivity disorder (AD/HD)* — often rears itself whenever someone has difficulty in school or work, can't sit still, or is unable to control his or her behaviors. The symptoms of AD/HD can affect anyone — children and adults, males and females, rich and poor. Because of this fact, and because the symptoms of AD/HD are simply extremes of everyday behavior, this condition is often misunderstood and misdiagnosed.

In this chapter, we introduce you to AD/HD. We give you a brief overview of the common symptoms, biological causes, diagnosis, treatment approaches, and life strategies for coping with AD/HD. This chapter gets you up to speed on the basics, and we deal with each of these topics in much more detail in the rest of the book.

As we point out in the Introduction, AD/HD is a complex condition that is estimated to affect between 3 and 6 percent of the people in the United States. Rest assured that there are many happy, successful people who live with AD/HD, including both of us.

Having so many people around you with AD/HD means you won't have problems finding quality information, support, treatments, and life strategies that can help minimize the negative affects and maximize the positive. (And yes, there are positive attributes to AD/HD. You can read about these in Chapter 17.)

Identifying Symptoms of AD/HD

If you have AD/HD, you may have trouble regulating yourself. This difficulty can exist in the areas of attention, behavior, and motor movements. AD/HD looks different in almost everyone. For example, one person may have no problem sitting still but gazes off into space unable to focus at all. Another person may constantly fidget but can spend seemingly endless amounts of time focusing on one thing, often to the exclusion of everything else in her life. Yet another person may not be able to stop himself from impulsive and often dangerous behaviors but may be able to sit calmly in school.

Peering into primary symptoms

In spite of all the different ways that AD/HD manifests, there are three basic symptoms:

- **Inattention/distractibility:** People with AD/HD have problems focusing. You may be able to focus sometimes but not others. This variable nature of being able to pay attention is one of the main features of AD/HD.

- **Impulsivity:** Many people with AD/HD have trouble regulating their behavior. In this case, you often act without thinking, perhaps talking out of turn or taking unnecessary risks.

- **Hyperactivity:** Someone who is hyperactive is frequently moving in some way. You may be able to sit but may need to move some part of your body when doing so. This hyperactivity is more of a problem with children than adults. This is because most AD/HD adults have less physical restlessness as they get older.

The term *attention deficit/hyperactivity disorder* (AD/HD) comes from the American Psychiatric Association's *Diagnostic and Statistical Manual of Mental Disorders* (DSM-IV). The DSM-IV outlines three types of AD/HD:

- **Inattentive type:** Having this type of AD/HD means that you have difficulty focusing but are able to sit still.

- **Hyperactive/impulsive type:** If you have this type of AD/HD, you struggle to sit still and have difficulty considering consequences before doing or saying something, but focusing isn't an issue.

- **Combined type:** If you have a hard time focusing, plus you also have difficulty sitting still or doing things without thinking, you have the combined type.

Seeing a few secondary symptoms

Aside from the basic three symptoms of inattention, impulsivity, and hyper-activity (which we discuss in the previous section), AD/HD has a ton of other symptoms. These symptoms can include, but aren't limited to, the following:

- ✔ Worry
- ✔ Boredom
- ✔ Loss of motivation
- ✔ Frustration
- ✔ Low self-esteem
- ✔ Sleep disturbances
- ✔ Hopelessness

In Chapter 3, we discuss these and other symptoms in detail.

These secondary symptoms are also connected to other common disorders. The overlap of symptoms among a variety of disorders is called *co-morbidity* and is one of the reasons that diagnosing AD/HD is so difficult. (See the "Getting a Diagnosis of AD/HD" section later in this chapter, or check out Chapter 5.)

Clueing in on AD/HD's Origins

Many people used to believe that AD/HD (before it even had this name) was merely a behavioral disorder and had no biological basis. However, research over the last 20 years has shown that people with AD/HD have something different happening biologically than people without the disorder. What exactly that biological basis is no one knows for sure. Some of the discoveries that researchers have made include the following:

- ✔ **Genetic links:** There seems to be a genetic predisposition to having the disorder. AD/HD runs in families — you're more likely to see a child with AD/HD born into a family where at least one parent has the disorder.
- ✔ **Neurological activity:** Some studies show that people with AD/HD have brain irregularities. For example, some studies have shown a lower level of activity in the front of the brain — the area that controls attention. Others have discovered abnormalities in other regions deep within the brain.

✔ **Chemical differences:** Certain chemical activity seems to be different in people who have AD/HD. Several studies suggest that there are differences in the responses when neurochemicals are created and released by people with AD/HD compared to people who don't have the condition.

We don't know the actual cause(s) of AD/HD. But despite this lack of completely detailed understanding of the causes, we do know a lot about how to treat the disorder. We give you an introduction later in this chapter in the section "Viewing Various Treatment Approaches," and we write about treatment options in detail in Part III of this book.

Getting a Diagnosis of AD/HD

Diagnosing AD/HD can be frustrating for some people because there is no definitive way to check for it. You can't see it in a brain scan. You can't test for it with a blood sample. The only way to diagnose AD/HD is to do a detailed evaluation of your (or your loved one's) past and present behaviors. This involves finding a professional who understands the subtleties and variations of AD/HD. The following sections give you an overview of this important process.

Choosing your professional

The first step to finding out if you have AD/HD involves finding the right healthcare professional. You may start with your family doctor, but in order to get an accurate diagnosis (as accurate as possible, anyway), you need to see a professional who understands all the different ways AD/HD looks and can review your history properly. Your options can include, but aren't limited to, the following:

✔ **Psychiatrist:** A psychiatrist is a medical doctor who specializes in mental illness and behavioral disorders. A psychiatrist can prescribe medication and often is up-to-date on the neurological factors of AD/HD.

✔ **Neurologist:** A neurologist is a medical doctor whose specialty is the brain. This person often views AD/HD from a biological basis and can prescribe medication. He or she may not be up-to-date on the best AD/HD life strategies or alternative treatments.

- ✔ **Psychologist:** A psychologist is trained in matters of the mind. Most psychologists understand the criteria for diagnosing AD/HD and can offer many treatment options, but they can't prescribe medication.

- ✔ **AD/HD specialist:** An AD/HD specialist can be anyone from a teacher to a therapist who has experience and expertise in working with people with AD/HD. Specialists likely have knowledge of many treatment and coping strategies, but they aren't able to prescribe medication and are often not well versed in the neurological factors present in AD/HD.

- ✔ **AD/HD coach:** Like an AD/HD specialist, a coach has expertise in working with people with AD/HD but usually can't prescribe medication and is not a medical doctor. A coach helps you improve your functioning in the world. Coaches can come from many backgrounds — education, business, psychology — and their focus tends to be on practical, day-to-day matters, such as skills training.

Choosing the best professional for you depends partly on the values you have regarding medication and partly on how open you are to unconventional ways of approaching treatment. This is because each professional will immediately recommend the approaches that he or she is most familiar with and that fit with his or her treatment philosophy.

In Chapter 4, we help you explore your values and how they fit with each type of AD/HD professional. You also find out how to question a professional to see if his or her philosophy fits with yours. Knowing this information prevents you from feeling pressured to attempt treatments that you don't agree with and helps you find treatments that fit your style.

Preparing for the evaluation process

After you've chosen a professional to work with, you can dig in to the actual process of evaluation. This process involves answering a lot of questions and looking at your past. Chapter 5 gives you a heads up on the types of questions you have to answer, as well as the official criteria for being diagnosed with AD/HD.

Diagnosing AD/HD is not easy, and a diagnosis either way is not the final word. AD/HD is one of many similar conditions, and it is possible for even the best professional to place you or your loved one in the wrong category. We recommend that you seek a second opinion, especially if you have any doubts about the diagnosis. Chapter 6 introduces you to many conditions and symptoms that can appear to be AD/HD or that can accompany it.

Viewing Various Treatment Approaches

AD/HD can manifest itself in almost limitless ways, and there seems to be no limit to the number of ways to treat it. In fact, one of the main struggles that most people have when they are diagnosed with AD/HD is to weed through all the treatment options and choose the best ones to try.

The most conventional treatment methods for AD/HD are medication and behavior modification. Both are useful and effective approaches, but many other types of treatment can work wonders with the right person.

Treatment options break down into several broad categories, which include the following:

- Medication
- Counseling and therapy
- Coaching
- Training
- Behavior management
- Nutrition and supplements
- Herbs and homeopathics
- Repatterning therapies
- Rebalancing therapies
- Social skills training

We discuss each option in detail in Chapters 8 through 13. Each treatment approach has a place, and many of them work well together. Knowing how to choose and what to combine can be difficult. Our goal is to make this challenge more manageable, which is why we wrote Chapter 7, where we help you develop and implement a plan for treatment success.

Recognizing AD/HD's Role in Your Life

One of the best ways to deal with the symptoms of AD/HD is to have a toolbox of strategies you can dig into when you run into difficulties. The more tools you have in this box, the easier life becomes. As we explain in the following sections, we dedicate an entire section of this book (Part IV) to helping you fill your box with the best tools possible.

Dealing with daily life

Whether you are at school, at home, or at work, you can develop ways to minimize the negative impacts of your AD/HD symptoms by using some strategies that have worked well for other people, including us. In Chapters 14 through 16, we offer you insights, tools, and ideas for making daily life as successful and stress-free as possible.

For example, we suggest ways to help you develop healthy family relationships, motivate your child with AD/HD to do his or her homework, know your legal rights at school and in the workplace, keep organized on the job, develop a solid career path, and much more. We hope that the information in these chapters also spurs you on to create your own unique ways of dealing with AD/HD in your life.

Accentuating the positive

Along with the challenges that AD/HD creates, there are some areas where people with AD/HD have certain strengths. When you understand these positive attributes — such as heightened creativity, high energy, and a willingness to take risks — you can discover ways to maximize and amplify them to help you succeed in the world. For example, you can identify your style of working to keep you on task and motivated to get a job done. We wrote Chapter 17 to inspire and encourage you to find your strengths and make the most of them.

Chapter 2

Exploring the Causes of AD/HD

●●●

In This Chapter

▶ Gaining some historical perspective

▶ Understanding the core issue with AD/HD

▶ Examining possible genetic causes

▶ Looking at the neurological factors involved with AD/HD

▶ Exploring chemical research

●●●

*N*o one completely understands the causes of AD/HD — yet. However, some enlightening research has been done, and solid theories exist about how AD/HD comes to be.

In this chapter, we review several theories about the causes of AD/HD — both those that have broken new ground and others that have severely missed the mark. We also explain some studies that indicate that AD/HD has a biological cause and demonstrate how all this research is essentially pointing to the same basic cause.

One of the immutable facts of life is that everyone has an opinion. Therefore, we also use this chapter to offer our opinion (whether you want it or not) of where all this AD/HD research is heading and what it means to the bottom line: What's the best way to treat this condition?

Reviewing Past Theories

Since the day in 1902 that British physician George Frederic Still lectured about patients he had seen with symptoms of AD/HD, numerous theories about the cause of AD/HD have been considered. Some of these theories have been based on behavioral problems (bad parenting, willful children), but many have viewed AD/HD as having some biological basis. (Dr. Still himself was one of the first people to suggest the biological nature of AD/HD.)

If you know someone with AD/HD (which we assume, or else you have curious reading habits), the focus on biological causes shouldn't surprise you. When you watch someone struggle with AD/HD symptoms, you know that this person wants to pay attention, sit still, or control his impulses. But try as he might, he isn't able to (as we discuss in Chapter 3).

We're guessing that you probably haven't had a chance to get caught up on all the past theories about AD/HD, so here we offer a brief overview of the more common ones. Presenting, for your elucidation, the highlights of AD/HD theories throughout the past 100-plus years:

✔ **Bad parenting:** Blaming parents for the behaviors that a child with AD/HD exhibits is, on the surface, logical. After all, plenty of kids act inappropriately when given the opportunity through insufficient supervision. The difference is that children with AD/HD can't be disciplined into not having the symptoms. They can be taught ways to cope and strategies to lessen their symptoms, but these strategies don't remove the AD/HD.

This theory is, without a doubt, the number-one misconception about AD/HD. Unfortunately, a lot of people still believe it. Don't buy into this theory — it's just not true.

✔ **Defiance/willfulness:** Like the bad parenting theory, the theory of defiance is based in logic, because when kids without AD/HD act out, they can be taught not to behave that way. The problem is that people with AD/HD can't concentrate better by trying harder, and they can't stop hyperactivity or restlessness by willing it away. This theory is still perpetuated among people who don't understand AD/HD, and it is hard to dismiss partly because many AD/HD children *are* openly defiant (see Chapter 3).

✔ **Moral defectiveness:** In early descriptions of children with AD/HD, the official-sounding term *moral defectiveness* was created to place the blame on the child and the parents. The grain of truth in the concept is that people with AD/HD can have problems with empathy and with following rules, so they may act in ways that other people see as immoral or amoral. Again, supporters of this theory believed that through effort and discipline, AD/HD could be overcome.

✔ **Poor diet:** After researchers realized that AD/HD was not caused by bad parenting or willful defiance, they started looking at other causes. Diet was one theory that garnered a lot of attention. A poor diet can, in fact, cause some AD/HD-type symptoms in people without the condition, and it can worsen the symptoms of AD/HD (see Chapter 11), but it doesn't cause AD/HD.

✔ **Allergies and sensitivities:** Much like a poor diet, allergies and sensitivities can create symptoms similar to AD/HD, such as inattention and forgetfulness. And these sensitivities can worsen symptoms for some people with AD/HD. People who have these symptoms (but not AD/HD) see them disappear when they get their allergies or sensitivities under control.

✔ **Brain damage:** One of the early, non-behavioral theories involved the idea that people with AD/HD have some sort of brain damage. This was partly a result of the 1918 influenza epidemic, when some children who had influenza encephalitis developed hyperactivity, inattentiveness, and impulsivity. This theory was later referred to as *Minimal Brain Damage* and eventually led to some of the cutting-edge research that's going on today.

✔ **Toxic exposure:** Exposure to lead, and the accumulation of lead in the brain, was once considered the cause of AD/HD. Studies have suggested that some people who don't tolerate lead exposure as well as others may display symptoms similar to AD/HD. However, lead exposure is not the cause of AD/HD for the majority of people who have it. Exposure to other environmental toxins during pregnancy or after birth can also cause AD/HD-like symptoms, but we don't subscribe to this theory as the cause of AD/HD.

✔ **Traumatic brain injury:** Similar to the brain damage theory, some people have believed that AD/HD stems from lack of oxygen during birth or a head injury early in childhood. While brain injuries can induce the same symptoms as AD/HD (depending, of course, on where the injury is), they are not the cause of AD/HD.

What's in a name?

AD/HD has been called many things since it was first observed. Two early names were *Minimal Brain Damage* and later — because at the time no one actually saw any damage in the brain — *Minimal Brain Dysfunction*. Both these names occurred before the American Psychiatric Association (APA) included this condition in its list of mental disorders. Since its inclusion in the APA listing, AD/HD has been officially called the following names:

✔ **Hyperactivity of Childhood.** This name was used in the first edition of the APA's *Diagnostic and Statistical Manual of Mental Disorders* (DSM).

✔ **Hyperkinetic Reaction of Childhood.** This name appeared in the second edition of the DSM.

✔ **Attention Deficit Disorder With or Without Hyperactivity (ADD).** This name was introduced in the third edition of the DSM. Its abbreviation — ADD — is still widely used outside the professional community.

✔ **Attention Deficit Hyperactivity Disorder (ADHD).** The third edition of the DSM was revised with this change of name.

✔ **Attention Deficit/Hyperactivity Disorder (AD/HD).** When the fourth edition of the DSM was published, it added a backslash to the name.

We expect this renaming trend to continue. Researchers are now discovering several different places in the brain where the symptoms of AD/HD seem to come from. This research is still in its early stages, but we predict that within a few years, what is now called AD/HD will be classified as at least five — maybe even seven — different disorders, or at least that many subtypes of AD/HD.

Several of these theories actually led to the identification of disorders that are distinct from AD/HD. This illustrates how the primary symptoms of AD/HD can be found in more conditions than just AD/HD. We discuss mental disorders that share the same basic symptoms as AD/HD in Chapter 6.

Searching for a Plausible Theory

Why is it so tough to pinpoint the cause or causes of AD/HD? In this section, we offer just a taste of the challenges researchers face.

If you consider just the name of this condition, you may think that AD/HD is primarily a problem of paying attention and sitting still. This belief may lead you to suspect that causes of AD/HD are rooted in parts of the brain that primarily work on these activities — say, the primary motor area and the primary attention area. Here are the problems with that detective work:

✔ Although a primary motor area exists, it mostly works to run individual muscles, and it doesn't even have much control over how active the muscles are. The ability to sit still is controlled by other areas of the brain that work with the primary motor area.

✔ There is no attention center in the brain. Instead, a group of centers work together to perform different tasks involved in attending.

Obviously, coming up with a reasonable idea of what is really going on in the brain of a person with AD/HD is about as simple as getting a straight answer out of an oracle.

So how do neuroscientists come up with a working hypothesis that can be turned into a theory? They start by trying to understand how the brain and the mind (your thoughts and memories, for example) interact to produce particular types of learning, emotions, and behaviors. Then they try to understand how the study group (in this case, people with AD/HD) functions differently from the general population, and they try to find evidence of some biological difference to explain the differences they have observed. As you can imagine, this requires a lot of guessing and trial and error before the scientists come up with a halfway-useful model.

In practice, all sorts of people are trying to attack the problem of understanding AD/HD from a lot of different directions. For example:

✔ Geneticists are looking for unique characteristics of the genes that people with AD/HD inherit.

✔ Doctors are trying to find biochemical or anatomical differences between people with AD/HD and those without it.

✔ Physiologists are trying to find differences in brain function between people with AD/HD and people without it.

✔ Psychologists (and others, such as speech–language pathologists and educators) are observing and analyzing behaviors to try to understand the nature of the differences in the ways people with AD/HD do things.

✔ Pharmacologists are studying how medicines interact with the body to produce different effects; by doing so, they shed light on what functions are involved in a condition, too.

When you get all these people talking, writing, and experimenting together, you have a chance of coming up with a good theory.

A good theory is an explanation of something that fits all the data currently known about that something. One of the big problems with science is that it has to categorize individuals in order to gather data about them. The category — or group — that a person with AD/HD is put into has to consist of people who have something in common (in this case AD/HD). If you don't have a category whose members are similar, you never get past the data collection stage, because you're comparing apples and mulberries with pineapples and fir trees — you'll never find anything that they all have in common. This is likely to be the problem with at least some of the research that has been done on AD/HD. Research seems to be showing that five or six different causes or types of AD/HD exist, so we probably need to have five or six models or theories to explain it.

Examining the Core Issue in AD/HD

The AD/HD research taking place today is rooted in the recognition that people with AD/HD have one core problem: the inability to consistently regulate their attention and behaviors. The following sections explore the nature of this problem and the various brain functions that contribute to it.

Recognizing the role of self-regulation

AD/HD may be primarily a problem with self-regulation. (Russell A. Barkley, PhD, has written a book titled *ADHD and the Nature of Self Control* [The Guilford Press] that discusses this topic at length.) Although anyone can struggle with self-regulation, especially when you're tired or uninterested, people with AD/HD are more likely to have problems controlling their attention, managing their impulses, modulating their moods, and managing their activity levels.

Self-regulation refers to your ability to attain and maintain particular states of functioning in a consistent and predictable way. This ability is a prerequisite for you to be able to plan, organize, and perform complex thoughts and behaviors as you wish, when you wish. Without it, you aren't confident that you can call upon the skills you already have when you need them, and you have no guarantee of being able to learn something new.

On the surface it may seem that self-regulation depends on your desire to control your behavior. While that is true, much more is involved than simple will power (as though *that* is an easy thing to understand!). All brain functions are partly hard-wired from birth and partly learned. (Learning is really just modifying the wiring through experience.) In other words, your ability to self-regulate is a characteristic of the brain you were born with as it developed through the experiences that helped you learn how to use it.

The areas that you try to regulate — such as sustaining your attention on a specific task or sitting still when you're asked — are things you can learn to do more effectively as you grow older if you get the right kinds of experiences. The ability to make use of your experiences to learn is partly dependent on your ability to attain and maintain consistent brain states — we've come full circle to self-regulation.

One characteristic of children with AD/HD (and one of the criteria for diagnosing AD/HD) is that their developmental age is younger than their chronological age; they perform at levels below their peers. This is one of the reasons that AD/HD is called a developmental disability.

Exploring executive functions

Executive functions are the brain functions necessary for you to be able to regulate your behaviors. Executive functions primarily cover these areas:

- **Response inhibition:** This term covers impulse control, resistance to distraction, and delay of gratification. According to researcher Russell A. Barkley, PhD, response inhibition is the core problem in AD/HD; the rest of the executive functions draw off of it.

- **Working memory:** Working memory is divided into two categories:

  - **Nonverbal:** This type of working memory allows you to refer to past events to gauge your behavior. For example, if you don't remember that interrupting someone while she's talking results in a negative social interaction, you may interrupt her.

  - **Verbal:** This ability allows you to internalize speech, which results in the ability not only to understand other people but to be able to express yourself clearly. (For more on this topic, see Julian Jaynes' *The Origin of Consciousness in the Breakdown of the Bicameral Mind* [Mariner Books].)

✔ **Motor control:** This function not only allows you to keep from moving impulsively but also helps you plan your movements.

✔ **Regulation of your emotions:** Without this function, you may find yourself getting frustrated easily or reacting extremely to a given situation.

✔ **Motivation:** This function helps you get started and persist toward a goal.

✔ **Planning:** This function works on many levels, but the most significant involves being able to get organized and to develop and implement a plan of action.

Executive functions are controlled in several areas of the brain, including the following (see Figure 2-1):

✔ Frontal lobe

✔ Basal ganglia, including the caudate nucleus (which is located deep inside the brain and, therefore, not indicated in the figure)

✔ Cerebellum

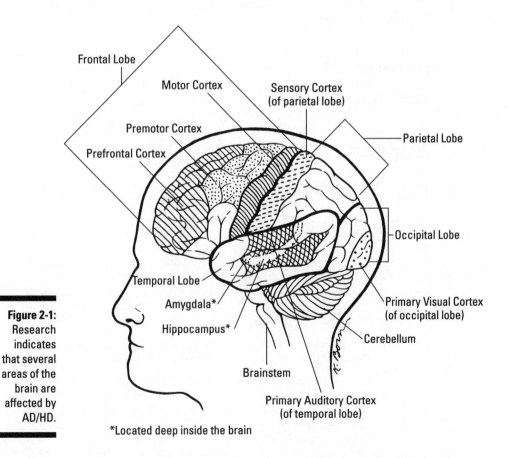

Figure 2-1: Research indicates that several areas of the brain are affected by AD/HD.

*Located deep inside the brain

As we discuss in the next section, current research is finding that in people with AD/HD, at least one of these brain areas seems to work differently than it does in people without AD/HD.

A ton of research has been done to try to determine the biological cause of AD/HD. Because we want to focus most of this book on ways to treat and cope with the symptoms of AD/HD, we have to limit the amount of research we cover. In the following sections, we include a sampling of studies to give you an idea of what researchers are looking at and what they're discovering. For a more comprehensive list of AD/HD research, check out coauthor Jeff Strong's Web site at www.reiinsitute.com and choose the "Resources" option at the top of the page.

Exploring Current AD/HD Research

Although the exact cause of AD/HD is still unknown, there is no shortage of research into the biology of AD/HD. This research fits into four broad categories: genetic, anatomical, functional, and chemical.

Genetic

AD/HD runs in families — so much so that when diagnosing the condition, an AD/HD professional's first step may be to look at the person's family to see if anyone else has it. We don't yet know what the genetic factor is, but recent research has identified a couple of genes that may contribute to AD/HD (which we discuss later in this section).

Many studies have examined AD/HD from a genetic perspective. These include studies that look at adoptive versus biological parents, the prevalence of AD/HD in families, twins' tendency to share AD/HD, and specific genes associated with AD/HD. Here's a short sampling of some of these areas of investigation:

- A study conducted by Dr. Florence Levy of the University of New South Wales, Australia showed that if one identical twin has AD/HD, 81 percent of the time the other one will as well. By contrast, only 29 percent of paternal twins share AD/HD. Because identical twins share the exact same DNA, this strongly suggests a genetic component to AD/HD.

- Several studies by Dr. Joseph Biederman and his colleagues at the Massachusetts General Hospital have shown that AD/HD runs in families. In one study, Dr. Biederman and his colleagues found that first-degree relatives (parents or siblings) of someone with AD/HD have a five times greater chance of also having AD/HD than someone who has no close relatives with the condition.

✔ Studies by Dr. Dennis Cantwell on adopted children with the hyperactive/impulsive type of AD/HD found that these children resemble their biological parents more than their adoptive parents in their hyperactivity. His studies suggest that the environment in which children grow up has less impact on the development of AD/HD than their genes.

✔ In a 1991 study, David Comings and his colleagues suggested that a mutation in the dopamine D2 receptor gene is connected to AD/HD. (We discuss dopamine, a brain chemical or *neurotransmitter,* later in the chapter in the "Chemical" section.) Research is underway now that is exploring several dopamine genes as possible links to AD/HD. A few researchers have suggested that two genes in particular — DAT1 and DRD4 — are the culprits. In fact, a recent study by researchers at the University of California, Irvine, suggests that the DRD4 7R gene may be associated with several AD/HD traits, such as novelty-seeking, increased aggression, and perseverance. By the time this book is published, chances are that more research will be completed supporting this possibility.

Anatomical

Researchers have conducted a few studies into the size and shape of the brains of people with AD/HD compared to people without it. A lot of conflicting data exists in this area, but a couple basic ideas have been suggested:

✔ One study suggested that the size of the *corpus collosum* (a bundle of nerves that ties the hemispheres of the brain together) is different in some people with AD/HD than in some people without it. Other researchers have suggested that this part of the brain operates differently in people with AD/HD than in others, so this observation may have some validity.

✔ Some research has indicated that asymmetry in the *basal ganglia* (a set of nuclei deep in the brain that are involved in regulation and control of the motor system) may be indicative of AD/HD. We discuss this further in the next section.

While anatomical research continues, most of the AD/HD research being done right now focuses on differences in brain activity between the AD/HD and non-AD/HD populations.

Functional

The brains of people with AD/HD seem to function differently than the brains of people without it. This area of research is buzzing right now, not only because it helps explain the cause of AD/HD, but also because these studies use relatively new technologies for imaging. (Boys — and girls — like their toys, you know.) Here's a sampling:

✔ A study by Alan Zemetkin, MD, using PET scans on adults with AD/HD discovered that when the subjects concentrated, the level of activity in the front part of the brain (the frontal lobe) decreased from its level at rest. People without AD/HD have an opposite response — an increase in activity in the frontal lobe when they concentrate. This study is generally credited with showing that AD/HD is a biologically-based condition.

✔ Dr. Joel Lubar at the University of Tennessee conducted several studies using quantitative EEG (electroencephalogram — see Chapter 5). The studies showed that when people with AD/HD concentrate, there is an increase in *theta activity* (slow brainwaves) in the frontal lobe of the brain. This finding corresponds to a lower level of activity in the region.

✔ Dr. Daniel G. Amen conducted extensive testing at his clinic using SPECT technology (Single Photon Emission Computed Tomography — see Chapter 5). He observed several variations in brain activity in people with AD/HD and has suggested that AD/HD is actually several different conditions, each with a different brain activity signature. According to his research, the areas affected by AD/HD include:

- **Frontal lobe:** Dr. Amen found a decrease in activity in this area when people with AD/HD are asked to concentrate. This corresponds with research done by Drs. Lubar and Zemetkin.

- **Limbic system:** The limbic system is located deep inside the center of the brain and is often involved with the way we feel and express our emotions. Dr. Amen's research found that some people with AD/HD have heightened limbic activity in addition to the decreased frontal lobe activity. This corresponds with a perspective put forth by researcher Paul Wender suggesting that the limbic system is at the center of the problems in AD/HD.

- **Parietal lobe:** Located toward the back of the brain (see Figure 2-1), this section is also referred to as the *sensory cortex.* Dr. Amen suggests that certain people with AD/HD have more activity in this area than other people.

✔ Dr. Robert Chabot and his colleagues at New York University found that 11 different patterns of *QEEG* (quantitative electroencephalogram — a device that measures surface brain wave activity and compares it to normal measurements found in a database) are associated with people diagnosed with AD/HD. They also found that some of these people could be predicted to respond well to certain medications and poorly to others.

Other researchers have been looking at AD/HD in more traditional neurobiological ways (such as anatomy imaging and chemical analysis), and their results have been confusing or conflicting in many cases. This isn't surprising; confusion is to be expected when people are trying to map out a new area of scientific knowledge.

With all this research available, it seems obvious that something unusual is going on inside the brains of people with AD/HD. It also appears that the frontal lobe usually has something to do with the unusual activity. The question yet to be answered, however, is what other areas of the brain are involved with AD/HD, and in what way. Some possibilities include the basal ganglia, the parietal cortex, and the cerebellum.

Chemical

For information to pass from one part of the brain to another requires the action of *neurotransmitters* — chemicals within the brain. A neurotransmitter is a small chemical messenger that allows one *neuron* (nerve) to communicate with another. When the upstream neuron gets excited and wants to pass on information to the downstream neuron, it releases the neurotransmitter molecules into a closed connection (like an airlock in a submarine or a space ship) called a *synapse.* The neurotransmitter then crosses the space to the downstream neuron's membrane and binds to specific receptors that cause an effect inside the receiving nerve.

Certain medications are generally effective for treating AD/HD symptoms (see Chapter 8), and most of these medications affect one of two neurotransmitters (or both): norepinephrine (also called noradrenalin) and dopamine. This is how we know that these two neurotransmitters are involved in causing the condition. These neurotransmitter systems are distributed throughout the brain in specific locations, and they have different effects based on the types of receptors that the downstream neurons have on their membranes. The receptors determine what effect a neurotransmitter has, and different types of receptors exist in different regions of the brain.

A ton of research has been done in this area showing a link between certain brain chemicals and the symptoms of AD/HD. Some of the more elegant theories about AD/HD consider the balance between norepinephrine and dopamine in the various areas they affect, including the idea that one neurotransmitter has more effect in one hemisphere of the brain than the other (see Figure 2-2). Most of the neurons that have norepinephrine as their transmitter are contained in one area of the brainstem, the *locus coerulius,* part of the reticular activating system. This is the area of the brain that controls the general level of activation of your nervous system (how aroused you are — whether you're awake or asleep). Dopamine is found in several different areas of the brain, but the area that seems most important for AD/HD is the part that projects to the prefrontal cortex and is probably responsible for significance, meaning, and motivation.

Median section through the left side of the brain

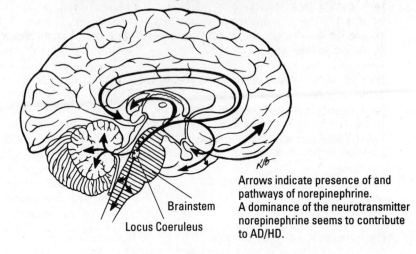

Arrows indicate presence of and
pathways of norepinephrine.
A dominance of the neurotransmitter
norepinephrine seems to contribute
to AD/HD.

Brainstem

Locus Coeruleus

Median section through the right side of the brain

Figure 2-2:
The
dopamine–
norepi-
nephrine
connections
in the brain
may have
a lot to do
with AD/HD.

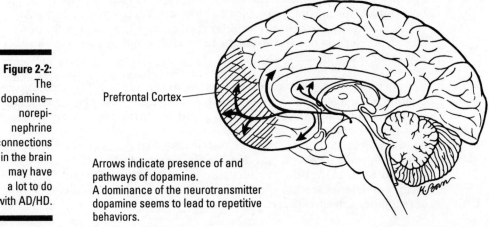

Prefrontal Cortex

Arrows indicate presence of and
pathways of dopamine.
A dominance of the neurotransmitter
dopamine seems to lead to repetitive
behaviors.

One way to think about AD/HD is that it is a problem of balance between the
activities of norepinephrine and dopamine. When you have too much norepinephrine working, you are agitated, and you can pay attention only to things
that may be threats or targets of opportunity (the "fight or flight" mechanism
is very active). When you have more dopamine dominance, you tend to get
stuck on repetitive activities, and you don't get bored doing the same things
over and over. AD/HD is associated with having too much norepinephrine.

Getting Down to the Bottom Line

No matter how you slice it, AD/HD has a biological basis. AD/HD is not primarily a behavioral problem, although the symptoms often involve problem behaviors. You can't fix AD/HD by just trying harder or by using more stringent discipline. The brains of people with AD/HD are different than the brains of people without it. The only problem is that no one yet knows exactly what the differences are, and the best ways to address them are still being investigated.

Several different areas of the brain and several different neurotransmitters seem to be involved in creating the symptoms of AD/HD. We'll go out on a limb here (a very short, sturdy one to be sure) and make a prediction that within the next few years what we now call AD/HD will actually be identified as several different conditions — having different physiological causes — that share many of the same core symptoms. As this all becomes clearer, you can expect that clinicians will have much better ways to help someone with AD/HD cope with the condition.

To effectively treat AD/HD, you need to not only deal with the psychological and social aspects of the symptoms but also the biological roots of the condition. In fact, biological treatment is the first line of defense against the symptoms of AD/HD because without it psychological and social treatments are often less effective (if not totally ineffective, depending on the person).

The term *biological treatment* doesn't necessarily mean medication, although medication is the most commonly used biological treatment approach. Other treatments address the biological end of things, and we cover many of them in Chapters 8, 11, 12, and 13. For a general overview of these approaches and more information about the three levels of treatment (biological, psychological, and social), check out Chapter 7.

Chapter 3

The Many Faces of AD/HD

In This Chapter

▶ Examining the primary symptoms of AD/HD

▶ Discovering secondary symptoms

▶ Looking at AD/HD in people of different ages

▶ Exploring the differences between the sexes

AD/HD can look different in everyone. One person may be able to sit still but can't focus, another may have very little trouble sitting still but constantly speaks without thinking, and yet another may not be able to sit still for any length of time while also having problems keeping focused on a task. Such is the nature of AD/HD and one of the reasons that many people have a difficult time believing this condition actually exists.

In this chapter, we list the primary symptoms of AD/HD and discuss how these symptoms often give rise to others. We also examine how gender and age create special issues for people with AD/HD.

Picturing the Primary Symptoms of AD/HD

AD/HD has three primary symptoms: inattention/distractibility, impulsivity, and hyperactivity. These symptoms don't all have to be present in order for you to have AD/HD, and if you do have one or more of them, they may not be present all the time. (Chapter 5 explains how this works.) The following sections explore these symptoms and many of the ways in which they manifest in people with AD/HD.

Inattention/distractibility

Inattention means you have a hard time focusing on something. *Distractibility* means your attention is easily pulled from one thing to another. Inattention is at the core of AD/HD — it isn't called *attention deficit/hyperactivity disorder* for no reason. However, inattention isn't as simple as never being able to focus; nothing about this condition is as clear-cut as that. Inattention is more accurately a problem in being able to control or regulate how and when you focus on something. (*Regulation* is a key word for people with AD/HD; check out Chapter 2 for more about regulation.) This is where distractibility comes in. External and internal stimuli pull on people with AD/HD much harder than people without it. As a result, they have a hard time staying focused on one thing.

A key thing to know about this symptom is that it can look different in almost everyone, and it can change from day to day in each person. But even with such variability, a few basic characteristics of inattention and distractibility are found in people with AD/HD. These are:

- ✔ **Not being able to concentrate:** Try as you may, keeping focused on something is difficult and, at times, impossible. The worst part of this is that the harder you try, the harder it is to concentrate. Your mind may go blank, or you may have other thoughts come into your mind.

- ✔ **Being able to focus well on some things but not on others:** This is one of the most confusing aspects of inattention in AD/HD. Many people think that just because a person can concentrate on something, she must be able to concentrate on everything if she just tries hard enough. This is not the case for people with AD/HD.

    For example, your coauthor Jeff recently worked with a 9-year-old boy who couldn't stay on task at school. He often stared out the window, spaced out, and sometimes almost dozed off. At home, whenever he had to do homework, he had the same difficulties. However, if you gave him a model rocket to build or a book about rockets, he was in his element and could often focus for hours. In fact, he would get so engrossed that he often forgot to eat or go to the bathroom.

    Some people with AD/HD claim that they don't have the condition because they can focus "as long as it's something I'm interested in." The criterion for AD/HD isn't about being unable to focus ever; instead, it's about not having control over when and how this focusing happens. This leads to another aspect of AD/HD, which we describe in the next bullet.

- ✔ **Being able to focus sometimes but not other times:** For many people, this is one of the most frustrating features of AD/HD. As an example, the same 9-year-old boy I mention in the previous bullet experienced many times when he couldn't even focus on the model building that he loved so much. Some days he would start putting a section together and lose track of what came next or end up gluing that section to the wrong part of the main model. This scattered thinking made it very difficult for him to tackle complex projects because he'd often lose track of what he was doing.

✔ **Being easily distracted by things happening around you:** Many people with AD/HD are unable to filter out all the things going on around them and are easily pulled away from what they want to focus on.

For example, your coauthor Jeff worked with a man in his 40s whose relationship was in trouble because he was unable to effectively listen to his wife when she talked, which led her to believe that he didn't care about her. This man explained that as he tried to listen, he found himself distracted by the sound of the refrigerator turning off or on, a passing car, or some other sound that his wife didn't even notice. For him, these sounds were irresistible. As much as he tried to ignore them, they seemed to draw him in. The result was that even though he genuinely wanted to listen to his wife, he caught only parts of the conversation and often ended up misunderstanding what she said.

Interestingly, this man was well aware of his tendency to get distracted when people were talking. He developed a system to deal with it at work; he kept a compact tape recorder with him and discretely used it during meetings or when he was given verbal instructions. Otherwise, he wrote everything down. Writing as he listened seemed to help him stay focused and pushed the external stimulus far enough into the background that it didn't pull his attention away as often.

✔ **Being easily distracted by your own thoughts:** For many people with AD/HD, it's common to have a series of unrelated thoughts flowing through their minds. Many people think of this as "daydreaming."

✔ **Losing track of your thoughts (spacing out):** An extension of being easily distracted is spacing out. This is common with people with AD/HD — it seems like they have gaps in their awareness.

✔ **Being forgetful:** A lot of people with AD/HD tend to lose their keys, forget appointments, and get lost.

✔ **Being late:** Because many people with AD/HD have trouble organizing their time, they are often late to appointments. Sometimes they are purposely early everywhere they go because they know they have a tendency to be late.

✔ **Being unable to finish things:** People with AD/HD are notorious for starting a project and then moving on to something else before finishing it. This is a common problem for another person your coauthor Jeff worked with. Jean, a woman in her late 30s, was extremely bright and ambitious, with tons of great ideas and the talent to back them up. The only problem was that every time she would work on one of her projects, she would leave it half finished. She always had an excuse for abandoning a project, such as another more important project coming up. As well, she had a long history of quitting jobs after just a few months even though she performed them very well.

✔ **Procrastinating:** Because people with AD/HD are often poor at organizing their thoughts and time, they often fail to even start something. Also, after repeated failures, many people avoid starting projects because of the fear that they'll fail again. Many people with AD/HD wait until the last minute to do things because the pressure helps them focus.

✔ **Not attending to details:** People with AD/HD are often "big picture" people. They can think up new and exciting ideas, but when it comes to actually dealing with the details needed to make those ideas happen, they just can't seem to follow through. As well, when given instructions on how to do something, they often miss important details.

✔ **Making careless mistakes:** Not attending to details leads to careless mistakes. This is a common problem with people who are easily distractible because they drift from one thought to another and lose track of what they've done and what needs to be done next.

This list can't even come close to detailing all the ways that inattention and distractibility manifest in people with AD/HD. The main aspect of inattention and distractibility for people with AD/HD is a reduced level of activity in the frontal lobe of the brain. The frontal lobe, as we describe in Chapter 2, is responsible for motor planning, organization, problem solving, attention, and impulse control, to name a few. When this part of the brain doesn't function properly, the symptoms of AD/HD appear.

Impulsivity

Impulsivity is the inability to consider the consequences of your actions beforehand — in other words, doing before thinking. When you have this symptom of AD/HD, it's almost as though you have an involuntary response to a stimulus. The response can take the form of actions or words.

Like the other symptoms of AD/HD, impulsivity looks different depending on the person. Some people have difficulty considering what they say before saying it, whereas others may act at times without thinking. Here are a few ways that impulsivity can manifest in people with AD/HD:

✔ **Blurting out answers before a question is finished:** Many teachers of children with AD/HD complain that the children shout out answers before questions have been asked. Many AD/HD adults have a habit of finishing other people's sentences.

✔ **Saying inappropriate things:** Having successful interpersonal relationships often involves being diplomatic — knowing when *not* to say something because it wouldn't accomplish anything useful. People with the hyperactive/impulsive type of AD/HD have a difficult time censoring themselves, and they respond to other people without considering the consequences of what they say. Most often, the person saying these things feels awful afterwards and wonders in amazement why he said what he said.

✔ **Butting into conversations:** Because of the inability to keep from saying the first thing that comes to mind, people with impulse problems often butt into conversations. This is partly due to the lack of impulse control but is also due to the difficulty that many people with AD/HD have in being able to "read" conversations. In other words, they cannot pick up on and interpret subtle signals (body language) and the rhythm of a conversation. When this person butts into the conversation, she may do so with a comment or story that doesn't fit with the current conversation.

✔ **Intruding on others:** Another characteristic of AD/HD sufferers is that they often don't know where their bodies are in space, so they tend to be somewhat clumsy. Couple this characteristic with the lack of impulse control, and you often find people with AD/HD intruding on others — bumping into them, grabbing at a toy, and so on.

✔ **Acting without considering the consequences:** Lack of impulse control often leads to doing something before thinking about whether it's a smart thing to do. Many people with AD/HD act from impulse to impulse. For example, your coauthor Jeff has worked with quite a few adults who, when at a mall, buy things they never planned on buying. They see something in a store and "have to have it," even though that item may not have any useful purpose for them.

✔ **Engaging in risky behaviors:** Because people with AD/HD often crave stimulus, they may get into situations where they do dangerous things. This is related to another aspect of AD/HD: thrill-seeking. Pushing life to the limits can really help some people focus and feel more in control.

✔ **Being impatient:** Impatience comes in many forms, some of which we cover in previous bullets, such as butting into conversations and blurting out answers before a question has been fully asked. One thing that is particularly difficult for people with AD/HD is waiting in line, which requires someone to stand relatively still. People with the hyperactive/impulsive type of AD/HD have symptoms that cover both impulsivity and hyperactivity or restlessness. As a result, they are more likely to fidget and squirm while waiting.

Waiting in line or for one's turn can be excruciating for people with AD/HD. For example, David, a man in his late 20s, finds waiting in line so unbearable that he won't even go into a store when it's busy. He does his food shopping after midnight at a 24-hour store, and if he sees a line at the cash register — even just one person — he mills around the store until he doesn't have to wait to check out. The pacing around the store instead of standing in line keeps him from feeling, as he describes, "caged in."

Some people with AD/HD can't stand to drive the speed limit or stop at stoplights. Your coauthor Mike has known people who would go out of their way not to stop in traffic. Your coauthor Jeff is one of those people.

✔ **Wanting things immediately:** This symptom can take many forms, such as wanting to have your needs met immediately, as in the case of a child who has a tantrum when you don't come running to his aid, or buying on credit.

Impulse control is regulated in the frontal lobes of the brain — the same part of the brain that controls attention. Because people with AD/HD often have less activity in this part of the brain, they have less control over their impulses. Often, their bodies react to a stimulus before the reasoning part of the brain can stop, choose the best response, and then act.

Restlessness/hyperactivity

Restlessness and hyperactivity are essentially the same thing — the inability to regulate your physical movements. For the person with this symptom of AD/HD, sitting still is difficult (especially at school or work where sitting for extended periods of time is expected), as is doing activities that require minimal physical movement, such as playing quiet games. Restlessness is subtler than hyperactivity because it's often internal rather than external.

Hyperactive children are probably the poster children for this disorder, even though only about half the people with AD/HD have the symptom of hyperactivity.

Keep in mind that most young children exhibit what would be called hyperactivity — frequent movement and activity. This isn't necessarily a sign that your child has AD/HD. Most children outgrow this level of activity by the time they're 4 or 5. And even before then, most kids have periods of time where they're able to sit quietly, such as when reading a book with a parent or older sibling.

Hyperactivity is easily seen in children running around, but in adults, it can be much subtler — so subtle, in fact, that many professionals have suggested that adults outgrow their hyperactivity. This suggestion is proving to be inaccurate. Adults don't outgrow their hyperactivity; they grow into their restlessness. And they often learn how to deal with the symptoms by disguising them.

Restlessness and hyperactivity are so variable in people that in one instance this symptom may be obvious, and in another it may be almost completely disguised. Following are a few of the ways this symptom can present itself:

✔ **Being unable to sit still for any length of time:** This is especially obvious in younger children. As children grow older, they often develop the ability to sit, although they may squirm in their seats or, as they grow older still, just fidget.

✔ **Being always on the go:** The classic descriptor is that people with this symptom of AD/HD seem to be "driven by a motor." As much as they'd like to stop moving sometimes, they can't seem to do so.

✓ **Feeling edgy:** Adults with AD/HD often have this form of restlessness. They are generally able to control their movements to the point of not drawing attention to themselves, but they still feel the need to move and release the energy that builds up inside them. For people with the combined type of AD/HD (inattention and hyperactivity/restlessness), these feelings of restlessness often make the inattention worse because the restlessness commands their attention. Restlessness can also manifest in the medium- and long-term parts of a person's life. It is quite common for people with AD/HD to move or change jobs frequently just because they are restless. These feelings of restlessness are not confined to adults, however; children can have them, too.

✓ **Fidgeting constantly:** When hyperactivity and the need to frequently move are internalized, this symptom often manifests as fidgeting. Fidgeting can take on a number of forms, from seemingly repetitive tapping to random movements. Fidgeting doesn't necessarily relate to restlessness in some older people with AD/HD. Some people fidget in order to try to focus on a task.

✓ **Talking nonstop:** Rather than move their bodies, some people with AD/HD run their mouths. Constant talking is simply another way to release the energy that seems to build up from AD/HD. Often this talking moves from subject to subject, following the somewhat random thought patterns that go through the person's mind.

Obviously, there are many other ways that hyperactivity and restlessness can manifest in people with AD/HD. The main thing to be aware of is that these actions are not voluntary. They aren't the result of defiance or bad behavior.

Studying Some Secondary Symptoms

Often the core symptoms of AD/HD (which we discuss in the previous section) are accompanied by additional symptoms, such as boredom, frustration, and low self-esteem. For many older people with AD/HD — adolescents and adults — these symptoms can be more of a problem than the primary symptoms of AD/HD. The sections that follow give you a glimpse into these secondary symptoms and how they can impact your life.

Anticipation of failure

Much of the anxiety that people with AD/HD feel is the result of repeated failures, such as losing track of thoughts, forgetting, being late, getting lost, saying the wrong thing, and so on. With a history of making these types of mistakes, many people get worried because they're afraid that they're going to make another one.

Worry

People with AD/HD often worry excessively. This worry is actually another expression of the pent-up feelings of restlessness. This makes worry both a symptom and a method for people with AD/HD to try to control how their minds work. If they can focus on a thought — in this case anxiety over some trivial thing — they can avoid spacing out.

Anxiety disorders have similar symptoms to AD/HD — restlessness, inability to concentrate, and hyperactivity — so someone who appears to have AD/HD may actually have an anxiety disorder. In order to rule this possibility out, you need to have a professional explore a differential diagnosis. We cover this subject in detail in Chapter 6.

Boredom

For people with the hyperactive type of AD/HD, almost any stimulus can become boring — especially something that happens repeatedly or is part of someone's everyday life. These types of people seek new and exciting stimulation to keep them interested, and they often partake in high-risk behaviors in order to quell the boredom that can so easily overtake them.

People with this symptom sometimes create conflict in their lives — whether at school, at work, or at home — in order to "spice things up." This behavior can look as benign as waiting to do a project until the very last minute, or it can take the form of instigating an argument. This need for stimulation can also be as risky as driving recklessly, seeking out high-risk sports, gambling, or compulsively overspending.

Loss of motivation/feelings of hopelessness

Many people with AD/HD feel as if they are failing in the world, which pounds their self-esteem and can lead to loss of motivation or feelings of hopelessness. Unfortunately, for many people these feelings exacerbate some of the other symptoms of AD/HD (such as forgetfulness, inattention, and spacing out), thus further reducing self-esteem and creating more social isolation. As well, these feelings can lead to depression (see Chapter 6 for details). Depression in people with AD/HD is a serious factor and needs to be dealt with by a professional.

Depression has many similar symptoms to AD/HD — inattention, poor memory, and negativity — so it can be confused with AD/HD. In fact, according to the American Psychiatric Association diagnostic manual (DSM-IV), depression has to be considered when diagnosing AD/HD. Chapter 6 details this process.

Frustration

Imagine not being able to control your ability to focus, to keep from moving, or even to keep from saying something stupid. This is a very frustrating situation. People with AD/HD not only have to deal with their inability to do these things but also — and probably more importantly — their inability at one time and their ability at other times. The symptoms of AD/HD, as we explain earlier in this chapter, can come and go. Sometimes you can concentrate, and sometimes you can't. Sometimes you can sit still, and sometimes you can't.

Not having control over one's attention, motor activities, or impulses leads to feelings of frustration, and people with AD/HD have a lower threshold for this frustration than others. Couple this with lower self-esteem (which we discuss next), which most people with AD/HD experience, and eventually the person with AD/HD may stop trying to do things altogether.

Low self-esteem

Years of not measuring up to others' or your own expectations, experiencing failures at home and school, and struggling in social situations often lead to low self-esteem. People with AD/HD generally struggle with low self-esteem, and this colors the way they view and act in the world.

People with low self-esteem have a hard time taking compliments. They often interpret what others say as criticism even though it may, in fact, be a compliment. Low self-esteem also leads to an overall negative outlook and can be accompanied by moodiness and eventually followed up by depression.

Sleep disturbances

Many people with AD/HD have trouble sleeping. Some have a hard time getting to sleep, others wake up often at night, and still others have a hard time waking up in the morning.

For some people, changes in sleep can be one of the side effects of taking medication. In this instance, you need to make adjustments to the dose and the time of day that you take your medication. Be sure to consult with your doctor before making any changes to your medication dosage or schedule.

Sleep problems can have many causes. Some people actually get hyper-focused on something and forget to go to bed. After a few times doing this, they may develop a sleep debt and need time to sleep longer than usual. This happens to many people with AD/HD: During the week they don't get enough sleep, and on the weekends they sleep most of the day away.

For other people — mostly ones with the hyperactive type of AD/HD in particular — getting to sleep may be difficult. Winding down is next to impossible, so it may take hours to fall asleep. For many people with AD/HD (regardless of the type), getting up and moving in the morning can be especially challenging. It may take an hour or so for the person to fully wake up.

The concurrence of sleep disorders and AD/HD is common, so a person with one condition may also have the other. To make matters more complicated, many sleep disorders share the same basic symptoms as the inattentive type of AD/HD — such as forgetfulness and inability to concentrate — so what looks like AD/HD may actually be a sleep disorder. Chapter 6 digs into this subject more deeply.

Substance abuse

Although substance abuse is technically a *co-occurring condition* with AD/HD (see Chapter 6), it is common enough among people with AD/HD that we include it in the list of secondary symptoms. Abusing drugs and alcohol may result from trying to numb feelings of failure and from trying to self-medicate. Certain drugs, such as cocaine, don't actually offer a high for people with AD/HD. Instead, these drugs work much like the prescription stimulants (such as Ritalin) used by people with AD/HD to reduce some of their symptoms. The problem with this approach — aside from the fact that it's illegal — is that it's impossible to get any consistency using street drugs to try to deal with AD/HD because you never know what's in them, and you don't know how strong they are.

Many people with AD/HD have drug or alcohol problems — probably due, at least in part, to a common biology between AD/HD and being prone to addiction. The good news is that people who are properly treated for AD/HD have less of a tendency to abuse alcohol and drugs than people who don't have AD/HD.

Facing AD/HD in Different Populations

Although AD/HD manifests differently in everyone, it can show some common characteristics within a given population. In some cases, it may benefit a person with AD/HD to know how other people of their same age or gender behave similarly.

Children

Almost all young children exhibit AD/HD characteristics, such as darting from one thing to another or climbing on everything in sight. This is why the DSM-IV (the manual for mental disorders) stipulates that in order for a child to be classified as having AD/HD, he must be acting in a way that is not appropriate for his age.

Regardless of age, kids without AD/HD can often sit still for periods of time — such as when reading a book — whereas kids with the hyperactive type of AD/HD can't.

Hyperactive children can be *really* active, which is why hyperactivity is most problematic when kids are young. As kids age, they mellow out a bit, and their hyperactivity turns more inward. By the time they're in their teens, they don't run around as much, although they often squirm or have feelings of restlessness.

Difficulties with attention and organization can have a lasting impact on children with AD/HD because AD/HD can interfere with learning the basic skills necessary for development into the next stages of education and life. Many children with AD/HD have difficulties learning to read, spell, or do arithmetic. These problems can be due to not being able to sustain attention and focus, or they can stem from specific learning disabilities that sometimes accompany AD/HD (see Chapter 6).

Some, but definitely not all, AD/HD children have difficulties getting along with others. A lot of AD/HD kids have problems taking instruction, being disciplined, or respecting rules. These problems can follow them into adolescence and adulthood.

Adolescents

For adolescents, the primary symptoms of AD/HD are often overshadowed by the secondary symptoms of low self-esteem, frustration, and boredom, to name a few. After years of not being able to get things "right" in school or at home, many teens with AD/HD are demoralized.

Dealing with these secondary symptoms in adolescents becomes a priority because they have the potential of causing many more problems down the road.

Adolescents with the impulsive/hyperactive type of AD/HD are often able to sit and don't exhibit the same level of activity as younger people. Generally, their hyperactivity manifests more internally as a general sense of restlessness and as fidgeting. This internalization does not indicate that the symptom of hyperactivity has lessened; instead, it indicates that the person is finding a way to release the kinetic energy in a way that is more socially appropriate. In other words, the hyperactivity is still there; it's just been transformed to be less obvious.

In school, adolescents with AD/HD may have a harder time than younger children with AD/HD. This is partly due to the way schools operate: After children leave elementary school, they often have classes in different rooms with different teachers and have access to fewer support services for kids who are behind in their study skills. Children with AD/HD also tend to be somewhat behind their peers in emotional development, and this delay continues into adolescence.

Because of the expanding world that adolescents inhabit, the effects of impulsivity can be far-reaching. Impulsive behavior that may have been relatively benign at a younger age can become downright dangerous as the person reaches his or her teens.

Another problem adolescents experience is that the hormonal changes occurring during puberty often coincide with an increase in the severity of the symptoms of AD/HD. (However, some adolescents actually have a decrease in AD/HD symptoms during puberty.) Add to this the fact that as the adolescent's body changes, his need for medication changes too, and it becomes increasingly important to monitor the dose and drug used. As well, many teens don't want to take medications and often sabotage a treatment regimen that would otherwise work for them. All these factors can create a very difficult period of time for families.

Adults

AD/HD used to be known as a childhood disorder. People assumed that after a child with AD/HD grew up, he also grew out of his AD/HD symptoms. This has proved to be a false premise — so much so that a plethora of books are now on the market addressing adult AD/HD.

AD/HD in adults does exist, but it often manifests differently than in children. Hyperactivity gives way to restlessness; most adults are able to find a way to sit reasonably still even though they desperately want to get up and move around. As we explain earlier in the chapter (in the section "Restlessness/ hyperactivity"), adults often develop ways to avoid running around — the classic sign of hyperactivity — and instead fidget much more.

Many of the inattention symptoms of AD/HD don't improve with age. Adults have often developed strategies to deal with the symptoms, but they still have them. Unfortunately, most adults with AD/HD still suffer from the effects of inattention/distractibility to the point where it impacts their lives. Money problems, frequent job changes, family problems, and so on can wreak havoc and cause the secondary symptom of low self-esteem or the co-occurring condition of depression to develop.

One of the most important and difficult things for adults with AD/HD to do is find the right occupation, and the right job within that sector. A large number of small business owners are adults with AD/HD. This is because many of the positive attributes of AD/HD, such as creativity, innovation, and risk-taking (which we discuss in Chapter 17), are essential attributes of entrepreneurs. In addition, many people with AD/HD are self-employed because they find it very hard to work for someone else and to meet the strict requirements of the corporate world.

Unfortunately, running their own businesses can be especially difficult for people with AD/HD because of the tendency to procrastinate, be unorganized and impulsive, and so on. For these people, life strategies, good assistants, and technological aids — such as PDAs and day planners — are invaluable tools. Chapter 16 has details about making the most of your work environment.

Women

One of the biggest challenges that women with AD/HD encounter is a lack of awareness about the condition, because the perception has been that AD/HD typically affects males. Add to this the fact that very little research has been done on females with AD/HD, and you end up with a lot less information about how the disorder affects women and how to best deal with it. Fortunately, awareness is growing, and more information is becoming available. (There are even a few books available that are written specifically for women with AD/HD.)

Research indicates that males are three to five times more likely to be diagnosed with AD/HD than females. Does this mean that fewer women have AD/HD? Or is it possible that many women with AD/HD are not being identified because the assumption has been that this disorder primarily affects males? With so little research available on AD/HD and females, it's hard to say. But one thing research has been discovering is that the women who are diagnosed with AD/HD have more serious cases. This suggests that many women with AD/HD may be falling through the cracks and not being identified.

Traditionally, more males are hyperactive than females. This doesn't mean that you don't see hyperactive or restless girls, but this symptom is less common among females and often doesn't manifest itself as extreme levels of activity — it tends to be internalized more. In young girls, hyperactivity may take the form of excessive talking, whereas boys tend to get up and move around.

Women with AD/HD are diagnosed with depression and low self-esteem at a higher rate than men.

Part II
Diagnosing AD/HD

The 5th Wave   By Rich Tennant

"It's my opinion that you suffer from a hyperactive disorder. And when you're done writing that down, I'd like my chart back."

In this part . . .

Part II examines how AD/HD is diagnosed, which isn't always an easy process. Accurately diagnosing AD/HD requires effort on the part of the person with AD/HD (or that person's parents) and the professional(s) involved. Chapter 4 introduces you to the many types of professionals who can diagnose and/or treat AD/HD. In Chapter 5, we walk you through what to expect from the evaluation process. And in Chapter 6 we help to explain why diagnosing AD/HD is tricky by exploring conditions that often share some symptoms with AD/HD.

Chapter 4

Finding the Right Professional for You

In This Chapter

▶ Exploring the different types of AD/HD professionals

▶ Considering your own beliefs about diagnosis and treatment

▶ Making sure that your diagnosis is as accurate as possible

▶ Determining what services your diagnosis provides

*T*he first step in getting diagnosed with AD/HD is finding a professional who understands the condition and can most accurately assess your situation. Not all professionals are the same when it comes to diagnosing and treating AD/HD. This chapter helps you understand the roles that different professionals play in AD/HD care and walks you through the process of choosing the best person(s) for you. As well, you discover how to ensure that your insurance covers the cost of diagnosis and some treatment.

Help Wanted: Searching for the Right Person (s)

You need to consider two primary aspects of AD/HD care when looking for an AD/HD professional: diagnosis and treatment. The right professional for one aspect may not be the best person for the other.

One of the most common questions we get asked is, "Which healthcare provider is the best for treating AD/HD?" As we show you in this chapter, there really is no single answer to this question. Essentially, your goal is to find a professional who has experience in diagnosing AD/HD and who is aligned with your personal beliefs. (We help you determine your personal beliefs in the section "Examining Your Values," later in this chapter.)

Getting a diagnosis for legal purposes

AD/HD is currently classified as a medical condition. As such, it can be diagnosed by any medical doctor, including family physicians, neurologists, psychiatrists . . . even dermatologists if they want to (although sunscreen isn't a very effective treatment for AD/HD!). AD/HD is also a psychiatric diagnosis, so any licensed mental health professional can make the diagnosis official.

The main reasons to have an official diagnosis relate to legal and financial matters. If you want to request accommodations at school or in the workplace, you need an official diagnosis. The same goes for getting disability status with the government. Most health insurance covers AD/HD treatments with a doctor, psychologist, or allied health professional if you have an official diagnosis. See the section "Being Eligible for Services" later in the chapter for more information.

In this chapter we refer to an *official* diagnosis as one that is legally recognized. This doesn't mean it's a more accurate diagnosis, only that it is made by a professional who is legally entitled to offer one, such as a medical doctor or mental health professional. An unofficial diagnosis can be just as accurate, but it doesn't afford you the same protections as its legally recognized counterpart.

Considering your professional options

Many different health professionals can look for the basic symptoms of AD/HD and let you know if you fit the profile for the disorder. However, only certain professionals can look at the nuances of your condition to see if AD/HD is the best diagnosis. Likewise, some professionals are good at diagnosing, while others are better suited to offer treatments or life strategies that can help you cope with the symptoms — regardless of what label is placed on them.

Bottom line: The best professional for you is one who has experience in your condition and who has the resources to effectively deal with the symptoms present. For some people, this person may be the family physician; others may determine that a psychologist or neurologist is best. In the section "Evaluating Your AD/HD Professional," later in this chapter, we offer tools for locating an individual whose experience, beliefs, and treatment approaches meet your specific needs.

In Table 4-1, we offer an at-a-glance overview of the types of diagnostic and treatment services provided by various health professionals. The sections that follow provide more detail and make generalizations about who may work best for you.

Table 4-1	Diagnosis and Treatment Capabilities				
	Diagnose (Officially)	Prescribe Medication	Counseling	Nonconventional Treatments	Life Strategies
AD/HD specialist	Yes (Sometimes)	Depends	Sometimes	Yes	Generally
Family physician	Yes (Yes)	Yes	Sometimes	Sometimes	Sometimes
Pediatrician	Yes (Yes)	Yes	Sometimes	Sometimes	Sometimes
Psychologist	Yes (Yes)	Sometimes	Not usually	Sometimes	Yes
Clinical social worker	Yes (Yes)	No	Yes	Sometimes	Yes
AD/HD coach	Yes (Sometimes)	No	Sometimes	Sometimes	Sometimes
Psychiatrist	Yes (Yes)	Yes	Yes	Sometimes	Yes
Neurologist	Yes (Yes)	Yes	Yes	No	No
Neuro-psychiatrist/ behavioral neurologist	Yes (Yes)	Yes	Sometimes	Sometimes	Sometimes
Educational diagnostician	Yes (Yes, according to school district)	No	No	No	Yes, but only for school situations
Speech–language pathologist	Yes (No)	No	No	Yes	Sometimes
Occupational therapist	Yes (No)	No	No	Yes	Generally

AD/HD specialist

An AD/HD specialist is a professional who specializes in working with patients with AD/HD (makes sense, huh?). An AD/HD specialist can be an excellent choice for diagnosing and/or treating AD/HD. The only problem is that anyone can call himself an AD/HD specialist; no licensing or certification is required for using this term. As a result, the term itself is hardly an indication that a person is qualified to treat or diagnose AD/HD.

The term *AD/HD specialist* in and of itself means virtually nothing. The main thing to look for when considering an AD/HD specialist is the background of the person using this label. You may find educators, psychologists, psychiatrists, or any of the other professionals listed in this chapter also calling themselves AD/HD specialists. Dig deeper than the label and find out what this person's educational background is to determine whether he is someone you want to work with.

One situation in which the AD/HD specialist may be your best choice is when you are dealing with a multidisciplinary clinic that specializes in evaluating and treating AD/HD and related conditions.

Family physician

Your family doctor is often a good place to start to look for AD/HD in you or your child. She can often spot the basic symptoms, and she may be able to perform some simple evaluations to quickly rule out AD/HD in most people. But when it comes to doing detailed evaluations and exploring the subtleties of AD/HD — and keep in mind that AD/HD is all about subtleties — a family physician may not be the best solution.

Family physicians have to focus on the big picture with their patients and often aren't as knowledgeable about current trends and research as specialists. Also, most family physicians don't have the time to perform the detailed evaluations necessary to rule out all the other possible conditions that look like AD/HD (which we discuss in Chapter 6). Some family doctors don't even believe that AD/HD is a legitimate disorder and may blame the problem on bad behavior or bad parenting. (This viewpoint is becoming rarer, but it does still exist.)

On the other hand, because your family doctor knows you or your child best, she can often get you started and then refer you to the appropriate professional if you need to dig deeper (assuming she believes AD/HD is real). She may also be able to rule out any physical conditions, such as thyroid problems (see Chapter 6), that can have the same symptoms as AD/HD.

To find out if your family doctor can help you with AD/HD, simply ask about her view of AD/HD as a disorder and what experience she has with the condition. Some family physicians have had enough experience dealing with patients with AD/HD that they're aware of the possible treatment strategies and current medications and their efficacy.

Pediatrician

Pediatricians often diagnose and treat AD/HD in children and adolescents. In many cases, they have a great deal of experience dealing with AD/HD. However, like the family physician, a pediatrician has little time available to do extensive evaluations and follow-up.

One subspecialty to consider when identifying the right person to evaluate your child is the *developmental pediatrician*. This person involves himself in all sorts of problems with development, including behavioral problems.

Like family physicians, pediatricians do their best to treat their patients as basically healthy rather than as carriers of pathology.

Psychologist

A clinical psychologist is a mental health professional who is well-versed in mental disorders and is often an excellent choice for someone to root out a diagnosis of AD/HD. There are also educational psychologists and neuropsychologists who may have even more capacity to analyze your situation and make a thorough assessment ending in diagnosis. These specialists sometimes participate in the diagnosis but leave the treatment to the clinical psychologist and the physician.

Most independently practicing psychologists have PhDs. A psychologist isn't able to prescribe medication like a psychiatrist, so if you think you want to try medication for your symptoms, you're better off going to one of the medical doctors listed in this section — a family physician, psychiatrist, or neurologist.

Where psychologists shine is in being able to help you deal with many of the secondary symptoms and co-occurring conditions of AD/HD, such as depression and low self-esteem. (Check out Chapter 3 for more on secondary symptoms and Chapter 6 for a discussion of co-occurring conditions.) These secondary symptoms and co-occurring conditions are often more of a problem for adults and adolescents with AD/HD than the primary symptoms of inattention, impulsivity, and hyperactivity, and they can make life very difficult unless they're dealt with effectively.

Some psychologists are also up-to-date on alternative treatments, such as neurofeedback (see Chapter 12), and can help you with other life strategies that can greatly ease your symptoms and make AD/HD less of an issue in your life.

Clinical social worker

Clinical social workers (and Licensed Independent Social Workers) usually have a master's degree and specific, advanced training in psychotherapy techniques. Because they are trained in social work first, they may have unique capabilities in terms of dealing with your interactions with other people, "the system," and society. In many respects, they work in the same ways that clinical psychologists do. Again, you have to find out whether your particular social worker is familiar or experienced with AD/HD.

Because LISWs are licensed mental health professionals, they can make an official diagnosis of AD/HD.

AD/HD coach

An AD/HD coach is someone who specializes in helping you improve your functioning in the world. AD/HD coaches can come from a variety of back-grounds, including counseling, psychology, business, and mediation. No official criteria for becoming an AD/HD coach exist.

AD/HD coaches often see themselves as being action-oriented. That is, they focus on practical skills and offer support for your everyday struggles. Most AD/HD coaches don't offer any kinds of treatment other than skills training and some minor counseling, but some may have a referral network in place to help you find other types of treatments to use.

Generally, AD/HD coaches are not able to provide you with an official diagnosis and can't prescribe medication.

Psychiatrist

A psychiatrist is a medical doctor who specializes in the mind. Psychiatrists are mental health professionals specifically trained to diagnose and treat psychiatric conditions, including AD/HD. The *Diagnostic and Statistical Manual of Mental Disorders* is published by the American Psychiatric Association, so you can be sure that a psychiatrist is qualified to explore whether you have AD/HD or not. Because psychiatrists are medical doctors, they are able to prescribe medications and are often very experienced in finding the best drug for each patient.

Some psychiatrists (especially child and adolescent psychiatrists) know a lot about AD/HD, and some even know a lot about adult AD/HD. On the other hand, some psychiatrists are still skeptical about the validity of AD/HD, particularly in adults.

A psychiatric diagnosis is most often made on the basis of information the psychiatrist gathers from interviews with the patient and his or her family members. Sometimes psychiatrists obtain test results from psychologists or physiological data from laboratory tests to help make a diagnosis.

The biggest advantages of going to see a psychiatrist for AD/HD are that psychiatrists are very familiar with the medications used to treat it, and they are very familiar with — and used to treating — other mental conditions that can accompany or mimic AD/HD. As with any healthcare professional, look for a psychiatrist who has experience working with people with AD/HD.

Neurologist

A neurologist is a medical doctor who specializes in diseases of the nervous system. Neurologists tend to use physical diagnosis, brain imaging, and physiologic testing to diagnose a disorder. Because AD/HD isn't diagnosed using these methods (yet), most neurologists don't do much work with people with AD/HD.

However, exceptions certainly exist. One situation in which the neurologist may be the best choice for you is if you or any of your family members have known or suspected neurologic disorders other than AD/HD (such as seizures or inherited mental retardation). Here again, as in the case of the psychiatrist and the psychologist, you can benefit from the specialist's knowledge of similar-appearing conditions that can be caused by different mechanisms.

Neurological testing has not yet been accepted as valid in making an AD/HD diagnosis. However, more and more professionals are finding differences between the brain functions of people with and without AD/HD and are getting closer to being able to use these types of testing as a way to diagnose AD/HD and determine the best treatment for a patient. Chapter 2 has more about the role of brain imagery in AD/HD research, and Chapter 6 details how brain imaging techniques are used in diagnosing (and sometimes treating) AD/HD.

As far as treating AD/HD, a neurologist is able to prescribe medication but generally isn't very well-versed in counseling or nonconventional treatments for AD/HD. However, a good neurologist who specializes in AD/HD will have a referral network where you can find these other resources.

Neuropsychiatrist/behavioral neurologist

Two subspecialties cross the boundaries of neurology and psychiatry: the neuropsychiatrist and the behavioral neurologist. These subspecialties are similar in that they emphasize problems of behavior that are known to result from abnormal nervous system function — problems like AD/HD. If you have one of these specialists in your area, he or she may be a good choice for an evaluation. Both are MDs, so they can prescribe medication.

The only drawback to these professionals is that they are often in great demand due to their expertise, so they may not have time to manage the case after the diagnosis is made. However, they should be well-connected to a treatment team that can do the case management.

Educational diagnostician

An educational diagnostician is trained to assess learning problems in students. These professionals are required to have master's degrees and, generally, several years of teaching experience. They also need to be certified by the state. Educational diagnosticians are employed by the school district and go by different titles depending on the state you're in. They can be called *educational consultants, learning consultants,* or *learning disabilities teachers* (not to be confused with *special education teachers,* whose job is to actually teach special education classes).

Educational diagnosticians usually work in concert with school psychologists and can do a good job of identifying learning difficulties (including AD/HD) in students. You won't get much from these professionals in the way of treatment approaches, except for maybe educational strategies and recommendations for your child's *Individual Education Plan,* or IEP (which we discuss in Chapter 15). However, an educational diagnostician can be helpful in first identifying that your child may have a problem in school and can offer insight into what that problem may be.

Speech–language pathologist

A speech–language pathologist (SLP) deals with issues related to speech, language, and hearing. Because many people with AD/HD have some problem understanding verbal instructions, an SLP can be helpful in rooting out the problem and offering some treatments and life skills that can minimize this issue. SLPs are in the best position to diagnose and treat a condition known as *central auditory processing disorder,* which often mimics parts of AD/HD and sometimes accompanies it (see Chapter 6). These professionals can also be very helpful if you are dealing with language delays or dyslexia as part of the problem.

While many SLPs claim to be able to diagnose AD/HD, they aren't specifically trained to do so, and many don't look nearly as deeply into the other possible diagnoses as other mental health professionals (such as psychologists and psychiatrists) do. This doesn't mean, however, that SLPs can't offer insight into your or your child's symptoms.

Speech–language pathologists often have quite a few nonconventional treatment plans that can help people with AD/HD (or at least the symptoms of AD/HD). These treatments include vision therapies and sound therapies.

Occupational therapist

An occupational therapist (OT) is trained to help people with everyday tasks (occupations) and can often help people with AD/HD deal with the sensory issues involved with the condition. OTs can have either bachelor's or master's degrees in occupational therapy, and many have a lot of experience with AD/HD.

OTs can often diagnose AD/HD, but that diagnosis is not official. They aren't able to prescribe medication, which is alright because most OTs prefer to use techniques they have learned to deal with the symptoms of AD/HD, most notably sensory integration, vision therapies, and sound therapies (see Chapters 12 and 13).

Other professionals you may encounter

You may work with a host of other professionals when trying to get a handle on your or your child's symptoms. These include homeopaths, acupuncturists, nutritionists, and others. Each of these professionals can offer some help for some people. In Part III, we detail many of the treatment approaches that these particular professionals offer, and we give you a heads up on what each can do. These professionals can often be found in the Yellow Pages listed under the name of the discipline they practice.

Examining Your Values

When you seek professional help for diagnosis or treatment of your or your child's AD/HD-like symptoms, it can be helpful to examine what you want from your relationship with a professional. In the following sections, we help you examine your values as they relate to diagnosis and treatment of AD/HD.

Digging into your ideas about diagnosis

Because a diagnosis of AD/HD can be difficult to pinpoint, and because many conditions share the same symptoms (as we explain in Chapter 6), you really must trust yourself and your professional to be able to identify the problem. Here are some things to consider:

- ✔ **How important is an official diagnosis to you?** (See the section "Getting a diagnosis for legal purposes," earlier in this chapter.) Some people want the label to make them feel as though they've done everything possible to get the "right" diagnosis or to receive services that may be available to them. Other people are happy just having some sense of what the problem is so they can get down to the work of minimizing their symptoms and maximizing their ability to function in the world.

- ✔ **How much are you willing to do to get this diagnosis?** Depending on which professional you go to, you may encounter a simple questionnaire or a whole slew of evaluations to root out the cause of your or your child's symptoms. You can be assured that an official diagnosis requires much more documentation and evaluation than an unofficial diagnosis. (Chapter 5 covers the evaluation process in detail.)

A diagnosis is a double-edged sword. On the one hand, it can offer you peace of mind, the best place to start looking for treatment, and possibly some much-needed services for you or your child. On the other hand, some people don't want to have a label placed upon them and don't have the desire to lobby for special services. As well, some people may be tempted to use a diagnosis as an excuse for their behavior rather than as a roadmap to making changes.

Tackling your thoughts on treatment

Successful treatment of AD/HD depends largely on identifying the right treatment for a specific person. This involves not only finding the potentially most effective treatment but also finding a treatment that the patient can stand behind and give his full attention. For example, even though a particular medication may have the potential to work for someone, that potential is wasted if the med is not taken according to the schedule prescribed by the doctor.

Many parents of children with AD/HD are adamantly opposed to using medication because they're unsure of the long-term effects on the delicate nervous systems of their children and don't want to take even the remotest chance of contributing to problems later in life. As a result, some children, who could respond well to the right medication, don't have the opportunity to try it.

Likewise, many people (even some professionals) don't believe that noncon-ventional therapies can have a positive impact on the symptoms and underly-ing causes of AD/HD. As a result, they reject these therapies outright without exploring them first.

We strongly encourage you not to dismiss any possible treatment approach without having at least explored the issue with a professional who is person-ally experienced with that approach. And before you agree to a specific treat-ment plan, take the following steps:

- ✔ Find out what's expected of you as a patient (or the parent of a patient) in order for the treatment to work its best. Honestly ask yourself if you have the time, energy, and desire to follow the necessary protocol.

- ✔ Make sure you understand the side effects of any treatment plan before starting it.

- ✔ Make sure your expectations for the outcome of the treatment plan are realistic.

Evaluating Your AD/HD Professional

When you choose a healthcare professional to work with, you invest a lot of time and effort in this relationship. Therefore, it's very important to find a professional whose experience, approaches, and beliefs fit with your needs and expectations. One way to determine the fit of a healthcare provider is to interview that person first. The following sections suggest some questions that you can ask a prospective professional.

Selecting a diagnostician

When you look for a professional to help you weed through the diagnostic process, here are some recommendations for finding the right person:

- ✔ **Take an active role in the diagnostic process.** Educate yourself (as you're doing by reading this book) about AD/HD and similar conditions, and come to your first meeting with a potential diagnostician armed with any questions you have.

- ✔ **Ask the professional you're considering how involved she wants to get in the diagnostic process.** In order to be relatively sure about the diagnosis, the evaluation needs to be fairly in-depth. The problem is that performing in-depth evaluations takes time and can cost a lot of money. Even if your insurance covers the cost of your evaluations, you don't want to have a more lengthy assessment procedure than necessary. On the other hand, some cases are a lot more complicated than others, and you don't want to quit the evaluation before the diagnostician knows what is going on.

An ethical diagnostician will use a "take it one step at a time" approach and perform only those evaluations that she deems necessary in order to root out the problem. This is where the information in Chapter 5 can come in handy; it lays out the process of evaluation so that you can go to a professional with a clear understanding of what to expect.

After you select a diagnostician, ask her to keep you informed about any diagnosis she makes and who this information is being shared with (such as your insurance company).

Partnering up for treatment

You may want to use the same professional to treat you as you did to diagnose your AD/HD, or you may decide to work with someone new. Either way, you can get a glimpse into a professional's treatment philosophy by asking a few simple questions:

- **What is your professional experience and training?** Knowing the educational and professional background of a professional can help you determine whether this person can offer you the service you require. For example, at the beginning of this chapter we jokingly stated that you could go to a dermatologist for treatment, but he probably doesn't have the skills to treat your AD/HD. As well, the experience and background of your professional will likely inform you about the types of treatment approaches that he can offer.

- **How do you generally treat people with AD/HD?** Expect a long answer here — one that essentially says, "It depends on the patient." Most healthcare providers have a few treatment approaches that are first on their list to try. Some prescribe medications, some look toward diet, and some use treatments such as sound therapies or neurofeedback (see Chapter 12). And some offer all these treatment options. Choose a professional who has an open mind and is willing to think outside the box.

- **Can you recommend other professionals for different treatments?** Most providers have a referral network of professionals who specialize in different treatments than the ones they typically use. The best professionals have the most complete lists and freely share this information while offering guidance along the way.

✔ **What if a treatment fails?** One reality of trying to treat AD/HD is that not everything works for every person, so you're going to have to make adjustments along the way in order to find the right combination of approaches for your situation. Knowing up front how to deal with these minor setbacks can keep your relationship with your provider on the right track.

Here are some other things to consider when choosing a healthcare provider:

✔ **Does your provider show up on time?** If you arrive on time for your appointment but have to wait a long time to be seen, that doesn't reflect very well on how the provider views you as a patient. A single instance is one thing — it could just be one of those days — but a pattern of running late speaks volumes about how the doctor values your time.

Some doctors, like other people, have trouble managing their time. They may be in the habit of spending extra time with all their patients, so don't be offended until you have some idea of what is going on. And be sure to extend the same courtesy to your provider as you would have him extend to you — show up on time and prepared for your appointments.

✔ **Is she respectful to you by listening to your questions and concerns and giving them the weight that you feel they deserve?** Good healthcare providers take the time to answer your questions and alleviate your concerns rather than brushing right past them.

✔ **How does your provider's staff treat you?** If staff members are impolite, or if all they're concerned about is how you're going to pay, this is a red flag. You should be treated with respect and politeness.

✔ **Do you feel comfortable with your provider?** Your provider could be the most qualified professional in the world, but if you're not comfortable in her presence, you probably won't get the most out of the relationship. Trust your gut (assuming it's trustworthy), and let that instinct rule over any intellectual reasons to use that provider.

Getting a Second Opinion

The AD/HD diagnosis is similar to that of other mental health conditions, such as anxiety and depression: It has its limitations. As we say many times in this book, there is no way to absolutely, positively determine whether someone has AD/HD — there is only a best guess based upon the information gathered. This best-guess basis will likely change as physiological testing procedures mature (which we discuss in Chapter 5).

As things stand now — before the magic physical test for AD/HD appears — the quality of your diagnosis is based upon the skills of your evaluator and the depths into which you and your caregiver dig while looking for an answer.

For most people, the first diagnosis they receive is usually sufficient to steer them in the best direction for treatment; even with a cursory evaluation, you may gain enough knowledge to get the help you need. Other people may find that their first diagnosis was inaccurate enough that they weren't able to find a treatment plan that worked. Or they may decide, after receiving an unofficial diagnosis, that they want a more detailed evaluation to make a diagnosis official in the eyes of their insurance company or child's school. In these cases, a second opinion and further evaluation are good ideas.

The primary reason for getting an official diagnosis is to be able to receive services, either in the form of insurance coverage or school support such as Individual Education Plans (see Chapter 15) for your child. We discuss these topics in the section "Being Eligible for Services" at the end of this chapter.

Managing Your Care

When you begin treating the symptoms of your or your child's AD/HD, you'll most likely work with more than one professional. In fact, we're willing to bet that you'll end up working with several people, each of whom will deal with different aspects of your care. For example, you may use your family doctor to handle your medications, a nutritionist to help you develop the best diet to minimize your symptoms, and a psychologist to help you deal with the secondary symptoms (such as low self-esteem). You may also have additional therapists for specific treatments, such as neurofeedback or sound therapies.

Keeping track of all these professionals and varying treatment plans is your responsibility — even if you hire a professional to help with this task — and it can require significant time and energy. The easiest way to manage your care is to document everything about each treatment you try. (Check out this book's appendix for a form for tracking your treatments.) Keep track of the following types of information:

- **The date the treatment started and ended:** This way, when you reflect on what changes you saw and how you felt at a certain time, you can see at a glance what you were doing.

- **The exact protocol of the treatment approach:** This is especially important for medications. You want to know how much you used and when.

✔ **The professional you saw:** It's important to keep all the professional contacts you've made handy because chances are that you'll encounter a lot of people while you seek out treatments that work. You can easily forget specifics about each person. Having an accurate record (including how you felt about this professional) can keep you from covering the same ground more than once.

✔ **The results you observed while trying each treatment program:** This includes both the good and the bad. This is probably the most important thing to keep track of. Having a detailed record of the effects of the various treatment plans you've tried offers invaluable information, not only to keep you from repeating an unsuccessful treatment but also to offer insights as to how new treatments may work.

✔ **What other treatments were going on at the same time:** Most of the time, you'll have more than one treatment happening at once. Perhaps you're trying nutrition and medication, sound therapies and homeopathics, or some other combination. Keeping track of overlapping treatments can help you avoid treatment combinations that don't work well together.

Be sure to share this information with the different professionals you work with; that way, they can design a treatment program around the other things you're doing or can advise you against trying one treatment while doing another. This information is especially important to share when you are taking medications. When you start making changes to your treatments, adjust one variable at a time instead of changing everything at once. This makes it easier for you to keep track of what works and what doesn't.

✔ **Why you stopped:** Sometimes you stop a treatment because the protocol for it has ended; certain treatments, such as the REI therapy program we describe in Chapter 12, are time-limited. Other times you may stop because the treatment isn't working, such as if you try a medication that has too many side effects.

Being Eligible for Services

As we note earlier in the chapter (see the section "Getting a diagnosis for legal purposes"), the main reason to receive an official diagnosis of AD/HD is to be eligible for services from your insurance company or your child's school.

Examining your insurance coverage

Some insurance providers cover AD/HD diagnosis and certain types of treatment — usually medication and counseling to some extent. To find out whether diagnosis or treatment is covered by your insurance company, you must contact your provider. Following are some things to consider when dealing with insurance and AD/HD (or any other mental disorder, for that matter):

- ✔ **How much coverage do you have for mental illnesses?** It is good to know which diagnostic and treatment services are covered and what to expect from your insurance company. Depending on your level of coverage, you may not receive many benefits, and you may be better off staying out of the system and paying out of pocket.

- ✔ **What types of treatments are covered by your insurance plan?** Many insurance plans cover only certain types of treatments, such as medication and a limited number of counseling sessions. You may find that you're not covered for the types of treatments you want to try. In this situation, you're probably better off not making a claim.

- ✔ **How does your insurance company classify AD/HD?** With some insurance companies, the classification of AD/HD carries less weight (and allows for fewer services) than a diagnosis of anxiety disorder, for instance.

- ✔ **How comfortable are you with having a label that will be permanently attached to your medical file?** After you file a claim with your insurance and have a diagnosis of AD/HD, this diagnosis becomes part of your permanent medical record. It's very hard (almost impossible, in fact) to have this diagnosis changed or removed. This label moves from insurance company to insurance company if you change policyholders.

- ✔ **How will filing a claim affect your insurance premiums and future eligibility if you change insurance plans?** Okay, we don't expect you to know this or even be able to find out. But we believe it can be a factor for many people, so it's worth considering before you make a claim on your insurance. Sometimes flying below the insurance company's radar can have benefits down the road.

Seeking out school services

Although we discuss school services for children diagnosed with AD/HD in detail in Chapter 15, we want to briefly mention how these services relate to the diagnosis you receive from your chosen healthcare professional. School services usually take the form of a *Section 504 plan* (accommodations under the Americans with Disabilities Act) or an *Individual Education Plan* (for children in need of special education due to a specific learning disability or behavioral disorder).

Before a school will even consider offering services for your child, you need to have an evaluation conducted by the school — usually from the school's educational diagnostician — or a complete diagnosis from either a psychologist or psychiatrist. (What constitutes "complete" in the eyes of a school varies from district to district.) Even with a psychologist's or psychiatrist's diagnosis, you probably still need to go through the school's evaluation process before it will recognize AD/HD in your child.

After the school acknowledges AD/HD in your child, you still need to petition for services for your child; these services are not guaranteed. Some schools bend over backward to help their AD/HD students; others don't. To be eligible for services, you must have a "proven" need for the services beyond the diagnosis. And guess who decides whether you need these services or not? Yep, you guessed it — your child's school.

This situation presents a potential conflict of interest because it costs the school money to put a child in the Individual Education Plan process. On the other hand, public schools get federal money to keep children in special education, and most schools nowadays are constantly short of money for these services. Your backup in dealing with resistant schools is the state board of education and the federal disability law (see Chapter 15).

If you want school services for your child, you may have a long and difficult battle to get them. Chapter 15 can help you with the process. You can also check out www.wrightslaw.com for information on receiving services for your AD/HD child.

Chapter 5

Navigating the Evaluation Process

In This Chapter

▶ Looking at psychiatric/psychological assessments

▶ Anticipating medical tests

▶ Discovering a variety of educational tests

▶ Finding out about functional tests

▶ Examining physiological evaluations

As we discuss in Chapter 4, AD/HD evaluations can be as simple as a single questionnaire and an interview that takes only a few minutes, or they can involve an elaborate series of tests that takes many hours to complete. The intricacy of your evaluation process depends largely on the professional you choose, the degree and makeup of your symptoms, and the depths to which you and your healthcare provider decide to go in assessing your condition.

This chapter lays out the full-blown (and then some) evaluation process for rooting out the cause of your or your child's symptoms. We explore the many types of assessments that an AD/HD professional may use to determine if you have the condition, including psychiatric/psychological evaluations, educational assessments, performance tests, and physiological tests. You probably won't have to endure all the different tests and diagnostic procedures that we cover in this chapter, but most likely you'll experience at least one in your quest to understand the reason for your particular symptoms.

Preparing for the Evaluation Process

When you hire a healthcare provider to conduct an evaluation on you or your child, you should be skillfully guided through the process. But it's important to remember that you're still half the partnership. In order to have a successful experience that causes as little stress as possible, you can do some things to prepare for your appointment.

Following are suggestions of things to do before your appointment to help the process move as quickly and smoothly as possible:

✔ **Write down any questions or concerns you have about the evaluation process and its eventual outcome.** Take this list with you because you'll likely forget these questions when you walk into the diagnostician's office.

✔ **Bring the results of any questionnaires you may have previously taken.** Doing so may shorten the evaluation process if the questionnaire is something your provider is familiar with.

✔ **Make a list of any allergies you have, all of your current and past medical conditions, and medications that you're taking or have taken in the past.** If you go to your family physician for an evaluation, you may not need to take this step if your doctor already has this information in your file.

✔ **Make a list of foods you commonly eat and any connections you've seen between these foods and your symptoms.**

✔ **Write down when you first noticed symptoms and how these symptoms have changed over time.**

✔ **Think about any strategies or coping mechanisms you've developed to help you deal with your symptoms.**

✔ **Make a note of any times that your symptoms seem to get better or worse.**

Be sure to arrive on time for your appointment and to bring these various pieces of information with you. When you're at your appointment, you can do a few things to help move the process along:

✔ **Be attentive when your provider is talking.** Depending on the level of your AD/HD symptoms, this may be difficult. If you know that you struggle in this type of situation, ask your provider if you can take notes or record what he says for later review.

✔ **Don't be afraid to assert yourself during the appointment.** It's often easy to give your power to a professional and have her control the direction of the conversation. If you have something to add during the conversation, speak up (politely). This helps keep the appointment going in the best direction and helps your provider to better understand you and your symptoms.

✔ **Reassure yourself that the appointment is necessary.** Cold feet are common at the first few appointments. Thoughts like "I'm fine, I'm just imagining my symptoms" are sure to pop into your mind as you're sitting in your first appointment. Trust that you made the appointment after careful consideration, and the appointment is important. You can assess the need for additional appointments after you've finished with the first one.

✔ **Be open and honest with your provider.** Without honesty about your experiences, behavior, and feelings, your provider can't get a clear picture of who you are or the challenges you live with.

AD/HD evaluations don't yet include a bullet-proof physiological test. (Notice we say *yet.*) However, with the interpretation of a skilled professional, the assessments that we list in the chapter can offer a pretty clear picture of what's going on and provide direction to help minimize the difficulties that you deal with in your life.

An adequate evaluation includes several different sources of information — for instance, home and school behavior, and performance reports. Also, the more professionals who assess your condition, the greater the likelihood of receiving an accurate diagnosis.

Psychiatric/Psychological Evaluations

Your first step in determining if you or someone you love has AD/HD is to do a mental health evaluation. This step usually involves completing a fairly simple questionnaire where you score your symptoms, rating them from being nonexistent to severe.

There are about as many AD/HD questionnaires available as there are people giving these questionnaires, but all of them use the basic criteria for AD/HD as outlined in the American Psychiatric Association's *Diagnostic and Statistical Manual for Mental Disorders* (DSM-IV). A few standardized questionnaires seem to be used over and over again in research arenas. The advantage of these questionnaires is that they are more scientifically developed than some simple questionnaires.

The most commonly used psychiatric/psychological rating scales include:

✔ **Conners' rating scales:** Several Conners' rating scales exist for both adults and children. The most widely used are:

  • **Conners' Rating Scales — Revised (CRS-R):** These rating scales are for children 3 to 17 years old. Children ages 12 to 17 complete the form themselves using the *Adolescent Self-Report Scales (CASS)*. Younger kids are scaled by a parent using the *Parent Rating Scales — Revised (CPRS-R)* or by a teacher using the *Teacher Rating Scales — Revised (CTRS-R)*. It takes only a few minutes to complete these forms.

- **Conners' Adult ADHD Rating Scales (CAARS):** These scales for adults come in three varieties: long, short, and screening. The long version has 66 items, the short form has 26, and the screening scale has 12. These scales are completed either by the person who may have AD/HD or someone close to that person, and they take only a few minutes to do.

✔ **Wender Utah Rating Scale (WURS):** This 61-question scale is used for adults and is commonly used in research.

✔ **ADD-H Comprehensive Teacher/Parent Rating Scales (ACTeRS):** This rating scale for adolescents and adults consists of 35 items that can be completed by the person thought to have AD/HD or by an observer. This form takes 5 to 10 minutes to complete.

Aside from evaluating your answers to these questionnaires, your healthcare provider must look at your past as well as your present behaviors in order to make a diagnosis. This makes it difficult to walk into a psychiatrist's office, have someone give you the once-over, and walk out with a diagnosis. So expect to spend a good deal of time talking with your healthcare provider about your (or your child's) past behaviors, academic performance, and social relationships.

For adults, the past can be a bit fuzzy; it's often helpful for an adult to have a close family member or friend offer his or her views because adults with AD/HD sometimes don't recognize their symptoms. If a child is being evaluated, the situation may be easier; parents often remember details of their child's behavior during the few years that can offer insights into the background of the symptoms.

Keep in mind that a questionnaire cannot rule out other conditions that share the basic symptoms of AD/HD. For details about these conditions, see Chapter 6.

Medical Testing

As we discuss in Chapter 6, some medical conditions share many symptoms with AD/HD. To determine whether one of these conditions is the cause of your symptoms or if you, in fact, have AD/HD, you may have to go through some medical tests, including tests for the following conditions:

✔ Lead poisoning

✔ Thyroid dysfunction

✔ Allergies or sensitivities

✔ Brain tumor

✔ Traumatic brain injury (including birth trauma)

✔ Connective tissue diseases

✔ Tourette's syndrome

✔ Fragile X

✔ Asperger's syndrome

Your healthcare professional will not need to order all these tests for you. Many of these conditions are very rare (such as a brain tumor), but they do need to be at least considered before making a final determination that you have AD/HD.

Educational Testing

Educational testing involves some sort of intelligence test and, for children, evaluations to check for age-appropriate functioning. These tests have less to do with trying to root out the symptoms of AD/HD than with evaluating the patient's intellectual functioning in terms of potential, balance, and performance in relation to potential. These measurements help to assess the likelihood of other causes of the symptoms, such as learning disabilities or medical conditions like brain damage.

Literally dozens of different intelligence tests are used, but the most common seem to be the following:

✔ **Kaufman intelligence tests:** Two types of Kaufman intelligence tests are used, depending on the age of the person being tested. These are:

- **Kaufman Brief Intelligence Test (K-BIT):** For ages 4 and up, this test quickly assesses verbal and nonverbal skills using two subtests. This test, like its name implies, takes very little time — only 15 to 30 minutes — and offers a pretty good assessment of your intelligence.

- **Kaufman Adolescent and Adult Intelligence Test (KAIT):** This test is more involved than the K-BIT and consists of two levels: the core battery and the expanded battery. The core battery takes about 60 minutes to complete, while the expanded battery takes 90 minutes. This test is designed for people 11 years old and up.

✔ **Wechsler intelligence tests:** There are three types of Wechsler tests, each for a different age group. These tests are:

- **Wechsler Preschool and Primary Scale of Intelligence — Revised (WPPSI-R):** This test is used for children ages 4 to 6½ and is designed to measure cognitive abilities. The WPPSI-R consists of 11 subtests that evaluate both performance and verbal abilities. This test takes between 50 and 75 minutes to complete.

- **Wechsler Intelligence Scale for Children (WISC):** This test is for children ages 7 to 16 and consists of six verbal and five performance subtests. The test takes 60 to 90 minutes to complete. This test scores for verbal and performance IQs, as well as a full-scale IQ based on these two results.

- **Wechsler Adult Intelligence Scale (WAIS):** This test is designed for people 16 and older. This test evaluates performance and verbal abilities using 11 subtests to determine verbal IQ, performance IQ, and full-scale (combined) IQ. This test takes about 60 to 90 minutes to complete.

✔ **Woodcock–Johnson III (WJ III):** This test consists of two sections — achievement and cognitive — covering academic achievement, general intellectual ability, oral language, scholastic aptitude, and specific cognitive abilities. This test is used for people ages 2 and up. Each subtest takes about 5 minutes to complete. The cognitive section contains 7 subtests (totaling about 35 minutes), while the achievement section consists of 11 subtests (totaling about 55 minutes).

All of these tests are commonly conducted by psychologists and educational diagnosticians. If you work with an educational diagnostician (see Chapter 4), keep in mind that you'll likely have to wait a while in order to get the school to schedule this type of test.

Making sense out of the results of educational tests takes some skill. These aren't tests that you can do at home in order to score yourself; you need a trained professional to score them for you. Fortunately, anyone who offers these tests has also been trained to interpret them properly and can offer guidance for what to do after you receive your score.

Skills Testing

Skills testing involves both motor and cognitive skills, including social skills. Motor skills evaluations are usually carried out by physical or occupational therapists. Cognitive skills may be assessed by speech–language pathologists or educational diagnosticians.

Social skills can be evaluated by psychologists or counselors who have expertise in social skills training. Some standard rating scales are used for this type of evaluation, including:

✔ **Novotni Social Skills Checklist:** This scale is available in two forms: the self-report version and the observer report version. These scales are used for adolescents and adults.

✔ **Reynolds Adolescent Adjustment Screening Inventory (RAASI):** This scale contains 32 items in 4 categories for 12- to 19-year-olds.

Behavioral Assessment

Behavioral assessments involve observation by a trained behavioral specialist. There are different protocols and methods for this evaluation, some of them more formalized than others. Often, a behavioral assessment is included in the academic/educational testing evaluation done by a school. Professionals use many standardized tests, the most common being:

✓ **Child Behavior Checklist for Ages 6–18 (CBCL/6–18):** This checklist is for children ages 6 to 18 and consists of 118 items. This scale is completed by a parent or close relative.

✓ **Adult Behavior Checklist for Ages 18–59 (ABCL):** This checklist is completed by a loved one of the person thought to have behavior problems and takes about 15 minutes to complete.

✓ **Child Behavior Checklist/1½–5 (CBCL/1½–5):** This checklist is for children ages 1½ to 5 years old and is completed by a caregiver.

Performance Testing

Performance testing involves assessing your ability to maintain attention. This assessment is usually done using a continuous performance test (CPT). CPTs are performed on a computer where the test-taker is instructed to respond to a repetitive and boring stimulus by either pressing or not pressing a key on the computer's keyboard in response to an image on the screen. Because this task is boring and repetitive, it requires sustained attention and control over impulsivity — both areas in which people with AD/HD have difficulties. Common CPT tests include the following:

✓ **Conners' CPTs:** The Conners' CPTs are available in two varieties covering different age groups. Each test assesses attention by using letters (CPT-II) or images (k-CPT):

  • **CPT-II:** This test takes 14 minutes to complete and is used for people 6 years old and up.

  • **K-CPT:** This test is for 4- and 5-year-olds and takes only 7 minutes to complete.

✓ **Integrated Visual and Auditory (IVA) CPT:** This test measures and evaluates both auditory and visual inattention and impulsivity. This test takes 20 minutes to complete and is designed for people ages 6 and up.

✓ **Test of Variables of Attention (TOVA):** This test for people ages 4 and up consists of two subtests — one focusing on visual processing and the other on auditory processing. This test takes between 11 minutes (for 4- and 5-year-olds) and 22 minutes (for ages 6 and up) to complete.

Physiological Testing

As far as we're concerned, physiological testing is the future of psychiatric diagnosis. Some clinicians are already using these types of tests, but so far there haven't been enough replicated studies to make this a widely accepted means to identify AD/HD. The following sections examine many of the current brain imaging approaches that are being used and how these different devices may fit in the future of physiological AD/HD testing.

EEG

Electroencephalogram (EEG) technology has been around for decades and consists of measurements of electrical activity in the brain, known as *brain waves*. These brain waves change when brain activity changes. The more activity in the brain, the faster the brain waves are; the lower the activity, the slower the brain waves are. EEG tracks only surface activity and can't see deep into the brain.

These brain waves are measured by placing electrodes on a person's scalp and sending the signal picked up by these electrodes to a device that amplifies the signal. The data can then be fed into a computer for viewing and analysis.

So far, research done with people with AD/HD suggests that there is an increase in slower, larger waves in certain parts of the brain when these people try to concentrate. (Chapter 2 covers some of the research done in this regard.) People without AD/HD tend to produce a different spectrum of activity in the same part of the brain when they concentrate. As a diagnostic tool, EEG can offer some guidance, but there really haven't been enough studies by enough different organizations to determine with certainty whether this lower level of activity observed is consistent with all people with AD/HD or just a certain percentage of them.

EEG is used quite a bit for treating AD/HD using a technique called *neurofeedback*. We cover this treatment approach in detail in Chapter 12.

ERP

This test consists of attaching the electrodes of the EEG device to your scalp, introducing a stimulus, and recording the changes in the brain's activity. This stimulus is repeated many times (up to 200), and then the signal from the brain is averaged. Taking multiple readings cancels out any background activity in the brain, leaving you with a discrete signal that's related to the stimulus event. This signal is called the *event-related potential* (ERP).

One of the ERPs that is looked for in people with AD/HD is called the *P-300,* and it happens about 300 milliseconds after the stimulus event. ERPs can also be used to help evaluate other conditions, such as primary reading difficulties or other learning disabilities.

MRI

Magnetic resonance imaging (MRI) uses a magnetic field to view the anatomy of the brain. MRI scans are useful for looking at the structure of the brain but don't actually record brain activity — they create only a static image. This isn't necessarily a bad thing because some studies have shown that slight differences in the size of certain parts of the brain exist in people with AD/HD compared to people without it. However, no standard of clinical diagnosis is in place yet for these measurements; in other words, these size differences are still under investigation.

The main problem with using MRI as a diagnostic device — aside from the static image it generates — is that the MRI machine is very noisy, and it takes a long time to get an image. While the image is being created, the patient is not able to move. Add to that the fact that they're stuck in a small space, and the testing process can get uncomfortable fast.

fMRI

Functional magnetic resonance imaging (fMRI) is like MRI on steroids with bifocals. Functional MRI can assess brain activity. This makes it much more useful for examining people with AD/HD because you can see what changes occur when someone is forced to concentrate.

The problem with fMRI, as with regular MRI, is that the device is loud, the space confining, and the time to get an image long. For now, fMRI devices likely won't be used clinically for people with AD/HD — the technology is still too new. Better diagnostic options are available, such as EEG and SPECT.

PET

Positron emission tomography (PET) detects the presence and movement of radioactive substances that are injected into the patient. As these substances travel to the brain, the PET device produces images of the brain, showing blood flow and glucose metabolism, which in turn offer information about the level of activity in the various parts of the brain. PET is part of a field called *nuclear medicine* and is being used in many areas to try to better understand how the brain functions. An advantage of PET over EEG, which also shows brain activity, is that PET scans can look deep into the brain, whereas EEG can view only surface activity.

PET scans offer medium- to high-quality images and provide invaluable information about activity in the brain. The problems are that PET scans are expensive, and the images take quite a while to capture. As with the MRI, the person being scanned has to sit completely still while the image is captured. This can take a while, and, for people with AD/HD, this time can be excruciating. In spite of this, there is a growing body of PET scan data about how people with AD/HD metabolize glucose when they try to concentrate.

The first PET study on people with AD/HD was done in 1990. This study showed that people with AD/HD experience reduced activity in the frontal lobes when they try to concentrate.

SPECT

Like PET, single photon emission computed tomography (SPECT) is a form of nuclear medicine, but SPECT is a little lower tech. SPECT still uses radioactive substances that are injected into the patient's arm, but these substances are less radioactive than those used for PET scans. Also, the SPECT device costs much less than a PET device and is easier to use. Although the images created by the SPECT device aren't as detailed as those from a PET device, they are clear enough to accurately assess blood flow and activity patterns.

SPECT imagery is being used extensively by some clinicians in the United States. Clinical SPECT studies have shown what other brain imaging devices have indicated: decreased activity in the frontal lobes when people with AD/HD try to concentrate. (Other anomalies appear as well.) Research by one prominent psychiatrist, Daniel Amen, MD, has also suggested that several variations in brain activity exist, depending on the type of AD/HD a person has.

Because of the degree of awareness this technique has gained over the last few years, we expect that you'll see more clinicians and diagnosticians using SPECT devices in their practices. The primary obstacle holding back SPECT imaging for the diagnosis of AD/HD at this time — similar to many of the other brain imaging devices — is the lack of third-party research validating the results of the few clinical studies that have been done.

Knowing What to Do after Diagnosis

Most people are somewhat relieved after they receive a diagnosis of AD/HD, if for no other reason than they feel like they finally have some sense of why things are the way they are. Even though on one hand you may be excited and relieved to finally have a diagnosis, on the other hand being slapped with a label can be somewhat disconcerting. This conflict is common and is something worth talking about with your therapist.

Ideally, after you finish your evaluations, you and your diagnostician should discuss what the results mean and examine some strategies to deal with your symptoms. Along with diagnosis often comes the first in what may be a long line of treatment plans. Most effective treatments for AD/HD involve a number of different types of approaches — some biological, some psychological, some social (see Chapter 7). The best treatments also are tailored to your particular needs and goals and are modified as those needs and goals change. Part III of this book deals with a variety of AD/HD treatment options.

You'll almost certainly run into some dead ends when you start trying to tackle the symptoms that caused you to seek professional help. Here are some things to keep in mind after you've received your diagnosis:

- ✔ **Don't feel rushed into any particular treatment plan.** You've lived a long time with your symptoms and can get by for a little while longer. Take whatever time you need to explore and understand everything involved in each treatment being offered, as well as what results you can expect, before you make a commitment to doing it.

- ✔ **Trust your instincts about a treatment approach.** If it doesn't feel right, don't do it — or at least request further explanations until you are satisfied that the treatment is something worth trying. On the other hand, if a particular approach seems to fit for you, don't be afraid to give something a try. No single treatment works for everyone; what works for someone else may not work for you, and what didn't work for someone else may make a big difference for you.

- ✔ **Be careful not to take on too many treatments at once.** You may feel like trying everything in the hopes that at least one treatment will work for you. This is okay, but don't do them all at the same time. Make a plan, and methodically work through the different treatments until you find the right balance. This allows you to keep better track of what works and what doesn't.

- ✔ **Disclose all treatments you're doing with each of your providers.** They need to be aware of any potential conflicts between therapies. This is especially true when you start mixing medications, diet, and other therapies that change your chemical makeup.

- ✔ **Allow yourself time to acclimate to the new you — the one with an official-sounding label.** Chances are you'll experience quite a few conflicting emotions about your new status. These can include (but aren't limited to) the following:

  - • **Relief:** Many people are glad to finally have a way to understand their symptoms and feel validation for the difficulties they go through.

  - • **Regret:** For older people, regret is a common feeling because of all the time they lost not knowing what was wrong.

- **Anger:** Some people feel anger because of what they've lost out on as a result of their symptoms.

- **Grief:** Grief is common when confronting the losses many people feel over the effects of their symptoms on their lives.

- **Hope:** After people get past the other emotions, they often come to a place of hope in being able to minimize their symptoms (through treatment) and maximize their strengths.

You need time to process all these emotions. Talk with people you trust who can offer perspective and help you move through these emotions, such as close friends, family members, or a qualified therapist.

Chapter 6

Conditions That Look Like or Overlap with AD/HD

*I*n this chapter, we outline disorders or conditions that can mimic AD/HD or that can accompany AD/HD symptoms. When you (or your child or loved one) go to a professional for an AD/HD evaluation (which we discuss in Chapter 5), these conditions should be considered as well. Around 75 to 80 percent of people with AD/HD also have one or more of these other conditions.

We start this chapter by explaining how a professional properly diagnoses AD/HD and similar conditions. The process of sorting through all the possible causes a group of symptoms can come from is called *differential diagnosis,* and this is what you are really asking a professional to do when you go for an evaluation.

The bulk of this chapter details conditions that can imitate AD/HD and explains why one of these conditions may be a more appropriate diagnosis for you.

Understanding Differential Diagnosis

One of the most difficult aspects of diagnosing AD/HD is weeding through what is called the *differential diagnosis.* This is industry-speak for "conditions that may be more appropriate for the person than the one you're currently considering."

When you see a mental health professional for your AD/HD-type symptoms, your professional also considers other causes for the symptoms that you're experiencing. This procedure ensures that the person making the diagnosis doesn't just assume that you have AD/HD when there is a better explanation available. The professional must consider many other conditions, including quite a few mental disorders, a handful of medical conditions, and a few conditions not necessarily recognized by the medical community that have the same basic symptoms as AD/HD.

Your mental health professional follows specific steps in making a diagnosis and ruling out conditions similar to AD/HD. These steps include:

1. **Discovering the symptoms comprising the main complaint.**

2. **Discovering secondary symptoms.**

3. **Exploring these symptoms in sufficient depth to evaluate their significance: when they started, how severe they are, and so on.**

4. **Making a mental list of all the conditions your professional knows about that are characterized by these main symptoms.** This list can get long, but most experienced professionals can narrow the list down pretty quickly.

5. **Asking about other information — symptoms or past events — that may suggest support for one or more possible diagnoses.**

6. **Narrowing the list down and prioritizing the related conditions according to the hierarchy of the symptoms and how they show up in different conditions.** Most likely your professional will have more than one possible condition in this list.

It's highly likely that you'll end up with a multifaceted diagnosis because your symptoms aren't easy to categorize and the many similar conditions overlap considerably. You may be told that you have elements of various conditions without receiving a clear diagnosis of any one condition. In fact, so much overlap exists that we believe in the future some of these conditions will merge and morph into new versions with new names.

How can you tell the difference between the many conditions we list in this chapter? You may not be able to — the differences are subtle, and all the symptoms are simply deviations on what's considered "normal." A good professional, however, often has enough experience to understand the subtleties and commonalities of the many conditions and will likely be able to recognize the core issues well enough to develop a treatment plan that works.

Looking at Conditions with Symptoms Similar to AD/HD

The basic symptoms of AD/HD — inattention, distraction, impulsivity, and hyperactivity — can be seen in other conditions. Not all of these other conditions are mental disorders; some are medical conditions, some are sensory processing disorders, and one is referred to as *pseudo-AD/HD*. In the sections that follow, we explore these other conditions in detail.

Mental disorders

According to the *Diagnostic and Statistical Manual for Mental Disorders* (DSM-IV), several mental disorders have features similar to AD/HD. We discuss each in the following sections.

Anxiety disorders

If you have an anxiety disorder, you have a significant, persistent fear or worry that occupies your mind and is difficult to control. Several types of anxiety disorders exist, but here are the three most common with symptoms similar to AD/HD:

- **Generalized anxiety disorder:** In a generalized anxiety disorder, the anxiety encompasses everyday events and issues, such as your job, finances, the health and safety of your family members, and minor things like appointments and household tasks.

- **Specific phobia:** A specific phobia is anxiety centered around a specific thing, such as heights, flying, or animals.

- **Social phobia:** A social phobia is fear of social interactions and the fear that you'll be embarrassed or humiliated around others.

Many people with these forms of anxiety disorders experience the AD/HD-like symptoms of restlessness, hyperactivity, impulsivity, excessive talking, scattered thinking, and forgetfulness. In addition, if you have an anxiety disorder, you may also experience fatigue, muscle tension, irritability, palpitations, sleep disturbance, dry mouth, abnormal sweating, and stomach upset.

What distinguishes these symptoms from the same symptoms in people with AD/HD is that in anxiety disorders the symptoms come and go with the anxiety (unless you have generalized anxiety disorder that is present all the time). When the anxiety itself isn't present, these symptoms generally disappear, whereas in AD/HD these symptoms remain relatively constant.

Many people with AD/HD also have some sort of anxiety, some to the degree that would constitute an anxiety disorder. If this is the case, you'll likely get a dual diagnosis — one of both AD/HD and an anxiety disorder.

Obsessive-compulsive disorder

Although obsessive-compulsive disorder (OCD) is technically a form of anxiety disorder, it occurs so frequently that we think it deserves its own separate heading. OCD is characterized by the following symptoms:

- **Recurrent anxiety-producing thoughts:** These thoughts are often ritualistic in nature, meaning that you feel driven to follow them over and over or are unable to get them out of your mind. As a result, these thoughts interfere with your daily life.

- **Persistent repetitive actions:** These behaviors are ritualistic in nature and often involve things such as frequent hand-washing that get in the way of your everyday life.

Many people with OCD also have symptoms similar to AD/HD, such as restlessness, problems with concentration, forgetfulness, and hyperactivity.

The key aspect that separates OCD from AD/HD is that the AD/HD-like symptoms are overshadowed by the obsessive or compulsive thoughts and behaviors. Many people with AD/HD also have OCD, and vice versa. These two disorders may be closely related biologically. They tend to run in the same families.

Bipolar disorder

Bipolar disorder, which is also called *manic-depressive disorder*, is similar to depression (which we discuss in the next section) except instead of just feeling down, you also have periods when you feel excessively up. Following are the two sides of bipolar disorder and their symptoms:

- **Depressive state:** The basic symptoms for people in this state are lack of interest in everyday things, profound sadness, fatigue, insomnia, or an excessive need for sleep. When you're in the depressive state, you also show symptoms similar to AD/HD, such as inattention, loss of concentration, distractibility, forgetfulness, and restlessness.

- **Manic state:** The manic state has the basic symptoms of inflated self-esteem, lack of sleep, excessive irritability, excessive talking, and goal-oriented focusing. (Sometimes irritability is the most pronounced symptom.) The symptoms of mania that are similar to AD/HD include hyperactivity, impulsiveness, and distractibility. This manic state generally lasts at least a week, but so-called *hypo-mania* (which is not quite as intense) can last from one or two days up to months at a time.

Over the last few years, bipolar disorder has been increasingly recognized in children. One of the main differences that seems to exist between AD/HD and childhood bipolar disorder is aggression. Bipolar kids are thought to be more prone to fighting and irritability in general. Also, their moods seem to be somewhat cyclic. However, one type of bipolar disorder called *rapid-cycling* can show changes in mood and activity levels on a daily, or even an hourly, basis.

Bipolar patients can have all the characteristics of AD/HD. Several studies of bipolar adults showed that more than 70 percent of them also qualified for the diagnosis of AD/HD. This is a conundrum that has yet to be worked out by the experts. Most likely, bipolar disorder and AD/HD are biologically related.

Depression

Depression is a very common disorder — more common, in fact, than AD/HD. Depression has the following basic symptoms:

- Depressed mood
- Lack of interest in everyday activities
- Profound sadness
- Excessive guilt
- Fatigue
- Sleep problems, such as insomnia or the need for excessive sleep
- Loss of appetite or weight

People with depression also have the following symptoms that are common in AD/HD:

- Inattention
- Loss of concentration
- Forgetfulness
- Social isolation
- Restlessness
- Distractibility

Distinguishing between depression and AD/HD can be easy with some people and very difficult with others. The difficulty exists partly because the conditions share many similar symptoms but also because the co-occurrence of AD/HD and depression is very common.

Pervasive developmental disorders

Pervasive developmental disorders (PDD) is a term that encompasses autism, Rett's disorder, childhood disintegrative disorder, and Asperger's syndrome. Children with these conditions show delays in communication and social interaction, and they have repetitive behavior patterns and restricted interests, among other symptoms.

These conditions can be confused with AD/HD because someone with PDD may also have symptoms of inattention, hyperactivity, restlessness, and impulsivity.

At the risk of gross overgeneralization, one way to tell the difference between people with AD/HD and those with PDD is that the AD/HD-like symptoms in PDD are not as pronounced as those symptoms are in children with AD/HD. As well, the developmental delays in children with PDD tend to largely overshadow the symptoms that overlap with AD/HD.

Learning disorders

Because AD/HD affects your ability to learn, one of the first things a professional looks for when assessing whether you have AD/HD is the presence of a learning disorder. Twenty percent of people with specific learning disorders have AD/HD, and 40 percent of people with AD/HD also have specific learning disorders. Distinguishing between the two requires using educational testing methods (see Chapter 5), as well as looking at how the AD/HD-like symptoms relate to the level of intelligence in the person.

Several different types of learning disorders are assessed by performing academic achievement tests and other tests of specific processing functions. For more details, see Chapter 5.

Oppositional defiant disorder

Oppositional defiant disorder (ODD) and conduct disorder are very similar to AD/HD, but they are characterized by defiant behavior that can range from disobeying rules to using violence. A person with one of these disorders often acts out in socially inappropriate ways. The problem is that many people with AD/HD, especially the hyperactive/impulsive type, also act out in socially inappropriate ways. The co-occurrence of AD/HD and ODD is considerable; it's not at all uncommon for someone to receive both labels.

In recent years, specialists have recognized a common progression in individuals from ODD to conduct disorder to antisocial personality disorder (which we discuss next). This progression seems to occur as the person gets older.

Antisocial personality disorder

Someone with an antisocial personality disorder often disregards the feelings of others, lies, defies authority, is aggressive and irresponsible, and lacks remorse. People with antisocial personality disorder also show some of the symptoms of AD/HD, such as recklessness, impulsivity, and irritability.

You find antisocial personality disorder in adults but not children. (Being over 18 years old is one of the criteria for a diagnosis of a personality disorder.) Children who have these behaviors are often diagnosed with oppositional defiant disorder instead.

Sleep disorders

Sleep disorders come in various forms, including the following:

✔ **Narcolepsy:** Narcolepsy is characterized by sleep attacks during the day, *cataplexy* (sudden loss of muscle tone), and *sleep paralysis* (not being able to move at night).

✔ **Insomnia:** This disorder involves not being able to fall asleep, waking frequently at night, or not getting quality sleep and feeling tired and unrested afterwards.

✔ **Obstructive sleep apnea:** Obstructive sleep apnea is disrupted sleep due to a blocked airway while you're asleep, which causes numerous arousals during the night. This poor quality of sleep leads to daytime drowsiness.

✔ **Primary hypersomnia:** Hypersomnia is defined as having excessive sleepiness. This means that you sleep for long periods of time or daily during the day, but the extra sleep doesn't make you feel more rested.

Regardless of the type of sleep disorder you have, they all produce levels of daytime sleepiness that can result in many of the symptoms of the inattentive type of AD/HD. These symptoms include:

✔ Trouble concentrating

✔ Forgetfulness

✔ Distractibility

✔ Spacing out

✔ Disorganization

These symptoms can also be present in people who have periods of disrupted sleep cycles but don't meet all the criteria for a sleep disorder. As we discuss in Chapter 3, many people with AD/HD also have problems with sleep. Some people may be diagnosed with both AD/HD and a particular sleep disorder.

Tourette's syndrome

Tourette's syndrome and other tic disorders are characterized by involuntary motor movements (called *tics*), such as blinking, grimacing, or jerking the head, arms, or legs. Older people with Tourette's sometimes also develop vocal tics, such as involuntarily saying insults or profanities. People with Tourette's syndrome also experience symptoms similar to AD/HD, including:

- ✔ Attention problems
- ✔ Impulsivity
- ✔ Restlessness

Tourette's and AD/HD are commonly linked; as many as 40 percent of people with Tourette's syndrome also have AD/HD. (Some people, such as researcher David Cummings, actually refer to Tourette's syndrome as "AD/HD with tics.")

Medical conditions

We feel a little strange separating these conditions from the ones we've been discussing so far in this chapter, as though the mental conditions we describe aren't also medical conditions! They certainly are, but what follows is a discussion of conditions that can be directly traced to a specific physical disorder or condition.

Several medical conditions produce the same symptoms as AD/HD. Before a diagnosis of AD/HD can be confirmed, these conditions may need to be ruled out.

Allergies and sensitivities

Allergies and sensitivities to toxins can cause some of the symptoms displayed by people with AD/HD, including the following:

- ✔ Poor concentration
- ✔ Distractibility
- ✔ Restlessness
- ✔ Forgetfulness
- ✔ Fuzzy thinking

Testing for allergies can be done by your family physician or by an *allergist* — a doctor who specializes in treating allergies. People who are allergic may show signs of AD/HD even if they don't have it. In addition, people with AD/HD who are also allergic to certain foods or chemicals may see their symptoms get worse in the presence of the allergen. If you show symptoms of AD/HD but don't have AD/HD, your symptoms should disappear after the allergen is dealt with. We discuss allergies and sensitivities in more detail in Chapter 11.

Cerebral palsy

Cerebral palsy (CP) is a type of brain damage that is usually caused by lack of oxygen to the baby's brain during or just before delivery. The damage can affect any combination of brain functions, so while most people think of kids with CP as having trouble with walking or talking, the damage can be really subtle and result in problems with learning or concentration with no visible difficulties in general functioning.

Similar kinds of problems can result from premature birth. Researchers are actively investigating these problems to try to better understand their possible nature and extent.

Epilepsy

Epilepsy is a condition that causes you to have repeated brain seizures. These seizures can vary in severity from full-body convulsive seizures (*grand mal* seizures) to simply spacing out for a few seconds (*petit mal* seizures). Because some types of seizures aren't very noticeable, they can often be confused with the symptoms of inattention and spacing out common in AD/HD.

Epilepsy is diagnosed by a neurologist; however, as with AD/HD, there is no definitive physiological test. Often, the person having the seizures doesn't remember them, so an eyewitness usually has to confirm that a seizure happened. Getting confirmation can be difficult with the petit mal seizures because there is no dramatic outward sign that a seizure is happening; usually an eyewitness just sees a blank look on the person's face and possibly fluttering eyelids.

Thyroid dysfunction

Your thyroid is a gland located in your neck that releases hormones that help determine the level of metabolic activity in your cells. An overactive thyroid (*hyperthyroidism*) or an underactive thyroid (*hypothyroidism*) can cause some AD/HD-like symptoms. These symptoms vary depending on whether your thyroid is over- or underactive:

- ✔ **Hyperthyroidism often includes symptoms of hyperactivity and inattention.** Other symptoms of hyperthyroidism include hand tremors, irritability, anxiety, diarrhea, erratic behavior, and intolerance to heat, among other things.

✓ **Hypothyroidism often includes symptoms of lethargy and inattention.**
Other symptoms include feelings of sadness, lethargy, fatigue, muscle
and joint pain, and intolerance to cold, to name a few.

Thyroid problems can be diagnosed by your family physician, often starting
with a simple test that measures your level of thyroid stimulating hormone
(TSH). For more information about your thyroid and its impact on your body,
see *Thyroid For Dummies* by Alan L. Rubin, MD (Wiley).

Brain diseases

Injury to the frontal lobe of the brain can cause the same symptoms you see
in AD/HD. (In Chapter 2, we talk extensively about the role of the frontal lobe
in AD/HD.) Trauma or disease to other parts of the brain can cause these
symptoms as well. Some possible causes of brain problems include the
following:

✓ **Traumatic brain injury:** This type of injury is a fall or blow to the head
that causes damage to the brain.

✓ **Frontal lobe disease:** A number of relatively rare conditions affect the
frontal lobes. A neurologist can tell you which ones affect different age
groups.

✓ **Brain tumor:** A tumor in the brain can cause many of the same symptoms
as AD/HD, depending on its exact location and size. Brain tumors are quite
rare, so don't start worrying about this as a very likely possibility.

✓ **Infections:** Leprosy, Lyme disease, parasites, fungus diseases, bacterial
and viral encephalitis, and meningitis can all cause a variety of symptoms, including ones that mirror AD/HD.

These conditions can be explored by a neurologist and aren't usually the
first place to look for the cause of your AD/HD symptoms. However, damage
to the frontal lobes of the brain is more common than most people would
expect. If your AD/HD symptoms seem to come out of nowhere — especially
after a fall — your doctor should check to see if you sustained any damage to
the frontal lobe.

Sensory processing disorders

Some disorders that can cause symptoms similar to AD/HD aren't classified
as either mental or medical conditions. Because they aren't classified in the
medical and psychological systems, they may receive too much or too little
attention, depending on who is doing the looking (see Chapter 4). For the

purposes of this book, we refer to these conditions as *sensory processing disorders.* The two most common are central auditory processing disorder and visual processing disorder.

Central auditory processing disorder

Central auditory processing disorder (CAPD) is a condition that causes you to have a problem understanding speech. Your ear hears someone talking just fine, but for some reason your brain can't completely make sense of the speech.

One of the distinguishing features of CAPD is that understanding speech is more difficult in noisy environments. You may be able to understand someone talking to you just fine in a quiet room, but in a noisy restaurant, very little may make sense. Another symptom of CAPD is confusing similar-sounding words, such as "air" and "hair" or "coat" and "boat." CAPD also shares some of the same symptoms as AD/HD, including:

- ✔ Forgetfulness
- ✔ Distractibility
- ✔ Inattention
- ✔ Failure to follow directions
- ✔ Disorganization

CAPD and AD/HD sometimes occur together, and it can be very hard to distinguish between the two. To find out if you have CAPD, the best professional to see is a speech–language pathologist or an audiologist who is well-versed in CAPD.

Visual processing disorder

Many people experience vision problems that cause them to see words on a printed page differently. The words may seem to fade away or to move as the person tries to read. This difficulty is called *Scotopic Sensitivity Syndrome* (SSS) or the *Irlen Syndrome,* named for the psychologist who first discovered the disorder. (Chapter 13 has more details about this disorder and how to fix it.) People with the Irlen Syndrome sometimes have the following symptoms similar to AD/HD:

- ✔ Loss of concentration
- ✔ Inattention
- ✔ Forgetfulness

Diagnosing this disorder requires seeing an Irlen Syndrome diagnostician. To find someone, go to www.irlen.com.

Other types of visual processing problems may exist that haven't even been discovered yet. One key to recognizing a particular sensory processing problem is that the person who has one usually has more difficulty doing things that rely to a great degree on that sensory modality.

Pseudo-AD/HD

The symptoms of AD/HD (and other disorders we discuss in this chapter) lie on a continuum. In other words, people without AD/HD may have the same behaviors and cognitive features of AD/HD, but these symptoms and features don't cause significant impairment in their ability to function in the world. Pseudo-AD/HD is a condition that features the same symptoms as AD/HD, except these symptoms are less profound and tend to vary in severity depending on your environment.

Unfortunately, our society breeds pseudo-AD/HD in a variety of ways, including the following:

- **Television:** Aside from being a sedentary activity, watching TV has an effect on the brain. The combination of the fast-paced visual content of today's TV and the relentless dual stimulus (visual and auditory) leads many children to expect that level of stimulation all the time. They don't get that type of stimulation in school, and they end up not paying attention, or being restless or hyperactive. According to a study done by the U.S. Department of Education in 1994, children who watch more than 10 hours of TV a week perform significantly lower in school and have shorter attention spans than those who watch less.

- **Video games:** The speed of TV is fast, but the speed of video games is even faster. The level of stimulation in video games is greater than in TV programs, and children who spend a lot of time playing them tend to have much shorter attention spans than children who don't play them.

- *Sound bite* **mentality:** We are a nation of sound bites. Everything is about the bottom line, and because we're not required to focus for a long time, we become unaccustomed to doing it. Attention is like exercise: If you don't practice focusing, you lose some of your skill in doing it. We are overstimulated by our everyday world and rarely allow ourselves the time to slow down.

- **Multitasking:** Many of us have to divide our attention among several things at once. Because most of us are short on time, we have to multitask. The problem is that doing so further breeds a short attention span and distractibility.

✔ **Sedentary lifestyle:** Lack of exercise tends to create many of the symptoms of AD/HD, including inattention, distractibility, and forgetfulness.

One of the best things you can do for your pseudo-AD/HD symptoms is to exercise. Exercise increases blood flow to the brain and raises serotonin levels, which helps your brain function at its best. We cover this topic in more detail in Chapter 14.

Each of these aspects of our society increases the AD/HD-like attributes in people who don't have AD/HD. And for people with AD/HD, these things make the symptoms much worse. In Chapters 14, 15, and 16, we talk about strategies to improve your functioning in the world. Minimizing the impact of these attributes of our society can go a long way toward decreasing your AD/HD symptoms.

Some people are more susceptible to these environmental influences than others; you don't need to cut TV and video games completely out of your life unless they seem to be creating problems for you.

Part III
Treating AD/HD

The 5th Wave   By Rich Tennant

"Is there a remedy for acute option shock?"

In this part . . .

Part III explores the many types of treatment available for AD/HD. Chapter 7 helps you understand the big picture: the role of treatment and the ways you can determine the best approaches for your situation. Then we jump into specific treatment options: medications; counseling, coaching, and training; behavior management; nutrition, vitamins, and herbs; repatterning therapies, which impact the way your brain works; and therapies that are designed to help rebalance your nervous system. Not all of these therapies are created equal — some seem to have success for larger numbers of people with AD/HD than others, and some have been researched much more than others — but all are worth reading about so you can make the best decision about what types of therapy you want to try.

Chapter 7

Choosing the Best Treatment Options for You

In This Chapter

▶ Recognizing the levels of treatment available

▶ Exploring multiple treatments

▶ Developing your treatment plan

▶ Keeping track of your experiences

*T*here is no shortage of possible ways to address your AD/HD symptoms. You can follow the conventional route of medication, counseling, coaching, and behavior modification; explore the growing trend of using vitamins, herbs, and supplements; and consider emerging methods designed to change your brain through experiential, sound, vision, or balancing therapies.

As you dig through Part III of this book, you may become overwhelmed with all the options. And chances are you'll want to explore many of them. This chapter can help you get off on the right foot in experimenting with these various approaches and help you stay on track as you try to get your symptoms under control.

In this chapter, we introduce you to the core levels of AD/HD treatment: biological, psychological, and social. We help you develop a plan for using the therapies that resonate with you and assist you in keeping tabs on your progress so that you can make changes as needed. We also provide resources that can keep you informed on new treatment options as they emerge.

Understanding the Three Levels of Treatment

Treating AD/HD involves looking at AD/HD from three levels: biological, psychological, and social. An effective treatment strategy explores therapies and strategies that address all three (see Figure 7-1).

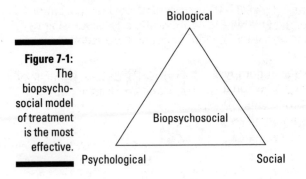

Figure 7-1:
The
biopsycho-
social model
of treatment
is the most
effective.

Biological treatments

Biological treatments change the way your brain works. This change can be accomplished in several ways and can be temporary or permanent, depending on the approach you take. The options we cover in this book include the following:

✔ **Medication:** In Chapter 8, we take a detailed look at the different types of medication commonly used to treat the symptoms of AD/HD. We also describe the best way to go about working with your doctor to find the right drug, dosage, and schedule for you.

✔ **Diet:** Certain types of foods work well for people with AD/HD, and certain food groups can actually make your symptoms worse. We cover diet in-depth in Chapter 11.

✔ **Vitamin supplements and herbal remedies:** The use of vitamin supplements and herbal remedies for people with AD/HD is becoming more commonplace and, although few controlled studies have been done, quite a bit of anecdotal support exists for using these methods to help reduce the severity of your symptoms. These subjects are covered in Chapter 11.

✔ **Experiential and repatterning therapies:** These therapies are designed to help facilitate a change in the way your brain functions over time. We explore several approaches in Chapter 12, including the following:

• *Neurofeedback:* Also called *EEG-biofeedback* or *neurotherapy,* this approach employs an EEG machine and specific exercises to help you learn how to change your brain activity over time.

• *Rhythmic Entrainment Intervention (REI):* Developed by coauthor Jeff Strong, REI uses targeted auditory rhythmic stimulation to influence brain function.

- *Auditory integration training (AIT):* AIT is also, obviously, an auditory program — one intended to improve auditory processing by having you listen to frequency reductions and enhancements in prerecorded music.

- *Vision therapy:* Vision therapy employs visual exercises, which may or may not be performed on a computer and are designed to help improve visual processing. You can find out about this type of therapy from a behavioral optometrist.

✔ **Rebalancing therapies:** Rebalancing therapies work to help you create a more balanced nervous system. In Chapter 13, we discuss several therapies that use this approach, including the following:

- *Acupuncture:* In this ancient Chinese technique, small needles are placed in specific points of your body to help correct the regulation and flow of *Qi* ("Chi"), also known as *life energy.*

- *Homeopathics:* Homeopathy has been around for about 150 years and consists of using very diluted amounts of substances that in stronger amounts could actually cause your symptoms. This practice uses the principle "like cures like" to influence a variety of symptoms, including some of the symptoms of AD/HD.

- *Manipulation therapies:* These therapies include osteopathy, chiropractic, and CranioSacral Therapy. These approaches are concerned with the flow of cerebrospinal fluid and the alignment of the spine. Chiropractic and osteopathy focus on the alignment of the bones. CranioSacral Therapy (which originated as a branch of osteopathy) focuses on the pulse of cerebrospinal fluid and ways to improve it.

- *Sensory integration therapies:* These approaches are designed to help your sensory system to better process stimuli.

Psychological treatments

Psychological therapies help you deal with the feelings that come from your symptoms — most often, the secondary symptoms that rise out of the core symptoms (see Chapter 3) — and help you understand ways that you can change how you think and act to improve your life. In this book we cover the following psychological treatment strategies:

✔ **Counseling and psychotherapy:** These approaches take many forms, including talk therapy, cognitive-behavioral counseling, and play therapy. In Chapter 9, we present some of the most common approaches to AD/HD counseling and therapy, including the following:

- *Insight-oriented:* This approach helps you understand what you do and why you do it.

- *Supportive:* Because people with AD/HD and their family members experience problems in many areas of their lives, supportive therapy can help you get perspective and allow you to feel, well, supported.

- *Cognitive-behavioral:* Here's a buzzword for you. Cognitive-behavioral counseling involves making changes to the way that you think and act using conditioning and association.

- *Play therapy:* Life without play is meaningless, and many children with AD/HD have little fun. More importantly, many children with AD/HD have difficulty realizing what they feel and think. This type of therapy uses play — in a planned way — to help children express feelings indirectly and to work with the negative emotions that accompany AD/HD.

- *Psychoeducational counseling:* This approach is designed to educate you on the effects of AD/HD, and it teaches you how to better handle the difficulties by offering strategies for coping with your symptoms and their effects.

✔ **Coaching:** Coaching focuses on helping you navigate the everyday issues that you may have with AD/HD. This approach shares a lot of common ground with skills training and psychoeducational counseling, but it's a discipline all its own.

✔ **Training:** Several types of training are available that can help you develop specific skills to improve your life with AD/HD. These include:

- *Skills training:* AD/HD often manifests in disorganization, procrastination, poor listening abilities, and similar difficulties. Skills training can help you develop some tools for improving these areas of your life.

- *Parent training:* This type of training is like a combination of supportive therapy, skills training, behavioral therapy, and psychoeducational counseling. It helps parents deal with their children with AD/HD in ways that improve the kids' chances of growing up with fewer problems.

  This type of training is particularly important if you or your partner have AD/HD as well. AD/HD parents often have difficulty with self-discipline and organization, and they may have been poorly parented themselves if their parents didn't know much about AD/HD.

✔ **Behavior management:** Behavior management is an important part of treatment for people with AD/HD. In Chapter 10 we offer several common approaches that can help you manage behavior. These approaches include:

- *Behavior modification:* Behavior modification is the most widely used method of managing behavior among children and involves a consistent use of rewards and consequences to encourage positive behavior and discourage problem behaviors.

- *Cognitive-behavioral counseling:* As we note earlier in this section, cognitive-behavioral counseling is a systematic approach to changing the way you think and act using conditioning and association.

- *Awareness training:* Awareness training involves discovering how to increase your awareness of yourself and your environment with the goal that you'll be more aware of how you act in certain situations. By developing this awareness you can figure out (among other things) how to stop and think before you act.

Each of these approaches can be used for improving your ability to deal with your AD/HD. Some help you reduce the impact of the main symptoms, while others allow you to get out from under the grip of the secondary symptoms.

Social treatments

To function effectively in the world, you need certain skills, which are often lacking in people with AD/HD. After the biological issues of AD/HD are being dealt with, you need to focus on developing the social skills and adding to your toolbox of coping mechanisms.

We cover many life strategies in this book, primarily in Part IV. We focus on the following areas:

✔ **Home:** AD/HD affects the entire family. Therefore, everyone needs to be involved in developing strategies to make family life more harmonious. These strategies — which we cover in Chapter 14 — include, but aren't limited to, the following:

- *Developing healthy family relationships:* These strategies focus on skills and techniques you can use within your family to reduce the conflict that is often part of everyday life when a family member has AD/HD.

- *Parenting a child with AD/HD:* You can use these strategies to increase your child's self-esteem and help him learn to act more appropriately.

- *Living with an adult with AD/HD:* Whether the adult is you or someone else in your household, we cover topics that can help, such as working together and taking time for yourself.

- *Developing good habits:* We also offer some strategies that can make everyday life a little bit better, such as getting enough sleep and doing aerobic exercise.

✔ **School:** Without a doubt, school is the biggest challenge for children with AD/HD. Being able to handle the issues that school creates takes some specific skills, which we discuss in Chapter 15. Strategies that we cover in this chapter include the following broad categories:

- *Understanding your legal rights:* Being able to navigate the legal process in school to ensure that your child gets the education that he deserves isn't easy. We explore the civil rights laws IDEA and Section 504 and let you know what you can expect from them.

- *Working well with your child's teachers:* Your child spends a lot of time with his teachers, and their attitudes about AD/HD can have a big impact on how well your child does in class. We offer you some ideas for cultivating a positive relationship with your child's teachers to help you recruit them as advocates for your child.

- *Finding the best school situation for your child:* Many types of schooling options are available, and understanding them is crucial so you can find the best place for your child to learn.

- *Dealing with the tough times at school:* Certain environments can pose extra challenges for a student with AD/HD. We explain many of these instances and offer suggestions for getting through them as easily as possible.

- *Working with your child at home:* You can use many strategies at home to make your child's experiences in school more positive. These strategies deal with the obvious homework issue but also others, such as supporting your child's self-esteem.

✔ **Work:** Life at work can be greatly improved when you discover the skills we discuss in Chapter 16. The areas we cover include:

- *Understanding your legal rights:* The Americans with Disabilities Act offers you some protections in the workplace. We explain what this law applies to and what it doesn't, and we help you make a decision regarding whether to tell your boss or coworkers about your AD/HD.

- *Managing your behavior:* We offer suggestions to help you manage your behavior so that you can conduct yourself in a professional manner at work.

- *Developing healthy work relationships:* Since many people with AD/HD have problems with social relationships, we provide some strategies that you can use to maximize your work relationships.

- *Creating daily success:* Many people with AD/HD have problems with day-to-day activities, such as getting and staying organized or effectively managing time. We offer strategies to develop the skills to tackle these particularly troublesome areas.

• *Following a career track:* Finding the right career and developing a long-term strategy for climbing the ladder of success are often problematic for people with AD/HD. We help you look at the big picture so you can find work that is satisfying to you.

The most effective treatment strategy is one that encompasses all three areas: biological, psychological, and social. Make sure that whatever treatment plan you develop contains at least one strategy from each category.

Trying Multiple Treatments Together

The best way to treat AD/HD is to use a *multimodal* approach. In other words, you use several different treatments that augment one another to give you the greatest reduction in your symptoms. For one person this may be a combination of medication, diet, exercise, and behavior modification. For someone else it may mean herbs, homeopathics, talk therapy, and neurofeedback. In addition, you may use some therapies for a short time and others for a long time. If you use medications, you may switch from one to another or change dosages over time.

Finding the right treatments and managing them take some research, planning, organization, and persistence. To make life easier, we recommend that you choose a medical professional who is very familiar with AD/HD to manage your treatment with you. If you use medication, you'll automatically have a professional to work with, and she may be a good person to help you with the rest of your treatment options. If you choose to go without medication, try to find a professional who is attuned to the types of treatments you want to use. This could be your doctor or any of the professionals we list in Chapter 4.

Developing Your Plan for Success

To effectively treat your symptoms, you need to first develop a plan. This process involves doing the following:

✔ Determining the areas where you struggle

✔ Understanding what you want to accomplish

✔ Discovering the best approaches to improve those areas

✔ Making a list of the various treatments

✔ Deciding which treatments to do and when

✔ Monitoring your progress to determine how well you're doing

Figure 7-2 shows how this process works, and the sections that follow walk you through the steps.

Naming your challenges

If you have AD/HD, you may have a hard time seeing your challenges clearly; many people with AD/HD don't recognize their own symptoms. We recommend getting the input of a professional (or at least a family member who can be honest with you) to identify areas where you struggle. This person may be able to help you better understand the impact of your symptoms on your life. Work with that individual, and make a list of your symptoms.

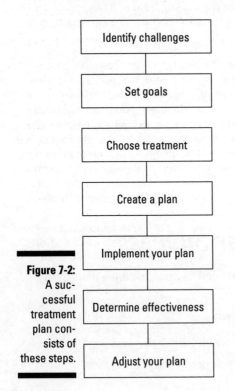

Figure 7-2: A successful treatment plan consists of these steps.

If your child or another loved one has AD/HD, you can help him make a list of the challenges he faces.

In most cases, treating AD/HD involves at least one professional. If you are working with more than one person, choose one of them to help manage your care. Having the guidance of a professional is essential to getting the best possible improvement in your symptoms. That professional can also prevent you from getting involved in treatments or combinations of treatments that can make your symptoms worse or that can be unsafe.

Identifying your goals

After you've identified your challenges, consider each one and make a list of the changes you'd like to see. Again, a professional can help you develop realistic goals. Optimism is great, but you don't want to be unrealistic about the progress you expect to see. On the other hand, you don't want to assume that you can't get better. Many people with AD/HD have taken hits to their self-esteem for such a long time that they may not be able to envision much progress at all. A professional can help you realize that you can make significant progress in a short time if you choose your treatment approaches well.

Sifting through the options

In Chapters 8 through 13, we present a variety of treatment approaches that are commonly used to help people with AD/HD. We cover a lot of ground, but our discussion certainly doesn't exhaust all the possibilities. Sifting through all the different treatment approaches could take a lifetime — especially when you consider that new approaches are being developed almost daily. Don't feel as though you need to look into absolutely everything available.

Do some research into the general categories of treatment approaches — medication, counseling, behavior management, coaching, vitamins and diet, repatterning therapies, and balancing therapies, for example — and figure out which ones resonate with you.

Once again, a well-versed professional can come in handy when sorting through your options, as can a network of other people who deal with AD/HD. Talking to people who have either professional or personal experience with the treatment you're considering can help you understand the results you can expect.

Prioritizing your plan

When you have a list of treatment approaches you want to try, you need to develop a plan to implement them. Doing so requires understanding the type of commitment you need to make for each one to be successful. A good first step is to discuss your treatment options with your peers or a professional to get a good idea of how long each approach will last.

Some treatments, such as diet, require an ongoing effort and a period of time before you start to see results. Others, such as medication, can produce results almost immediately but still need to be used for an extended period of time.

Some treatments are used for a finite period of time — for example, Rhythmic Entrainment Intervention, which takes between 8 and 12 weeks. In these instances, you know in advance how long you'll be committing yourself to the course of treatment. The course for some other time-limited treatments, such as neurofeedback, can't be determined exactly from the start. With neurofeedback, your progress determines the final length of the program, so you must be flexible.

As you create your treatment plan, you must decide when you want to do each treatment you've chosen, and you must understand the implications of doing two or more treatments at the same time. You need to make sure that various treatments are compatible and know whether combining them creates the potential for problems. Again, your AD/HD professional should be a good resource.

Don't be in a rush to try everything at once. Combining too many treatments may be unsafe, and it certainly makes it difficult to keep track of what you're doing. (We discuss combining treatments in the following section.) Even the best treatment won't work if it isn't done properly. For example, if you take medication, you need to make sure that you take the pills when you're supposed to. If you choose neurofeedback, you need to show up at your appointments and practice regularly at home.

Combining approaches safely

Some AD/HD treatments, such as neurofeedback and Rhythmic Entrainment Intervention (see Chapter 12), are perfectly safe to use in combination with any other treatment approaches. But chemical treatments, such as medications (see Chapter 8), herbal remedies, or supplements (see Chapter 11), need to be monitored carefully by a professional who knows all the possible side effects of combining treatments.

Careful monitoring is required because these chemicals interact within your body and, although most combinations are perfectly safe, some are not. For example, taking the supplement 5-HTP in combination with a prescription antidepressant can cause some serious side effects.

In the chapters on chemical treatments, we let you know when certain combinations have been shown to be unsafe. However, we strongly encourage you to do your own research — and consult a professional who is well-versed in the chemical treatments you intend to use — to make sure that what you take doesn't interact in a negative way.

Following Your Progress

Most people with AD/HD try a variety of different treatment programs in the hopes of finding the right balance of symptom control. If you choose to take this approach, you need to be committed to keeping a log so you can follow the progress of your efforts and understand the outcomes of the various treatments. This task can be daunting in itself. This section lays out some suggestions for keeping tabs on what you're doing and how each treatment is working. Also, see this book's appendix for sample forms to use to help with this process.

If you use more than one treatment at a time (which includes each of the vitamins you may take), knowing which part of your combination is providing which effects can be very difficult. In fact, it can be virtually impossible. We strongly recommend that when you make modifications to your treatment plan, you limit the changes to one or two strategies at a time and take careful notes.

Here are some suggestions for following your treatment plans and their effectiveness:

✔ **Get a good calendar with enough room on each day to enter notes.** A business appointment planner may work, or look for a planner specifically created for following your health status, which is often called a *personal health journal.*

Journaling can be an effective treatment modality in itself. That means that you may not be able to tell whether the other treatments are having an effect, or whether the discipline required to keep track of your treatments is helping you.

✔ **Write down all the specifics about the treatment.** Include the time a treatment takes and the amount of treatment that you use, take, or undergo.

✔ **Record your observations of your AD/HD symptoms for the day.** Include any changes that you see throughout the day. This is especially important in the case of medication because the drug's effects change over time.

✔ **Do a quick review of your status once a week.** Pick the same day every week to do a quick assessment of your plan. Make sure that you're following the proper protocol for each treatment and that you don't have any serious side effects that are making your life more difficult than it already was.

✔ **Once a month, perform a more careful analysis of your progress.** Compare where you are to where you were a month ago and to where you thought you'd be given the plan you drafted for yourself. Be honest with yourself about the results of what you're doing to treat your symptoms, and make adjustments to your plan based on what you see.

If you're the one with AD/HD, you may find it difficult to accurately assess your progress (or lack thereof). In this case, you need the input of someone else to help you see how you're doing. This could be a family member or a professional. Make an appointment with this person every month to discuss your progress.

✔ **Adjust your plan as needed.** After you do your weekly review or monthly assessment, if you see things you don't like, don't be afraid to make adjustments to your plan. If a medication isn't working, meet with your doctor and discuss changing it. If the diet you're trying makes you feel worse, change it.

Don't just a drop a treatment from your plan if things aren't happening as fast as you'd like. Change takes time. So before you stop — unless the side effects are getting in the way of your life — consult the professional you hired to help you with that treatment. If the treatment is something you decided to try on your own based upon a recommendation or some research, talk to people or do more research into this treatment to see if you're doing something wrong. Look for ways to adjust the treatment before you give up on it.

Keeping Up-to-Date on New Therapies

When it comes to AD/HD treatments, we can guarantee one thing: change. The available treatments will evolve, and new approaches will be developed.

As the professional community learns more about the causes of AD/HD, it also discovers better ways to deal with the symptoms. The sections that follow show you how to keep up with the pace of change.

Attending conferences

AD/HD conferences are conducted around the country. These conferences can be an excellent way for you to discover more about AD/HD and get a chance to talk to AD/HD professionals and other people with the condition. Topics covered in these conferences include treatment options, life strategies, and current research findings.

For the most part, conferences by each sponsoring organization are held once a year. The most prominent are the conferences sponsored by the groups ADDA and CHADD. You can find out about these conferences and discover other useful information (such as audiotapes of previous conference presentations) on the ADDA and CHADD Web sites:

- **ADDA:** ADDA stands for *Attention Deficit Disorder Association.* ADDA is a clearinghouse for AD/HD information and resources. You can find ADDA at P.O. Box 543, Pottstown, PA 19464. Phone: 484-945-2101. Fax: 610-970-7520. Web site: www.add.org.

- **CHADD:** CHADD stands for *Children and Adults with AD/HD.* You can contact CHADD at 8181 Professional Place, Suite 150, Landover, MD 20785. Phone: 800-233-4050. Web site: www.chadd.org.

You may discover that your local area hosts a chapter of CHADD. If that's the case, you may want to participate in local meetings, which can serve as a resource for information as well as support.

Conferences on autism and learning disabilities seem to be more prevalent than conferences focusing on AD/HD. (Perhaps the disorganization inherent in AD/HD is the culprit?) You may find that conferences on autism or learning disabilities include sessions that have valuable information for you. To find such a conference, type "autism conference" or "learning disabilities conference" into your favorite Internet search engine. These days, most national and international conferences have a Web presence.

If you have a child with AD/HD, you may want to look into special education conferences. Most states have at least one of these conferences each year. They're often geared toward educators, but they can offer parents some useful information as well. Call your local college or university special education program and ask if it sponsors a conference; even if it doesn't, someone in that program may know about conferences being organized in your area.

Browsing the Internet

The Internet is a great source for information — it isn't called the information superhighway for no reason. The only problem with the Internet as a research tool is that it can be tough dodging all the junk that's floating around in cyberspace.

As a starting point, check out the ADDA and CHADD Web sites listed in the previous section. Each site has a list of informative links. You can also simply use "AD/HD" as your criteria in your favorite search engine and take what you read with a grain of salt.

Reading professional journal articles

Several professional journals print studies on treatments for AD/HD. Following are some examples:

- **The journals from the American Psychological Association (APA).** The APA publishes quite a few journals, including *Neuropsychology,* which often contains studies on AD/HD. The organization's contact info is 750 First St., NE, Washington, DC 20002-4242. Phone: 800-374-2721 or 202-336-5500. Web site: `www.apa.org`.

- *The Journal of Neuropsychiatry and Clinical Neurosciences* **and** *The American Journal of Psychiatry.* Both are both published by American Psychiatric Publishing, Inc. You can contact the Circulation Department at 1000 Wilson Blvd., Suite 1825, Arlington, VA 22209. Web site: `http://neuro.psychiatryonline.org/`.

You may not want to subscribe to these journals because studies on AD/HD aren't included in every issue. Also, many of the most recent (and, dare we say, groundbreaking) therapies don't show up in these journals until long after they've been in use. It takes time to do the research that these journals report, and these studies are generally conducted after a fairly large body of evidence from case studies has been completed. Still, these journals are a great source of information about the more established treatment approaches. You can likely find copies of these journals in a university or medical school library.

Perhaps a better resource to know about is medical search databases. By using these databases, you don't have to subscribe to professional journals in the hopes that you'll find an article or two on AD/HD throughout the year. (However, you may have to pay to access a particular article.) With these

Web sites, all you have to do is enter a search — such as "AD/HD" — and articles from a variety of publications appear. Following are some of the best Web sites we've found for this purpose:

- ✔ **U.S. National Library of Medicine,** www.nlm.nih.gov: This site, sponsored by the U.S. government, has links to several databases, such as Medline, one of the best medical databases available.

- ✔ **HighBeam Research,** www.highbeam.com: This site has a powerful search engine that pulls articles from many sources.

- ✔ **MedBioWorld,** www.medbioworld.com/index.html: This site has links to thousands of medical journals and articles.

You can also do a search using one of the more popular Internet search engines, such as www.google.com. In addition to (possibly) locating professional journal articles, this type of search engine may locate newspaper and magazine articles of interest to you. However, if you go this route, you increase the chances that you'll get a bunch of unrelated hits. We suggest that you perform a narrow search — for example, "AD/HD homeopathy study" — to reduce the volume of responses.

Attending support group meetings

Support groups can be very helpful for a variety of reasons. Not only do they offer much-needed moral support, but they can be great sources of information. You can talk with people who have AD/HD and have tried or heard about new treatments. We offer some advice for finding or starting a support group in Chapter 20.

Chapter 8

Managing Medication

. . . .

In This Chapter

▶ Considering pros and cons of taking medication

▶ Understanding how medications work

▶ Examining different types of medications

▶ Enhancing your success with medication

. . . .

*M*edication intervention is often the first line of defense against the symptoms of AD/HD. This chapter informs you about the types of medications that are commonly used in treating the symptoms of AD/HD and shows you how to work with your doctor to find the best drug or combination of drugs for your situation.

Because medication is not always the best solution for every person with AD/HD, we first discuss how to determine whether drug treatments are the right option for you or your child.

Determining If Medication Is Right for You

If you consult a medical doctor about AD/HD, medication will most likely be part of your initial treatment plan. With the right drug and optimal dosage, the success rate of medication is high: It can work for at least 80 percent of people with AD/HD. Even so, medication is not for everyone, and starting a treatment program requires more involvement from you than simply taking a pill. Before you go down the pharmacological path, here are some things to consider:

✔ Finding the right medication, amount, and dosage schedule can take a while.

✔ Every medication has side effects. Balancing them with the positive effects of the medication is an art and may take time to perfect. (See the section "Singling out side effects" later in the chapter.)

✔ You must keep in communication with your doctor and follow your doctor's advice (or let her know if you are doing something different). If you don't communicate with your doctor, she can't help you get the most out of your medicine.

✔ Medication can be a quick way to help you out of a crisis and give you time to develop life strategies to lessen your symptoms and their impact. You still want to undertake other aspects of a multimodal treatment plan, which we describe in Chapter 7.

✔ Medication isn't a magic bullet. Medication helps manage the symptoms of AD/HD; it does not cure AD/HD.

Medication is not your only biological treatment option; you can change your brain by learning how to use it differently. One of the methods we recommend for such learning — and thus getting away from the need for medication — is to try one of the repatterning therapies we describe in Chapter 12. Also, many people get similar results to medication using a combination of diet and supplements, as we describe in Chapter 11.

Periodically, AD/HD medication gets a bad rap — you may hear or read some scary things. But be sure to evaluate the source before determining how much credence to give the negative reports. Most of the medications that are used for AD/HD are safer than the majority of medications used in modern medicine.

Understanding How Medications Work

Medications for people with AD/HD focus on affecting brain chemicals called *neurotransmitters* (see Chapter 2). This section explores the types of neurotransmitters involved in AD/HD and how medications can change the levels of these chemicals in your brain.

Recognizing medication's impact on brain chemicals

The medications that work for AD/HD generally impact either the norepinephrine-containing *neurons* (nerve cells) or the dopamine-containing neurons (see Chapter 2). (Note that norepinephrine is another name for noradrenalin.)

These medications tend to work by increasing the amounts of these neuro-transmitters in the *synapses* — the areas between transmitting and receiving neurons. The increase allows the brain to rebalance the activities of these two systems and, consequently, the activities of other transmitter systems. Dopamine is responsible for the strength of signals coming into the brain and for the filtering capacity of the areas that select out what you pay attention to. Norepinephrine is responsible for your arousal level (how aware or drowsy you are) and the clarity of your brain processes. Both have some-thing to do with your level of motivation.

Medications called *selective serotonin reuptake inhibitors* (SSRIs), which we discuss later in the chapter, don't usually have a direct effect on AD/HD. However, they can be useful for other conditions that you may experience along with AD/HD, such as depression or anxiety. The serotonin system (whose chemical shorthand is *5-HT* because 5-hydroxytryptamine is the chemical name for serotonin) is involved in calming other processes in the brain — it smoothes out the rough edges. In many parts of the brain, sero-tonin inhibits the activity of dopamine and norepinephrine neurons, and dopamine and norepinephrine inhibit serotonin activity. The actual result is a rather complex balance that we don't yet completely understand. Often times, people take stimulants or other AD/HD meds and SSRIs together.

Connecting symptoms and brain chemicals

Neuroscientists and pharmacologists are starting to understand brain chemi-cals well enough to say a little bit about which chemicals are associated with specific AD/HD symptoms. For instance, depression has been associated with a lack of activity — or a decreased activity — in the dopamine, norepinephrine, or serotonin system. Distractibility is often a result of too much norepinephrine activity in relation to the amount of dopamine activity. Impulsivity may be related to too much norepinephrine or too little dopamine. Obsessiveness can be a sign of too much dopamine in relation to the amount of serotonin.

With many symptoms, the actual amounts of chemicals in the nerves are normal, and the problem is how the chemicals are released or how the recep-tors bind to them. Medications work in ways that can be difficult to under-stand. Sometimes, it seems the relevant mechanism is just increasing the amount of transmitter in the synapses. Other times, the medications seem to be conditioning the receptors to react a certain way, and the reaction has the desired effect. In still other cases, the balance of different systems seems to be important.

Exploring Medication Types

It used to be that the only way to effectively treat AD/HD with medication was to use a stimulant, such as Dexedrine or Ritalin. This isn't the case anymore. A veritable smorgasbord of options is available to help with your symptoms. The trick is to know which types of medication work for which types of symptoms. Although you obviously need to have this discussion with your doctor, that discussion may be more effective if you have a general idea of what the different medications are and how they work. This section provides you with that information.

Because many of the medications we discuss in the following sections share similar side effects, we discuss those effects *en masse* later in the chapter, in the section "Singling out side effects." If a medication has an unusual potential side effect, we note that in the discussion of that substance.

Stimulants

Stimulants work by causing more dopamine or norepinephrine (or both) to be released into the synapses, and by causing more of the transmitter(s) to be retained in the synapses for a longer time. Stimulant medications are the most popular drugs for treating AD/HD and include the following brand names:

- **Dexedrine (d-amphetamine):** This is the oldest medication used for AD/HD and still one of the best. Both short-acting and sustained-release forms are available.

- **Adderall (salts of d-and l-amphetamine):** This medication is similar to Dexedrine but contains both left- and right-handed forms of amphetamine, so it supposedly works a little more on norepinephrine-containing neurons than Dexedrine. Both long- and short-acting forms are available.

- **Desoxyn (methamphetamine):** This is the same as the *meth* that is causing so much trouble in our society right now. It is relatively expensive as a pharmaceutical and still works better than anything else for some people. Currently, only a short-acting form is available.

- **Ritalin, Concerta, Metadate, Focalin (methylphenidate):** This is still the most widely used medication for AD/HD. In many ways, it is like Adderall and Dexedrine, but its effects are slightly different in most people. The big difference among the brand names is the delivery system — how the drug is released in the intestinal tract, and how long it lasts in the body. Some people find that one brand works for them, and the others don't.

✔ **Cylert (pemoline):** This medication releases only dopamine, and it is a little trickier to use because it can cause damage to the liver; you have to have liver function tests periodically when you take it.

✔ **Provigil (modafinil):** This drug is prescribed mostly for narcolepsy. It may not work through the dopamine or norepinephrine systems, but in research trials with people with AD/HD, it has shown some success.

Non-stimulant AD/HD medication

As we go to press, Strattera (atomoxetine) is the only medication that is not a stimulant that is specifically approved by the FDA for the treatment of AD/HD. Strattera works like an antidepressant in that it is a reuptake inhibitor, but it targets norepinephrine and not the other neurotransmitters. Some synapses in the prefrontal cortex have both norepinephrine and dopamine receptors on them. In those synapses, Strattera has an effect on dopamine, too. This is a once-a-day medication, and it takes four to six weeks for the full effects to be established.

Monoamine oxidase inhibitors (MAOIs)

These medications prevent the breakdown of *monoamines* (the neurotransmitters norepinephrine, dopamine, and serotonin), thus keeping them around longer in the synapses. The big drawback to these otherwise-useful meds is that they can cause some nasty reactions if you take them with certain foods. The good news is that a patch is on its way (containing the MAOI selegiline), which probably won't cause the same problems. Here are some MAOIs on the market:

✔ Nardil

✔ Parnate

✔ Eldepril (selegiline)

Selective serotonin reuptake inhibitors (SSRIs)

SSRIs slow down the removal of serotonin from synapses. These medications are used primarily to treat depression and various forms of anxiety (including obsessive-compulsive disorder), but they are also useful for helping people modulate anger and aggression. Each SSRI is slightly different, and some people may do better on one than another, but (despite what advertising may say) they all work on the same conditions.

One big difference between the SSRIs is how long they last in the body. This information is usually expressed in terms of *half-life*. The half-life of a medication is the time it takes for the medication to get to one half of the peak level after taking a dose. The longer the half-life, the longer it takes for the medication to be in equilibrium (which is called *steady state*) in your body. The shorter the half-life, the more important it is to take the medication on time in order to maintain the same conditions in your body throughout the day.

Although SSRIs don't have a direct effect on AD/HD symptoms, they can be taken along with the medications that do. Here's a list of the SSRI brand names available:

- ✔ **Prozac (fluoxetine):** This is the oldest SSRI used in the United States. Prozac has more potential drug interactions than most SSRIs but is still a very good choice most of the time. Because of its long half-life, missing a dose of Prozac isn't as great a concern as missing a dose of another SSRI.

- ✔ **Paxil (paroxetine):** This is a shorter-acting SSRI, so there is more potential for *discontinuation syndrome* — an unpleasant effect that can last for weeks and includes insomnia, dizziness, irritability, ataxia, and general malaise.

- ✔ **Zoloft (sertraline):** This medication may have a slight advantage for people with AD/HD because it has some dopamine activity, so it may have the same effects as the stimulant medications we discuss earlier in the chapter. It has a fairly short half-life.

- ✔ **Luvox (fluvoxamine):** Luvox has a medium-long half-life and fewer drug interactions than Prozac.

- ✔ **Celexa (citalopram); Lexapro (escitalopram):** These medications have a longer half-life than Zoloft or Paxil and may have fewer side effects and fewer drug interactions than most of the other SSRIs. Lexapro generally works better than Celexa; it's stronger and has fewer side effects.

Don't take an SSRI at the same time you're taking an MAOI; these two types of medications make a *deadly* poisonous combination.

Serotonin/norepinephrine reuptake inhibitors

These medications work on both serotonin and norepinephrine (noradrenalin), so they may help depression, anxiety, and AD/HD. In practice, they usually don't have as much effect on AD/HD symptoms as most people would like, so they are often prescribed along with a stimulant. Serotonin/norepinephrine reuptake inhibitors come with these brand names:

- ✔ **Effexor (venlafaxine):** This medication is energizing, yet calming, for most people. It has a fairly short half-life, so people using it are more prone to discontinuation syndrome (see the Paxil bullet in the previous section).

- ✔ **Serzone (nefazodone):** This medication is often prescribed by primary care doctors, but your coauthor Mike hasn't had much success with it in his patients.

- ✔ **Remeron (mirtazepine):** Remeron is good for stimulating appetite and inducing sleep. It works on seratonin, norepinephrine, and histamine.

Tricyclic antidepressants (TCAs)

This group of medications was the first of the modern drugs used to treat depression. Most TCAs also have a positive effect on AD/HD. They have some potential for problems with the conduction system of the heart because they slow the electrical impulses from the upper to the lower chambers of the heart. This can cause problems such as heartblock and arrhythmias. These medications can also cause some side effects, such as dry mouth, light-headedness, and constipation. Each TCA affects norepinephrine, dopamine, and serotonin to varying degrees. Besides being useful in treating AD/HD and depression, these medications have applications in a variety of other medical conditions, such as bedwetting and heart arrhythmias. TCAs come as the following brand names:

- ✔ **Tofranil (imipramine):** This was the first TCA and is often used as the gold standard to which other antidepressants are compared. It's also potentially useful as a cardiac drug.

- ✔ **Nortriptyline:** This medication is probably the safest middle-of-the-road TCA and is not too sedating. This medication also has fewer side effects for most people.

- ✔ **Sinequan (doxepin):** This TCA is slightly sedating and has good, balanced effects on the transmitters.

- ✔ **Anafranil (clomipramine):** This medication is used for obsessive-compulsive disorder because it has lots of serotonin effects.

- ✔ **Norpramine (desipramine):** This medication is rarely used in children because several years ago it was associated with some sudden deaths. It can be quite useful for AD/HD in low doses in adults, but it still has more side effects than most people like.

- ✔ **Elavil (amitriptyline):** This TCA is very sedating for most people but can be useful for some headache conditions.

Atypical antidepressant agents

Some other antidepressants are often used for people with AD/HD. These include:

- **Wellbutrin (bupropion):** This medication is useful for treating depression and has fewer sexual side effects than SSRIs. It can be quite helpful in treating AD/HD, especially for impulsivity and motivation.

- **Desyrel (trazodone):** This mild antidepressant is often used when people have sleep problems.

Dopamine agonists

Dopamine agonists increase dopamine transmission. Two of these medications may be used for people with AD/HD:

- **Parlodel (bromocriptine):** This medication is mostly used to treat Parkinson's disease and *hyperprolactinemia* (a neuroendocrine condition resulting in too much prolactin — the hormone that makes the breasts secrete milk), but it is sometimes useful in treating AD/HD as well.

- **Symmetrel (amantadine):** Again, this medication is mostly used for Parkinson's patients, but it can help AD/HD symptoms. Symmetrel is also useful for treating traumatic brain injuries.

Antihypertensives

These medications affect the norepinephrine system in various ways. Psychiatrists use them to treat some anxiety conditions, and they are sometimes used to control hyperactivity or anger. Antihypertensives used for people with AD/HD include the following:

- **Catapres (clonidine):** This medication is somewhat sedating and short-acting. Catapres is sometimes used to induce sleep in children and adults and is also helpful for hyperactivity and impulsivity.

- **Tenex (guanfacine):** This medication is similar to clonidine but is longer-acting and less sedating.

- **Inversine (mecamylamine):** This is a nicotinic receptor antagonist — originally a high blood pressure medicine — that is being used to treat Tourette's syndrome and has promise for use in AD/HD, depression, and bipolar affective disorder.

✔ **Beta blockers: Attenolol, inderal, nadolol, metoprolol:** Dr. John J. Ratey (coauthor of *Driven to Distraction*) uses inderal along with stimulants in some patients to get even more improvement of their AD/HD. Beta blockers are useful for migraine prophylaxis, as well as for anxiety, anger, and high blood pressure.

Anticonvulsants

These medications are primarily designed to reduce or prevent seizures, but they are used in psychiatry as mood stabilizers and to treat anger problems. The use of anticonvulsants for behavior disorders other than mood swings and anger control is probably going to increase as we understand more about the causes of these other disorders. For instance, prominent MDs such as Dr. Daniel Amen (author of *Healing ADD*; see Chapter 20) and Dr. Stephen Suffin and Dr. W. Hamlin Emory (directors of CNS Response) all recommend the use of anticonvulsants for certain types of AD/HD. Anticonvulsants on the market include the following:

✔ **Depakote (divalproex):** This is the most widely used mood stabilizer now, except for lithium. Some potential for liver toxicity exists.

✔ **Neurontin (gabapentin):** This medication is used as a mood stabilizer, to treat neuropathic pain, and to treat traumatic brain injuries.

✔ **Tegretol (cabamazepine):** Despite a high incidence of unpleasant side effects, such as dizziness, clumsiness, nausea, and some liver toxicity, this medication is still in use.

✔ **Klonopin (clonazepam):** This anticonvulsant is used in certain seizure disorders and to treat anxiety.

✔ **Lamictal (lamotrigine):** This medication is good for bipolar depression. (Some people say all the anticonvulsants are useful for some depression.)

One more for the road

One medication used to treat some people with AD/HD doesn't fit into any of the other categories in this chapter:

✔ **Buspar (buspirone):** This serotonin stabilizer is used for anxiety and anger control. It can also help with impulsivity in some people.

Finding Success with Medication

As you can see, a lot of different medications are used to treat AD/HD and associated conditions, so it can be tricky to find just the right one and just the right dose for your symptoms. Just to make it more interesting, many people often need to use more than one medication. With a good doctor on your side — one who has experience in working with a variety of people with AD/HD — your chances of finding the right fit increase.

Often the medication does not last for the entire day. Even the long-acting formulas often fade in six or eight hours. Some people take multiple doses throughout the day or combine a long-acting with a shorter-acting medication in the evening to get complete coverage.

Because the effects of different medications can vary and the side effects can run from mild to severe, you need to make sure that you're diligent in following your progress. Your doctor can only know how well your medication is working if you provide feedback on your experiences. The best way to do this is to understand the positive results you're looking for and to be aware of the potential side effects that can accompany them.

This section gets you up to speed on potential positive and negative results of your medication trials. We offer some guidelines to help you follow your progress with each medication you try, so that your doctor has the information she needs to find the right combination of drug and dosage.

Even the best medication at the perfect dose does you no good if you don't take it when you're supposed to. People with AD/HD are notorious for forgetting their medication, and many children with AD/HD resist taking medication at all. Before you write a medication off as not working, make sure that you give it its due by strictly following the doctor's instructions on how and when to take your pill(s), and then discussing the results with the doctor.

Recognizing positive results

Many people don't know what constitutes a positive result with medication. Obviously, you're hoping to see changes in your symptoms, but what exactly does that mean? Some of the results you should see when a medication and dosage level are working for you include the following:

✔ Better control over attention

✔ Decreased distractibility

- ✔ Better ability to remember things

- ✔ Decreased hyperactivity or restlessness

- ✔ Improved ability to control emotions. Irritability, impatience, and moodiness are common symptoms. The proper medication can reduce these considerably.

- ✔ Improved motivation level. This can be as simple as being able to start and finish projects that you couldn't before, or it could be an increase in your desire to so something.

- ✔ Increased ability to think before acting

- ✔ Improved school or job performance

For some people, these effects can be hard to see right away; for others, they can be immediate. Also, a medication may improve some symptoms without touching others. Keeping a log of your daily experiences can help you see how well your medication program is working for you. (See the upcoming section "Charting your progress.")

When you get positive results, you may think that you should try to minimize the amount of medication you take. However, the National Institute of Mental Health multi-center trial (MTA), whose results were published in the *Archives of General Psychiatry* in 1999, showed that the biggest difference between people who were treated in the community and those treated by AD/HD specialists was the percentage of people whose performance was normalized. Guess who got the best results? That's right: the folks under the specialists' care. The best treatments with medication can make a person function in the normal range about 85 percent of the time.

You may be one of those people who has a fine tuning point of medication that gives you optimal results. (If you take just a little less or more than you should, you don't function nearly as well.) You won't know that unless you allow the doctor to try different doses (and maybe different medications).

Sometimes too much of a good thing can be a problem. When you take your medication, look for signs that the dose is too strong, such as:

- ✔ Feeling anxious, jittery, or overly drowsy

- ✔ Developing symptoms that you didn't have before

- ✔ Experiencing mood changes that get worse and worse

Singling out side effects

If you take medication to treat your AD/HD, you may experience side effects. These side effects may be so mild that they don't discourage you from taking your medication, or they may outweigh the benefits you see from the drug. Still others may be downright unhealthy for you even if you could stand them long enough to give the medication a fair trial.

Some of the most common side effects of AD/HD medications include the following:

- **Loss of appetite:** Most of the time, stimulant medications cause a brief decrease in appetite, which then returns to normal. In some people, appetite actually increases. Working your meals around your medication schedule can help you get the food you need throughout the day. Because medication is scheduled to wear off before bedtime, you can usually plan an evening snack — or even a full dinner. Another good solution is to plan a healthy protein-rich meal in the morning before you take your first dose for the day.

- **Insomnia:** Difficulty falling asleep or winding down at night is fairly common in AD/HD, even when medication isn't in the picture. If your medication causes sleep problems, sometimes they can be reduced by adjusting either the strength or the timing of the last dose of the day. Some hyperactive people need a dose right before bed to help them calm down, while other people without hyperactivity respond to a lower afternoon dose or even an elimination of it. If these changes in medication don't work (or don't work well enough), try practicing good sleep *hygiene* (habits). We cover sleep hygiene in Chapter 14. Occasionally, it is necessary for the doctor to prescribe something to induce sleep.

- **Rebound symptoms:** About half to two-thirds of AD/HD patients who take stimulants experience some rebound effects as the medication wears off. The rebound symptoms can be moodiness, irritability, increased distractibility, or other increased AD/HD symptoms that last for half an hour to an hour. This is usually worst when the medication is wearing off before the evening meal, because that is a low point in most people's day anyway. The rebound symptoms can be reduced in a variety of ways. Sometimes difficulty falling asleep is a rebound symptom when the medication wears off in the hour or two before bedtime.

- **Stomach upset:** Taking your medication with food usually cuts down on the incidence of stomachache or nausea.

- **Headaches:** For most people, ibuprofen or acetaminophen alleviates the pain until this side effect disappears.

✔ **Changes in personality:** This side effect can take the form of irritability, moodiness, or depression. If these things happen, you probably are going to want a different medication.

✔ **Increased heart rate or blood pressure:** The symptoms are generally mild, but if your heart rate is very high or if you experience chest pains or a fluttering feeling in your chest, call your doctor right away.

✔ **Skin rashes:** Some people are allergic to ingredients in certain medications, such as the dyes used to color them. The allergy often shows up as a rash. The only way to get around this side effect is to change medications.

✔ **Tics (abnormal muscle twitches):** Some people with AD/HD have tics either because they have a co-morbid condition, like Tourette's syndrome, or for some other reason. Stimulants and other AD/HD medications can affect tics either for the better or for the worse, depending on the individual.

Don't let this list frighten you; in most cases, you won't have to tolerate any side effects at all. And if you do, most side effects can be eliminated by either changing the dosage or the medication itself. Work with your doctor closely to find the optimal combination of the medication, the dosage level, and the time of day that you take it.

Sometimes side effects decrease after a week or two of taking a medication. Talk with your doctor, and try to stick with your planned medication for a few weeks before making a change based on side effects.

Stunted growth

Some children taking stimulants for AD/HD have been reported to experience slowed growth. Obviously, slowed growth isn't a side effect that you'll be able to notice right away; only after a few years of continued medication use will you know if it's a concern. Generally, growth speeds up as soon as the medication is stopped. As a result, many doctors try to find times when the medication can be eliminated, such as during school vacations.

This problem has been studied quite a bit, and the consensus is that very few children are stunted by stimulants. Even if they continue to take the medications, most children meet or exceed their projected growth. If you think you want to take your child off medication in the summer and on weekends to counteract the possibility of slowed growth, consider how much his AD/HD affects his and your life during the periods when he is off medication. Also, keep in mind that it can be difficult for a child to readjust to medication after being off it, especially if that readjustment is required on a weekly basis.

Charting your progress

To get the most out of medications, you need to keep track of your progress and create a log that you can review with your doctor. Although keeping a log does take some time and organization, it makes getting the right drug, dosage, and schedule much easier and keeps you from retracing your previous steps.

Here are the things to keep track of when you try a medication:

- **Medication name:** Usually the brand name of the drug is sufficient (such as *Ritalin*).

- **Dosage amounts and schedule:** Make sure you note whether you remembered to take your dose when you were supposed to.

- **Observed positive effects:** This includes any of the bullet points we list in the "Recognizing positive results" section earlier in the chapter. Also include when these effects start (how soon after taking the medication) and when they stop.

- **Side effects:** Note any negative effects you feel from the medication and include when these effects appear and disappear. These negative effects consist of both the side effects we list in the "Singling out side effects" section and any worsening of your symptoms over the course of the day.

- **Comments from other people:** If you're the one taking the medication, you may not be able to see some of its effects. We recommend that you have a loved one make notes regarding your symptoms and behavior. As well, we suggest that you write down any comments you receive from other people throughout the day, such as praise you get at work.

You can find a medication log in this book's appendix or at www. reiinstitute.com/resources.html.

Knowing when to call it quits

Finding the right medication, strength, and dosage schedule is a trial-and-error process. With the right doctor on your side — one who understands your symptoms and all the different medications available — you can experience significant success using medication for your symptoms.

Unfortunately, finding just the right combination can be frustrating for some people, especially if side effects come into play. In this case, you have a few options:

- ✔ **Stick it out:** You have a lot of alternatives for medications, strengths, and time schedules, so if you don't see success right away, chances are you'll find it eventually. Don't get discouraged if your first attempt (or second or third) doesn't work. The odds are in your favor for finding the right medication.

- ✔ **Take some time off and try again later:** Sometimes just giving your body a break can do wonders. Take a few weeks or months off from using medication, and try it again later. New drugs come out all the time, one of which could be just right for you.

- ✔ **Look for other alternatives:** Medication is effective for most people, but it's not the only way to treat the biological side of AD/HD.

- ✔ **Find a new doctor:** Sometimes a new professional with a fresh perspective can help you find the right medication (and dosage) for your symptoms. If you go this route, make sure that you take all your notes about what you've tried, when, and what your experiences were. Be sure to include the medication types, dosage times and amounts, and when you tried them.

Drug therapy is not the magic bullet that some people would like to think. Keep in mind that biological treatment is only one part of treating AD/HD. As your coauthor Mike likes to tell his medical students, if the medication did all the work, we'd just send the pills to school, and the students could stay home.

As you are discovering in this book, you can take other avenues to treat your AD/HD symptoms. Don't give up if medication doesn't work for you. We can confidently say that at least one treatment option presented in this book will have a positive impact on your life.

Chapter 9

Queuing Up Counseling, Coaching, and Training

● ●

In This Chapter

▶ Exploring types of counseling and therapy

▶ Examining AD/HD coaching

▶ Discovering training options

▶ Locating a professional to work with

● ●

*C*ounseling, coaching, and training are parts of the core treatment strategy for many people with AD/HD. Combined with biological treatment approaches (see Chapters 8, 11, 12, and 13), counseling, coaching, and training can do wonders in helping you develop the necessary awareness and skills to handle the symptoms of AD/HD and the other conditions that occur along with AD/HD.

In this chapter, we examine the roles of counseling, coaching, and training in treating AD/HD. We discuss many of the types of counseling that are commonly used for people with AD/HD, such as insight-oriented and cognitive-behavioral. We introduce you to an emerging discipline called *AD/HD coaching* and present several types of training to help you develop essential life skills. This chapter also guides you through the process of finding the right therapist and presents some other options, such as group therapy and AD/HD support groups.

Adding Counseling to Your Treatment Plan

Even though AD/HD is a biological disorder (see Chapter 2), counseling can do a lot to help you deal with the symptoms that accompany the condition.

Counseling can help you develop skills to deal with many of the primary and secondary symptoms (which we discuss in Chapter 3), although it won't eliminate the symptoms altogether.

Counseling comes in many different forms and, as a result, can offer differing levels of success for someone with AD/HD. In order to choose the right type of therapy for you and your goals, you must understand how counseling fits into your AD/HD picture. Here are some things to consider:

- ✔ **Understand that you'll need to make adjustments.** Chances are that before you ever got a diagnosis, you developed coping strategies to deal with problems caused by having AD/HD. With a diagnosis in hand, you may need to replace your original coping strategies with skills that will work better in the long run. Even if medications help you substantially (see Chapter 8), you probably need to make adjustments to the way you live. Counseling can help a lot.

- ✔ **Manage the label.** For many people with AD/HD, putting a label on their symptoms is complicated. On one hand, it's nice to have an explanation for why you act the way you do. On the other hand, identifying too much with the label can cause problems of its own, such as feeling limited in what you can do because you have a "disorder." For this reason, many people benefit from examining what being labeled with AD/HD means.

- ✔ **Recognize the biological basis for the condition.** When you understand a bit about the cause of AD/HD — the fact that AD/HD has a biological basis (see Chapter 2) — you can begin to look at your symptoms differently and remove some of blame and shame that you may have about the way your brain works.

- ✔ **Examine your attitude about therapy.** Many people are prejudiced against any kind of therapy because they associate the word with psychiatry and psychology, and thus with being mentally ill. Unfortunately, a stigma is still attached to the whole idea of dealing with problematic emotions, thoughts, and behaviors, so people tend to avoid seeking help for problems like having AD/HD.

- ✔ **Deal with denial.** Some people with AD/HD want to deny their condition or the severity of their symptoms. Part of the difficulty is that AD/HD is a neurobiological condition, and research indicates that many people with neurobiological conditions have a limited understanding of their problems. The stigma that we discuss in the previous bullet is obviously another factor.

In order to find the best type of counseling, you need to understand the areas you want to work on, as well as your views and feelings about different types of therapy.

Exploring Counseling and Therapy Options

Many options for counseling and therapy are available to help you with your AD/HD. Each type has its strength and weakness, and not all are right for you. This section presents many of the common types of counseling and therapy and offers a realistic view of what each type can and can't do for you.

People often use the terms *counseling* and *therapy* interchangeably when referring to psychotherapeutic techniques, but there is a difference. In rough terms, *counseling* refers to help in the form of conversation and discussion with someone who has general training in problems of emotions, behavior, and relationships. A counselor may or may not have detailed, specific training in a particular set of therapeutic techniques and usually doesn't have as much advanced training as a clinical psychologist or social worker. *Therapy,* in this context, usually refers to the application of specific theories or techniques by someone who has advanced training in those theories and techniques.

Understanding yourself through insight-oriented therapy

Insight-oriented therapy is one of the oldest forms of psychotherapy. Based on what amounts to a long, extended conversation with a knowledgeable therapist, it is intended to help you better understand what makes you tick. Insight-oriented therapy helps you uncover your unconscious motivations so that you can understand why you do what you do, and you can make better choices about how to behave.

Bringing the unconscious to light

This type of therapy works on the belief that our actions have many causes, some of which we're aware of and some of which we're not. For example, as a person with AD/HD, you may procrastinate because putting something off until the last minute adds external pressure that gives you motivation (stimulation) to do the work. Or maybe you procrastinate because you don't like the job you have to do and want to avoid it as long as possible. Or maybe both factors (and some others) are at play. By knowing what causes you to wait until the last minute to do your job, you can develop ways to stop procrastinating. For example:

✔ If you unconsciously want or need the stimulus of a tight deadline to get to work, you can set up several interim deadlines for yourself. You can use the pressure of each deadline to avoid having to do the entire project at the last minute.

✔ If your unconscious motivation for procrastination is that you really don't like the job you have to do, you can change your relationship to the work and avoid having to suffer at the last minute and end up doing a bad job. In this case you could set up a system of small rewards to encourage yourself to get a little bit of work done each day.

The bottom line is that by understanding your motivations you can design ways to work through the problems. Without a clear idea of why you act the way you do, finding a way to change is like shooting in the dark. You may by chance hit on a solution, but the odds are much better if you turn on the light and take aim first.

Realizing the limitations

One of the problems of using insight-oriented therapy for AD/HD is that some of your behaviors are not only unconscious but also hard-wired into your brain. Because these behaviors are not learned in the usual ways — instead, they're biologically determined — this type of therapy may not help with all your symptoms. In this situation, be careful not to take on responsibility for something that you really can't control. Just because you know why you act a certain way doesn't always mean you'll be able to change your behavior. For example, you may not be able to change your impatience with standing in lines if that is part of the pattern of your AD/HD. And even with the help of a therapist, you may not be certain whether a behavior is under your control or not.

But therapy didn't work for me

Many people with AD/HD try therapy before they even learn they have the condition. And many of them experience few, if any, positive benefits. Also, with the preponderance of self-help books available, we can safely say that nearly everyone (okay, everyone) we've worked with has tried self-help strategies and been disappointed with the results.

Chances are, if you're one of these people, you're probably ready to just skip over this chapter because you didn't see any results before.

We encourage you to try counseling and therapy again even if it didn't seem to do much for you before you knew you had AD/HD. The knowledge of having AD/HD can help you identify areas where counseling and therapy can help. But more importantly, by addressing the biological end of things (through one or more of the biological treatments we present in this book), you'll more than likely find that you're able to make some real headway with the right therapy or combination of therapies.

Digging deep

The process of identifying your hidden motivations obviously involves look-ing within yourself. Done with the help of a skilled therapist, this process can uncover many things that are painful to deal with. For this reason, you must work with a good therapist who can help you cope with the emotions that emerge.

This type of therapy can help you deal with the grief of having missed important parts of your youth or with the difficulties of accepting the reali-ties of being "different." (Supportive therapy, which we discuss next, can do the same.) Insight-oriented therapy can be useful for alleviating co-occurring conditions, such as depression and anxiety, and for coping with secondary symptoms of AD/HD, such as low self-esteem.

Benefiting from supportive therapy

Think of supportive therapy as your personal cheerleader. Supportive ther-apy not only offers you encouragement; it often also helps you keep a healthy perspective on your progress.

The purpose of supportive therapy is to help you see your life in perspective and maximize your ability to mobilize your internal resources to help your-self. (Because many people with AD/HD have low self-esteem, they can't see their strengths or abilities objectively.) Supportive therapy can also help you find solutions to problems you're having. One thing that is not emphasized in supportive therapies is substantial analysis of what you can't immediately see or know about yourself — that's why insight-oriented therapies exist.

Most integrated programs of treating AD/HD include some aspects of sup-portive therapy. You won't likely find a therapist who uses *only* supportive therapies, so the best way to find out if a particular therapist incorporates this approach is to ask. If your therapist describes her practice as humanist psychotherapy, Rogerian therapy, or Eriksonian therapy, you can bet she has supportive therapy in her repertoire.

Considering cognitive-behavioral counseling

Cognitive-behavioral counseling (which is also called cognitive-behavioral therapy) is a systematic approach to helping you change your behavior. The cognitive aspect of this approach consists of figuring out what your internal dialogue is and how it relates to your moods and actions. The behavioral aspect consists of using various methods of manipulation to change your behavior.

Unlike insight-oriented therapy, the focus isn't on your motivation or even trying to understand your beliefs. Instead, this approach focuses on identifying thought and behavior patterns and using techniques to change them. Proponents of this type of counseling believe that by changing your thoughts and behaviors, your underlying beliefs change, too. (But you can either believe that or not!) The point is that your behaviors are learned through a combination of thought processes and conditioning, and they can be altered using the same methods.

The process of doing cognitive-behavioral counseling usually involves some type of homework. Here's what's involved in the traditional form of cognitive-behavioral counseling:

- ✓ **Record your thoughts.** You write them down as they appear. (Well, not always right at the moment, but as soon as you have time.) The key thoughts are the ones that occur before a negative behavior.

- ✓ **Record your behaviors.** What you're trying to do is create a record of how many times your behavior is a problem, how your behavior relates to your thoughts, and what exactly happens from moment to moment in the unfolding of a behavior.

- ✓ **Qualify and scale your emotions.** It may be that certain behaviors are associated with particular emotions or that you experience certain emotions more frequently than others. To discover this, keep track of the types of emotions you experience. In addition, note their intensity: Use a 100-point scale and assign a level to each of your emotions. Doing so usually helps you to understand how strong the motivation is for a particular behavior and makes it easier to see how what you think relates to what you do.

- ✓ **Look for connections.** The information you have collected so far should lend itself to finding patterns of relationships between your thoughts, feelings, and behaviors. Identifying these patterns prepares you to strategize about modifying them.

- ✓ **Create alternative ways of thinking to change the behavior.** This involves replacing the negative thoughts with positive ones and using conditioning principles to change your behavior.

For the left-brain, intellectual type of person, these steps aren't too cumbersome. But for many people, especially disorganized people with AD/HD, these steps can represent a challenge. Fortunately, most cognitive-behavioral therapists use a more organic, dynamic approach to these steps that makes discovering your thoughts and changing your behavior much easier (and faster).

For the most part, cognitive-behavioral counseling is a good fit for people with AD/HD. For adults especially, it's much more effective than the old standby, behavior modification (which we discuss next). In fact, we believe in the cognitive-behavioral approach so strongly that we cover it in more detail in Chapter 10.

Exploring behavior modification

Behavior modification is the most common type of behavior therapy, especially for children with AD/HD. This type of therapy involves using a structured environment to provide rewards to reinforce positive behaviors and consequences to minimize the possibility for negative behaviors. If you have a child with AD/HD, because of the need for consistency and structure, behavior modification often requires modifying your *own* behavior as much as your child's.

As we explain in Chapter 10, behavior modification is applied differently to address AD/HD than to address other problems. Behavior modification is particularly helpful for children who have discipline problems and for children with AD/HD under the age of 12.

As with most of the other approaches to counseling and therapy we discuss in this chapter, the best results are achieved when behavior modification is combined with other types of therapy (see Chapter 7).

Expressing yourself through play therapy

Many people with AD/HD have difficulty knowing how they feel. If this describes your child, play therapy is designed to help him get in touch with his emotions in a nonthreatening way. This type of therapy uses structured play to help children express their feelings.

Play therapy is basically a children's version of insight-oriented therapy. It doesn't seem very effective at helping people reduce the actual symptoms of AD/HD, but it works very well for children with emotional problems who are cut off from their inner world or their ability to express their emotions.

Seeking psychoeducational counseling

This type of counseling educates you on the effects of AD/HD and teaches you how to better handle the difficulties by developing strategies for coping with your symptoms and their effects. Psychoeducational counseling is all about helping you understand your condition and giving you skills and strategies to work with it.

Psychoeducational counselors are essentially teachers, instructing you about AD/HD and providing coping strategies and problem-solving skills. When you leave a good psychoeducational session, you should take with you new tools for dealing with your AD/HD, as well as a better understanding of why you do the things you do.

This counseling approach is very practical, focusing on education and skills rather than underlying emotions or beliefs. Psychoeducational counseling is often helpful for people who like to gather information and need new skills but don't need or want to dig deeply into their emotions.

Considering family therapy

AD/HD and its associated behaviors are a family problem. The person with AD/HD may have the symptoms, but the people he lives with are all affected by them. For this reason, you may want to get your entire family involved in therapy.

For example, if you have a child with AD/HD, therapy can help you discover how to best interact with him to promote the types of behaviors you want to encourage and reduce the behaviors you want to avoid. If your spouse or partner has AD/HD, going to therapy with him or her can help both of you deal with communication and interpersonal problems that stem from AD/HD.

A therapist with specific experience in AD/HD is, obviously, the best choice. Like individual therapy, family therapy can take many forms. But the basic goal of each is to try to clear up communications between family members and to balance influence and power so everyone can get more of what he or she needs. Often, a crisis is the catalyst for a family entering therapy together. However, we encourage you to make use of family therapy before things get to the boiling point.

Getting into group therapy

Group therapy entails a group of people who have similar issues meeting (usually regularly for a set period of time) under the guidance of a therapist. Group therapy often focuses on helping you develop specific skills and allowing you to share your experiences with other people who have AD/HD. This type of therapy can take many forms, including the following:

 ✔ **Ongoing:** Some therapists facilitate an ongoing group that may have members who cycle in and out. The constants are the facilitator of the group and the overall structure that the therapist provides.

✔ **Time-limited:** Some groups are scheduled to meet for a specific amount of time. Many therapists find that having a group that lasts, for example, ten weeks is beneficial because each member is likely to attend each session. This allows members to feel comfortable with one another and to create bonds. Obviously, this setup has real advantages, especially if establishing and maintaining relationships is part of the group's focus. A set agenda can also be established for each session.

✔ **Skills-based:** Sometimes a therapist will set up a group to address specific areas of struggle and to focus on problem solving or skills training. For example, a group could work specifically on social skills or on financial management.

✔ **Supportive:** As the name implies, these group sessions generally focus on participants sharing their experiences and offering support. This type of group may or may not emphasize learning coping skills or problem-solving techniques.

Of course, a single group can combine two or more of these approaches. If you're interested in group therapy, your goal should be to locate a group that is structured in a way that is congruent with your needs and desires.

Using support groups

AD/HD support groups offer you a chance to commiserate with other people who face some of the same challenges that you do. Doing so can help you gain a healthy perspective about your struggles, as well as about areas where you excel.

If you're looking for an informal way to meet with other people with AD/HD, a support group may be the answer. These groups are generally open to anyone and scheduled to meet every week or so. To get the most out of a support group, you need to understand what it can and can't do for you. Here are some facts about support groups to help you keep their role in perspective:

✔ **Support groups are often informal organizations created by nonprofessionals — usually people with AD/HD.** This means that some groups do not have an AD/HD professional facilitating the discussion. The risk here is that you may end up getting some questionable ideas and misinformation from someone else in the group. (A lot of misinformation about AD/HD is floating around.)

✔ **People can come and go as they please, which means that the members of the groups change often.** This can be either a good or a bad thing. If, for example, you don't get along with someone in the group, the problem may not be long-term if that other person decides not to attend regularly. On the other hand, a constantly changing group dynamic can make it difficult for some people to feel comfortable.

✔ **There's no commitment — you can choose to attend only when you want or need to.** This flexibility can be an asset, considering how busy most of our lives are. On the other hand, it means that the group can fall apart for lack of support. Support groups are often very dependent on the few stalwart people who found them and make the effort to keep them going.

Chapter 20 contains suggestions for locating support groups in your area.

Considering Coaching

Working with a coach can be very useful if you have AD/HD. A coach is, among other things, part cheerleader, part taskmaster, part personal assistant, and part teacher. No specific training is required to become an AD/HD coach, and coaches come from a variety of backgrounds, including psychology, counseling, and teaching. The main attribute a coach brings to the table is specialized knowledge about the challenges facing people with AD/HD and the skills that help overcome those challenges.

A coach may use techniques related to counseling or training approaches, such as psychoeducational counseling, supportive therapy, or skills training, but her goal is to help you improve your life. A coach may help you do the following:

✔ Develop structures for organizing your life

✔ Make plans and set goals

✔ Deal with mundane tasks, such as paying bills

✔ Get and stay motivated

✔ Develop time and money management skills

A good AD/HD coach works with you to identify the areas where you struggle and helps you find ways to improve on these deficits. A coach wants to see you succeed, and she roots for you every step of the way.

The way an AD/HD coach works varies depending on the coach and your needs and desires. Some coaches meet their clients only occasionally and stay in frequent contact by phone. For example, this type of coach may schedule 15-minute calls with you each day to check on your progress and guide you along your way. Other coaches focus more on face-to-face contact; some even come into your home to help you with specific tasks, such as organizing or working on social skills.

Taking a Look at Training

Training approaches focus on helping you develop specific skills that you may be missing or areas where you could stand some improvement. Training covers many areas and isn't necessarily specific to people with AD/HD. By the same token, training is performed by a variety of professionals from teachers to psychotherapists, from foremen to coaches.

Examining awareness training

Awareness training consists of developing skills to gain a greater awareness of who you are and of the world around you. (Makes sense, huh?) Awareness training can take many forms, but the most common is meditation. By meditating and exploring your inner life, you can gain insight into how you operate — why you act the way you do and how you can change your behavior.

If you have AD/HD and think you could never sit still or quiet your mind long enough to meditate, don't despair! This type of training can take many forms and some of them (for example, Kundalini yoga or Sufi dancing) are much more active than the Zen-like practice that many people imagine.

We believe that awareness training can be of considerable benefit for people with AD/HD. Therefore, we spend some time in Chapter 10 exploring this approach in more detail.

Taking parent training

If your child has AD/HD, parent training offers a combination of therapies that we discuss in this chapter — such as supportive therapy, skills training, behavior modification, and psychoeducational training — to help you work with your child effectively and reduce the problems he has to deal with. The skills you learn in this type of training are particularly important if you (or your partner) have AD/HD as well; parents with AD/HD often have difficulty with self-discipline and organization, and they may have been poorly parented themselves if their parents didn't know much about AD/HD.

Parent training can take many forms, from small classes run by a psychologist to commercial curriculums, from one-on-one study sessions to workshops led by traveling professionals. The content of each training program can vary considerably as well. Some programs can be very basic, teaching young parents how to take care of their children, while others may be targeted at particular problems or types of children (or parents). If this type of training interests you, you need to do some research to determine what is available in your area that offers the information and skills you need.

Before you sign up for a training program, make sure it focuses specifically on parenting a child with AD/HD — not any other condition. Also, keep in mind that you may need to take more than one class in order to get all the information and skills that you need.

Improving yourself through skills training

If you have AD/HD, you may lack some basic skills. These can include social, organizational, or academic skills, to name a few. If this is the case, skills training can help because it focuses on the areas where you need to develop your abilities, rather than focusing on your emotions.

For someone with AD/HD who doesn't want to do talk therapy, skills training can be a valuable approach. With this type of training, you focus on improving your deficits without having to dig deeply into your motivations for why you may act a certain way. Also, this approach is very practical in that you focus only on skills you want to work on.

Skills training won't address the emotional challenges you may have, except the skills of recognizing and expressing what you feel. This type of training won't necessarily result in changing your behaviors; then again, you may find that having new skills to deal with what you have to do may change the way you conduct your life.

Finding a Counselor, Coach, or Trainer

The single most important aspect of counseling, coaching, and training — even more important than the type of approach you choose — is the professional you work with. A good professional who understands the issues facing someone with AD/HD and who can help guide you through the many difficulties you face can do wonders for your ability to function successfully in the world.

You may have to work hard to find the right professional for you. In Chapter 4 we discuss how to find a healthcare professional and how to work with one to get your needs met. These suggestions are also valid for choosing a counselor, coach, or trainer, so we encourage you to flip back to that chapter. (Go ahead — we're happy to wait.)

In addition, here are some ways to go about finding a good professional:

- ✔ **Ask your other healthcare professionals for a referral.** Most healthcare professionals have referral lists and are happy to make recommendations to their patients.

- ✔ **Ask other people you know who've been dealing with AD/HD.** Referrals from friends can be very helpful, but keep in mind that a therapist, coach, or trainer who is a good fit for your friend may not be the best person for you. If you know several people with AD/HD, ask each of them for suggestions.

- ✔ **Attend a support group.** If you don't know many other people with AD/HD, a support group is a great place to meet people who can offer suggestions for professionals such as therapists, coaches, or trainers. See the section "Using support groups" earlier in this chapter.

- ✔ **Check with your insurance company.** If you rely on insurance to pay for your care, your choice of professionals may be limited. You may also have restrictions on the number of times you can see a therapist in a year.

- ✔ **Consult the phone book.** You local phone book has listings of counselors, therapists, and psychologists. Some may have ads in the Yellow Pages saying that they specifically work with AD/HD.

- ✔ **Search the Internet.** Like the phone book, the Internet is a source of names of potential therapists. In your favorite search engine, type in the approach you want to try (such as "cognitive-behavioral therapy" or "AD/HD coach") and your location, and you should find some leads.

The Internet can be helpful in other ways as well. If you find an article about AD/HD written by a therapist whose ideas resonate with you, try contacting the author and asking if he or she has suggestions for therapists in your area. You can also find a state-by-state listing of professionals on Web sites such as www.add.org and www.addconsults.com.

Finding a good counselor, coach, or trainer requires the same combination of networking, tenacity, and luck as finding a good professional of any sort. Don't get discouraged if you don't find someone right away; the upfront effort required will definitely pay off.

Chapter 10

Managing Behavior

*W*ithout a doubt, the main aspect of AD/HD that you're going to deal with — whether in yourself, your child, or another loved one — is the behaviors that accompany the symptoms. Since the beginning of AD/HD treatment, these behaviors have been targeted with specific approaches. By far the most popular and long-standing approach is behavior modification, but other techniques have been developed that work well for most people. These alternatives include cognitive-behavioral counseling (therapy) and awareness training.

This chapter explores all three techniques and offers you some insight into how they are used for people of all ages in treating the many problem behaviors that are part of AD/HD. We offer suggestions for using these approaches and for finding a professional who can help you fit them into your overall treatment strategy.

The treatment strategies we discuss in this chapter cannot alleviate every AD/HD symptom and should be just one part of a complete treatment program that involves biological, psychological, and social approaches. See Chapter 7 for ideas of how to approach treatment from a variety of angles.

Taking Behavior 101

Let's get theoretical for a minute: One traditional psychological theory hinges on the belief that behavior is simply a mechanical process of connecting reflexes together. According to this model, learning involves conditioning, and teaching involves setting up situations that encourage desired behaviors and extinguish undesired behaviors (through conditioning). The methods promoted by this model are the stock in trade of behavior modification.

Another way of looking at your behavior is to see it as the result of motivation and the connections between what you think and feel about yourself and your world. Behavior gets shaped and refined over time by several processes, including *cognitive* study (intentional teaching and learning through language) and the more subtle and mostly unconscious activity of *modeling* (copying other people's behaviors). Treating behaviors involves using teaching techniques, such as the ones we discuss in this chapter, and other types of techniques that are based on the way we think our (and other animals') brains work.

Association

The internal mechanisms of the brain are largely based on *association* — connecting one thing with another. These connections occur both in the "wiring" of the brain and in the meanings we assign to things in our minds. If two things happen at the same time, for example, we tend to associate them with each other, and a weak connection is made. If they happen at the same time on a regular basis, the connection becomes stronger; their happening together becomes a pattern.

The pattern can be modified to varying degrees by using the same methods of association that caused it to develop. Usually this involves connecting an *intrinsic motivation* (something you naturally want to do anyway) with a desired behavior. The mechanisms involved in accomplishing this connection are probably more complicated than we describe here, but Pavlov's dog is a great example to keep in mind. In human terms, by connecting a behavior you want with a specific reward — for example getting to play video games after completing homework — you encourage the behavior that you want.

Feed forward/feedback

Behavior occurs as a process called *feed forward/feedback*. The name may sound complex, but the process is fairly simple and involves the following steps:

1. **Make a plan.** You decide on a course of action. For example, if you hear a sound, you want to see what's going on. You plan to move your eyes to look. This is the first part of the feed forward.

2. **Execute your plan.** Your eyes move to look in the direction of the sound. This is the second part of the feed forward.

3. **Evaluate the outcome.** You get feedback. For example, you see whether you are looking where you meant to look.

4. **Make adjustments.** You try a new feed forward.

5. **Repeat the process.**

For people with AD/HD, the *feed forward* (making a plan and executing it) and *feedback* (seeing how your plan worked and making corrections) system doesn't work very well. The pre-frontal lobes of the brain use this system, and that same part of the brain is affected by AD/HD, as we discuss in Chapter 2.

If you have AD/HD, the feedback part of the process doesn't work properly. You may be able to formulate a plan and execute it, but you probably struggle to see the effects of your actions and make adjustments. In addition, you may lose track of your plan (because of distractibility) and make a new one instead of modifying the old one. This makes it difficult to learn new behaviors. For this reason, many AD/HD people find that they make the same types of mistakes over and over, even though the feedback is a costly penalty or some other painful outcome. Because the feed forward/feedback process is not working properly, and correcting your actions is difficult, you may struggle to create a practice of correct behaviors.

The basics of behavioral therapies

The purpose of behavioral therapies, such as those we describe in this chapter, is to help you gain skills to develop better behaviors and help you become better able to learn from the results of your actions. In the simplest sense, behavior modification attempts to accomplish these goals by creating a very structured environment with specific *motivators* (rewards and punishments) to help you learn to behave a certain way in a certain situation.

The other two approaches we present in this chapter — cognitive-behavioral counseling and awareness training — support an internal process of understanding your motivations and response (behaviors) and helping you to change the results of those motivations into more desirable behaviors.

By consciously working on understanding the process your brain uses to create behaviors, you can develop skills to help you improve the feedback, which then helps you determine how to adjust your behaviors as they occur.

Looking at Behavioral Treatments

Behavioral treatment strategies consist of specific approaches that are designed to correct misbehavior and support positive behavior. No single approach can work for everyone, every time (even though some experts may make this claim). In this section, we present three common (and often effective) approaches. In addition to describing each approach, we offer our views on when and where each can work best.

Behavior modification

Behavior modification is one of the standard treatments for AD/HD. It is used in other conditions — such as eating disorders and drug abuse — in both children and adults. For AD/HD, it is most often used by parents or teachers working with children. It involves directing the child's behavior by doing the following:

- **Creating an environment conducive to good behavior:** By reducing the possibility of misbehavior, you make it easier for your child to act the way you would like him to.

- **Reinforcing positive behaviors:** Positive feedback for good behavior is the surest way to perpetuate this positive action. By praising and rewarding your child when she behaves the way you want, you both reinforce her self-esteem and encourage more of this positive behavior.

- **Providing consequences for misbehavior:** By providing clear consequences for misbehavior, you discourage this type of behavior. The consequences need to be logical to the situation, and they must be clearly understood by your child.

- **Being consistent:** You need to apply the corrective methods as consistently as possible. As we discuss in the previous section, people with AD/HD have trouble making the connections (associations) you want them to make. If you are inconsistent about your expectations and the consequences for good and bad behaviors, you add to the confusion. At the same time, you can't expect yourself to be perfect, which is fine because the rest of the world isn't perfectly consistent, either.

Making behavior modification a success

Behavior modification has been around a while, and there is no shortage of experts claiming to have the best method to implement this approach.

Because we have this 360-page soapbox to stand on, we thought we'd offer our ideas for using behavior modification for your child. (Would you expect anything less?)

- ✔ **Use both rewards and consequences.** Some behavior modification plans use either rewards or punishments, but you really need both to get the best possible results.

- ✔ **Act quickly.** Studies have shown that if the reward or consequence is delayed, even for a short time, it doesn't work as well. Make sure that you provide the feedback (reward or consequence) for your child's behavior as soon as that behavior happens.

- ✔ **Keep it going.** Behavior modification takes a long time to be effective. Don't expect that you'll see lasting improvements after just a few weeks or even months. Keep up the program for the long haul, and make adjustments as you need to. Which brings us to the next suggestion . . .

- ✔ **Change the rewards and consequences as needed.** Your AD/HD child will get bored with the rewards and consequences quickly. (After all, people with AD/HD need change.) If you don't change them before boredom sets in, your child will lose interest in following the program.

- ✔ **Use positive reinforcement.** As much as possible, try to reward desired behaviors. Sometimes just a word or two to show you noticed your child doing the right thing is enough.

- ✔ **Use positive cognitive messages.** For example, if you're a teacher and you ask your misbehaving student to write a statement about his misbehavior, make it a positive statement, such as "I will leave other students' things alone," instead of "I won't take Johnny's pencil."

- ✔ **Use concrete reinforcements.** People with AD/HD have a hard time with abstractions, so instead of putting a star on a chart for a positive reward, give the child a poker chip or penny. Providing something that involves the tactile sense can make the reinforcement more real.

Behavior modification is as much about changing *your* behavior as it is about changing your child's. In fact, you may very well end up doing the most changing. Take another look at the list above and notice that most of the burden is placed on you — the parent or teacher — to make this system work. You need to make sure that you act in a certain way if you want your child to respond as you expect. So whose behavior is being modified?

Understanding possible downsides

For many AD/HD professionals, behavior modification has become the standard behavioral treatment and is often seen as being flawless. In our opinion, this isn't the case. Behavior modification is only as good as the people involved in it and can be applied too rigidly if you're not careful.

Here are some things to be careful of when you use behavior modification:

✔ **A power struggle can develop.** Some experts advise parents and teachers to make sure they always win power struggles. We think it's better to avoid them by thoughtful preparation and creative adjustments. Although you create and enforce the rewards and consequences, their effectiveness relies on your child agreeing to abide by them. If your child determines that he doesn't want to obey your rules, what do you do? The only way to avoid this situation is to set up your rewards and consequences so that they are agreeable to both you and your child. Consider involving your child in the process of deciding rewards and consequences for his behavior.

✔ **Beware of the idea that AD/HD is a disorder needing external correction.** This is the main problem that behavior modification can create. By its nature, this approach suggests that in order to behave correctly, a person with AD/HD needs to have her behavior controlled (modified) externally. This implies that without the rewards and consequences, the person has little chance of learning to act properly. If you accept this idea, you set up a situation where you have to be there all the time to make your child perform correctly. (This is called *negative reinforcement.*)

✔ **Avoid being coercive.** Using rewards and consequences to control someone's behavior can be seen as a form of coercion. The degree that behavior modification is coercive and oppressive is determined by the degree and range of modifications you are trying to make and by the level of control you try to have over your child. Even at its most benign, behavior modification models coercive, manipulative behaviors through its external control.

To minimize these possible problems, consistently reevaluate the goals and objectives of your behavior modification plan and your child's progress. By being mindful of the dynamic between yourself and your child, you can make adjustments to keep these problems from occurring. If problems develop in spite of your vigilance, you may find that cognitive-behavioral counseling is better suited to your situation (see the next section).

Because of the possibilities for abuse, we recommend behavior modification only in instances when a very structured environment is required — for example, in children or teens who also have oppositional defiant disorder (see Chapter 6) and are out of control. In this case, a very rigid form of behavior modification is often used, such as a token system that regulates all facets of the person's behavior (see the sidebar "The token system").

Many teachers — especially in special education — have training in using behavior modification in the classroom. Your therapist should also be able to help you tailor-make a plan that works for your family.

The token system

Parents of children with serious behavioral issues, such as those with oppositional defiant disorder (see Chapter 6), may use a strict interpretation of behavior modification that involves issuing tokens for every positive behavior and taking some away for every negative behavior, including rudeness and resistance. If the child doesn't comply with a parent's request promptly, the cost for misbehavior goes up — he loses double or triple tokens.

When using this system, your child earns tokens by fulfilling his responsibilities, such as doing homework and chores. If he wants to do anything beyond those tasks, he must pay for the privilege with his earned tokens. For example, in order to go to the movies he has to have earned enough tokens (through positive behavior) to pay for it.

If you're going to undertake behavior modification with your child, make sure that you do it with compassion. You want to be authoritative without being an authoritarian. In other words, set up a system that's clear, fair, and doesn't control to the point of not allowing your child to make some decisions on his own. The goal is to help your child develop self-discipline and behavioral competence. As your child grows and improves his behavior, make adjustments and allow more freedoms. Try to keep the rewards more prevalent than the consequences. (In other words, catch your child doing things right as often as possible.)

Cognitive-behavioral counseling

Cognitive-behavioral counseling (also called *cognitive-behavioral therapy*) is a systematic approach to helping you change your behavior. This approach (which we introduce in Chapter 9) involves changing the way you think and is based on the idea that the way you feel and act is related to the way you talk to yourself. It is bolstered by techniques of conditioning and association, as well as environmental control.

The *cognitive* aspect of this therapy consists of figuring out what your internal dialogue and thought patterns are and understanding how they relate to your moods and behaviors. The *behavioral* aspect consists of using conditioned responses to these internal dialogues to change your behavior. Unlike with behavior modification, where your behavior is essentially controlled by external rewards and punishments, your behavior is moderated by understanding your thoughts and using preconditioned approaches. This approach is more cooperative than behavior modification and is very effective for older children and adults.

Applying cognitive-behavioral counseling

Cognitive-behavioral counseling is usually implemented by a therapist who can work with you to find your problem behaviors — your motivations and the circumstances under which they appear — and develop strategies for changing these behaviors. The basic construct of cognitive-behavioral counseling involves the following steps:

1. **Choosing a behavior:** Only one behavior is examined at a time because each behavior is complex and exploring more than one confuses the understanding of motivations and circumstances.

2. **Exploring a situation where this behavior manifests:** This step involves exploring two key elements, motivations and circumstances.

   - *Motivations:* By understanding what your thoughts and feelings are before and during your behavior, you can better find a way to change the behavior using strategies that diffuse the emotions and change the thoughts that cause it.

   - *Circumstances:* Taking a look at when a behavior happens can help you understand the motivations for it.

3. **Developing a strategy:** After you understand (or at least think you do) when a behavior happens and what your thoughts and feelings are during this time, you can look for ways to change your behavior.

4. **Implementing your strategy:** Armed with a list of possible strategies, you can use one of them whenever you encounter a time when the behavior tends to happen.

5. **Assessing your results and making adjustments:** Chances are that you won't be completely successful in eliminating a behavior with the first strategy you try. By assessing the results of your strategy, you can make adjustments to how you approach a behavior until you end up with a strategy that works. You may end up with several different approaches to the same behavior depending on the circumstances that bring that behavior forward.

As an example, suppose that young Johnny throws a tantrum every time his teacher asks the students for their homework. Using cognitive-behavioral counseling, you want to find out what happens in Johnny's mind when his teacher says the word *homework* — what does Johnny hear, feel, and think?

Next, you want to find out how Johnny's teacher goes about asking for his homework. For example, does she single him out from the rest of the class? Compare this to what Johnny *thinks* is happening. Most likely, a difference of perception exists.

Also, you need to ask Johnny's parents how he approaches doing his homework. Does he finish his work? Does he remember to take it to school with him? What are his expectations of his performance? What messages are his parents sending him about homework?

As you can see, a lot of digging may need to be done in order to find the best ways to deal with the behavior.

The answers to these questions determine what type of strategy you use. For example, say that Johnny regularly finishes his homework, generally hands it in on time, and gets about average grades. However, he describes that he feels anxious and uneasy — he's afraid that he'll fail — when his teacher asks for the homework. His teacher tells him regularly that he's a smart kid and would do so much better if only he'd try harder, and his parents often remind him that if he wants to go to college he needs to do well. At this point, the strategy may be threefold:

1. **Help Johnny relax and develop a realistic expectation of his home-work performance.** Johnny may benefit from working on some physical relaxation techniques, such as deep breathing. He may also need to work on creating an internal dialogue where he tells himself that he did the best he could and his grades in the past have been satisfactory, so his homework is likely good enough.

2. **Gently remind his teacher that telling him to try harder isn't exactly what he needs to hear.** This is a classic mistake that teachers make. Even though their intention is to give their student motivation, in the case of many people with AD/HD, trying harder is not the answer. Johnny's teacher may need to take his homework without any commentary about how hard he worked.

3. **Let his parents know that their expectations are causing Johnny to feel anxious and afraid.** They can still have a goal of helping their son get into college, but they need to put less emphasis on the grades and more on his educational growth.

The bottom line is that cognitive-behavioral counseling involves looking for the pattern in your behavior and finding ways to change this pattern. The really tricky part of this behavioral approach is finding the best ways to change the behavior. As you can see in the example above, you may need significant time to explore and experiment.

The advantage with this approach is that after you get some experience with it and have some successes, it becomes pretty easy to get to the heart of the matter. And when you find the right way to change a behavior, you see significant results.

Understanding when to use cognitive-behavior counseling

This approach to managing behavior is effective for most people with AD/HD. The only real exceptions are very young children — those who are unable to articulate their thoughts and feelings — and people who need a much more structured approach, such as those who are exceptionally defiant and unwilling to cooperate in managing their behaviors.

Awareness training

In awareness training, you learn how to increase your awareness of yourself and your environment. The goal of this approach is to help you pay attention to how you think, feel, and behave. It's a bit like cognitive-behavioral counseling, except that you're examining what's happening in your head at this very moment. Instead of analyzing your thoughts, feelings, and behaviors after the fact, you monitor them all the time and make conscious decisions about how to behave as a result.

A simple way to illustrate the way awareness training works is to imagine that you build skyscrapers for a living. In order to do your job — and not fall off — you need to be constantly aware of where your body is and how each of your actions is going to affect your ability to stay on the building. You need to know if reaching too far to your right means that you'll fall off balance. You can see that this is not just a process of thinking, "I can't fall off! Don't step there! Watch out!" It involves actually paying attention, not just thinking and talking to yourself.

Through constant attention, awareness training tries to fix the feed forward/ feedback mechanism (which we discuss earlier in the chapter) that's spastic in people with AD/HD. In the example of the skyscraper, the sheer level of physical danger is enough for most people with AD/HD to maintain their attention on not falling. However, when your environment is not so dangerous you need to apply techniques that help you develop the awareness and keep your attention where you want it. This is where awareness training comes in.

Many approaches to awareness training exist, and more are being developed every year. This approach holds a lot of promise for people with AD/HD, both because the techniques are varied (there's an approach to fit just about everyone) and because the techniques can benefit anyone.

Here are a few ways to develop your awareness:

  ✔ **Mindfulness meditation:** Several types of mindfulness meditation training exist, but the easiest one for most people with AD/HD is a walking meditation. This approach consists of the following steps:

    • *Find a quiet place free of distractions where you can walk quietly.* This place can be your backyard or a park.

- *Stand up straight.* Keep your back straight, your shoulders back, and your head looking down at a point a few feet in front of you.

- *Breathe deep, slow breaths.* Breathe in a relaxed manner from your stomach.

- *Take a step slowly.* Focus on the sensation of lifting your foot, moving it forward, and putting it down. In this meditation, you focus on your walking instead of your breath. Follow each foot as you lift and place it in front of you.

- *Release your thoughts.* As you walk, let go of any thoughts other than the moving of your feet. Release any thought that comes into your mind by thinking "Lift, move forward, and put it down." Watch, listen, feel, taste, and smell. Do not talk to yourself about what is going on as you are walking.

✔ **Martial arts:** Many types of martial arts, such as aikido, can help you become aware of your body and keep your mind in the present moment.

✔ **Tai chi and certain forms of yoga:** These techniques are useful for helping people become more aware of themselves and their surroundings.

✔ **Sensory integration:** Sensory integration techniques vary, but at their core they involve helping you become more aware of your body in space. We cover this approach in detail in Chapter 13.

Most of these techniques focus on developing body awareness, but one of the main aspects of awareness training is to help you learn to be in the present moment and be aware of more than just your body. Ultimately, you want to learn how to focus your attention on how you feel, what you think, and how you act. Knowing these things can help you see where your behavior comes from and help you develop ways to change it.

Awareness training is much easier to do with the help of a coach (see Chapter 9). A coach can not only show you techniques and make sure you do them correctly; she can also offer gentle reminders to keep you on track.

Also, for many people, a combination of cognitive-behavioral counseling and awareness training can be very effective.

Chapter 11

Narrowing In on Nutrition, Vitamins, and Herbs

*M*any people find that making changes to their diet and using vitamins, herbs, and combination supplements called *nutraceuticals* judiciously go a long way toward reducing the symptoms of AD/HD. While definitive research doesn't exist to demonstrate the effectiveness of these treatments, we expect our understanding of these treatments to grow extensively in the near future as researchers and AD/HD professionals devote serious attention to them.

In this chapter, we cover the many ways that diet, vitamins, and herbs are being used to manage the symptoms of AD/HD. In addition, we discuss how controlling your physical environment may impact AD/HD. We try to stay as objective as possible, presenting the various options available to you and explaining potential benefits and risks. But we admit that sometimes we get a little biased: After all, eating a balanced diet and drinking enough water are just good common sense, whether you have AD/HD or not!

For treatments that are more complex, such as taking vitamins or herbs, we strongly suggest spending time up front finding qualified professionals to help you. Frankly, these treatments can get pretty involved, and we simply don't have space in this book to go into the detail you need before making a decision to ingest one or more of these substances.

We see some similarities between the treatments discussed in this chapter and treatments that involve medication (which we cover in Chapter 8). Changing your diet, or taking vitamins, herbs, or nutraceuticals, changes the chemical makeup of your body and brain. And just as you must be careful how you're using medications, you must be careful how you use vitamins, herbs, and nutraceuticals, or else you can throw your system further out of whack and worsen your symptoms.

Just because something is natural doesn't necessarily mean it's safe. And a substance that may be helpful at a low dosage may cause problems in a higher dose. Likewise, one herb or supplement may be safe by itself but toxic if taken in combination with something else. Be aware of potential effects before you start any of these treatments by seeking professional help.

Digging Into a Healthy Diet

Let's face it: So much information is tossed around about diet these days that it's becoming nearly impossible to figure out what the words *healthy diet* actually mean. Should you focus on reducing fat? Eliminating carbohydrates? Following the food pyramid?

Part of the confusion stems from the fact that we all have different dietary goals. Maybe you want to lose 20 pounds, your brother needs to reduce his cholesterol, and your best friend wants to bring her blood pressure down. The best diet for you may not be the best diet for your brother or best friend.

In the sections that follow, we discuss diet strategies that seem to make sense for everyone and may have a particularly positive effect for people with AD/HD.

Defining healthy eating habits

One of the main challenges that people with AD/HD have is eating well. Many people with AD/HD eat fast food or snack foods to get by and never get around to eating a balanced meal. For some people, the organization required to buy all the necessary groceries in advance and prepare and cook them into a good, nutritious meal is too difficult. No matter what the causes of unhealthy eating are, we can all use some reminders of what constitutes a healthy diet.

Drinking more water

About two-thirds of your body is made up of water. This water is used for everything from metabolizing food to eliminating wastes to hydrating your cells (every last one of them). Many people don't drink enough water. An adult needs at least eight glasses a day in order to avoid dehydration. Most people wait until they're thirsty to take a drink, but the problem is that if you feel thirsty you're probably already dehydrated.

Another big issue is that many people drink coffee or soft drinks instead of water to quench their thirst. Why is this a problem? When you drink a beverage that contains caffeine, it has a diuretic effect on your body — it causes your body to lose water. So when you drink coffee or caffeinated soft drinks, you may actually be taking water away from your body instead of adding water to it. (We don't mean to be nosy, but have you ever noticed that you urinate more when drinking caffeinated drinks than when you drink water?)

 We know we promised to try to be objective in this chapter, but we have to step out of that role for a minute. We strongly recommend that you consider how drinks such as coffee and soft drinks affect you and consider replacing them with water. You may have been told that if you have AD/HD, caffeine can improve your symptoms. But research hasn't proved this to be true for the majority of people with AD/HD.

Alcohol is another issue: It may make you feel relaxed, but alcohol has been shown to make the symptoms of AD/HD worse. It also tends to dehydrate you and can produce alterations in sleep.

If you're used to flavored drinks, you may find water a little, well, tasteless at first. Try a squeeze of lemon or lime to add some flavor. After you get used to how it feels to be hydrated, you'll probably actually enjoy drinking water and have fewer cravings for sugary, caffeinated drinks.

Adding essential fatty acids

Essential fatty acids are fats that help our brains to function properly. (Did you know that your brain contains a lot of fat?) Research is showing that a proper level of fatty acids can help with the symptoms of a variety of neurological and mental conditions, including AD/HD.

Essential fatty acids come in two forms: Omega-6 and Omega-3. We need some of each in our bodies, but we can't manufacture these fats ourselves; we have to ingest them. (Sounds like a good excuse to have a snack, doesn't it?) You can find Omega-6 fatty acids in the following foods:

✔ Fruits

✔ Nuts, such as pine nuts and pistachios

✔ Grains

✔ Seeds, such as sunflower, flax, pumpkin, and hemp

You can find Omega-3 fatty acids in the following foods:

- ✔ Fish, such as salmon, mackerel, sardines, anchovies, and tuna
- ✔ Flax, sesame, and pumpkin seeds
- ✔ Walnuts and Brazil nuts
- ✔ Avocados
- ✔ Some dark leafy green vegetables, such as kale, spinach, mustard greens, and collards
- ✔ Some oils, such as canola oil, soybean oil, and wheat germ oil. The oils need to be *cold-pressed* and *unrefined* (check the label for these terms).

Cooking with oils such as the ones noted in the above bullet doesn't add essential fatty acids to your diet because these fats are very unstable and break down under heat. For the same reason, you must eat nuts and seeds in their raw form — not roasted.

You need more Omega-6 than Omega-3 in your diet — two to four times as much, in fact. But most people have no trouble getting enough Omega-6; where they struggle is with Omega-3. Adults need about 1.5 grams of Omega-6 a day and anywhere from one-third to three-quarters of a gram of Omega-3. This isn't a lot, but the foods listed in this section don't contain a large amount of these fats.

While you're working on taking in enough essential fatty acids, be sure you aren't counteracting their effects. Certain foods you eat — primarily simple carbohydrates, such as junk food and sugar — make it difficult for your body to use the Omega-3 and Omega-6 fatty acids.

Recent research has confirmed that getting enough Omega-3 fatty acids can help protect people against the recurrence and worsening of a variety of psychiatric and neurological problems, including AD/HD.

Being alert to allergies and sensitivities

Many people with AD/HD find that certain foods make their symptoms worse. For example, many people with a gluten sensitivity have a hard time concentrating after eating foods such as bread or pasta that have gluten in them.

You can find out if you have sensitivities to particular foods by performing an elimination program. This is not easy to do, because some types of triggers can be *additive,* meaning amounts of different substances that wouldn't trigger a reaction by themselves can add together to cause a reaction. So you must start with an extremely limited diet in order to try to get rid of your symptoms. Consult with a professional dietitian or your physician before taking this step; you don't want to waste your time on a half-hearted or poorly designed elimination diet.

It may take a while to identify the foods or ingredients that create a negative reaction in you or your child. You may have to hunt around and experiment to see exactly what part of the food is causing the reaction. For example, some people react strongly to the dyes in foods, while other people react strongly to a whole category of foods, such as dairy products.

When you identify an offending food and stop eating it, you may find that you can later add a small amount of that food back into your diet. Just be sure to watch closely for any reaction to that food, and be prepared to cut it from your diet again if necessary.

Following are some ingredients that people with AD/HD may be sensitive to:

- ✔ Dairy products, including milk, cheese, butter, yogurt, sour cream, cottage cheese, whey, casein, and ice cream (darn!).

- ✔ Wheat products, including breads, pasta, flour, and baked goods. People affected by these foods are said to have *gluten sensitivity*.

- ✔ Corn products, including corn chips and tortillas, popcorn, and any product containing corn oil, vegetable oil, corn syrup, or corn sweetener.

- ✔ Eggs and any products containing eggs, including almost all baked goods.

- ✔ Citrus fruits (and foods containing them), such as oranges, grapefruits, lemons, limes, and tangerines.

- ✔ Artificial ingredients, preservatives, and dyes. We discuss this topic in detail in the "Figuring out the Feingold diet" section later in this chapter.

A variety of tests are available to check for allergies or sensitivities, with names like the RAST, skin prick, and VEGA tests. Each can be useful for finding the foods that you may be allergic or sensitive to, but to be honest these tests can't check for everything. The substance you're sensitive or allergic to may not be on the list of things these tests check for. The most surefire way to determine if a food creates a reaction in you or your child is to monitor your diet closely and take deliberate steps (preferably under the guidance of a professional) to find and eliminate the culprit(s).

Cracking down on carbohydrates

Not all carbohydrates are bad, but unfortunately people with AD/HD (and people without AD/HD, for that matter) often go for the kind of carbs that can cause problems: the simple carbohydrates. (We discuss the other kind, complex carbohydrates, later in this section.) Simple carbohydrates include white flour, pasta, potatoes, corn, white rice, and other refined foods. Junk snack foods, which many people seem to live on these days, are simple carbohydrates as well.

These types of carbohydrates metabolize quickly in the body and create a quick burst of energy — not a good thing for a person with hyperactivity. Because simple carbohydrates metabolize quickly, they trigger an overproduction of insulin, which tends to produce exactly the types of symptoms that appear in AD/HD. These symptoms include:

✔ Inattention

✔ Tiredness

✔ Scattered thinking

For people with AD/HD who already experience these symptoms, they often get worse either immediately after eating refined foods or within an hour or so.

To prevent creating or worsening these symptoms, the solution is simple: Eat complex. Carbohydrates, that is. You want to eat complex carbohydrates rather than simple carbohydrates as often as possible. What's the difference between the two? Whereas simple carbohydrates are refined foods, complex carbohydrates contain all the fiber and nutrients of the whole food, so they take a lot longer to convert into energy in your body. This offers a sustained level of energy that doesn't create the quick burst followed by the crash. Table 11-1 shows examples of simple and complex carbohydrates.

Table 11-1	Examples of Simple and Complex Carbohydrates
Simple Carbohydrates	*Complex Carbohydrates*
White bread	Whole wheat bread
Pasta	Lentils
White rice	Brown rice
Potatoes	Beans
Processed cereals	Whole grains

Providing plenty of protein

As you get rid of those nasty simple carbohydrates, you may want to add some more protein to your diet. Not only are proteins important to the structural integrity of your body, but the amino acids that make them up are used as the raw materials for *neurotransmitters* (chemicals that transmit nerve impulses). Some people with AD/HD find that eating meals rich in protein can help with their ability to concentrate and to sit still.

Finicky eaters

Quite a few people with AD/HD are picky about what they eat. This fussiness has less to do with stubbornness or cravings for junk food than it does with the textures of certain foods. If your child or you are bothered by food textures, there may be a sensory integration issue. To avoid having a limited diet, you have to work at providing yourself or your child with a good variety of nutritious foods with enjoyable textures. Or you can undertake a sensory integration therapy program to help reduce the aversion to the bothersome textures. For details about sensory integration therapies, check out Chapter 13.

Good-quality proteins include the following:

- ✔ Lean meats, such as chicken, turkey, and lean cuts of beef. (Preparation counts: Opt for baking or grilling over frying as often as you can.)
- ✔ Rice and beans.
- ✔ Soy products, such as tofu (unless you are among the unfortunate who have an allergy or sensitivity to soy).
- ✔ Fish.
- ✔ Protein powders. Be careful with these, though, because some are made with pea protein that can cause an allergic reaction if you're sensitive to peanuts.
- ✔ Dairy products, such as milk or cheese. Again, some people have sensitivities to dairy products, so be cautious. Also, you don't want to make dairy products the number one source of your protein because they often have high fat content.

Saying goodbye to sugars

Because sugars are simple carbohydrates and they metabolize fast, they can give you what's often called a *sugar rush*. This rush is often addicting to people with AD/HD because it can help them have increased energy for a (very short) while. The problem is that this increased energy is short-lived, and after it fades the person's concentration is even worse — sometimes much worse.

Many people benefit from cutting sugar out of their diet. But to do so successfully, you need to be a good detective because sugar is contained in almost all processed foods in one form or another. For example, you want to avoid foods that list any of these ingredients:

- ✔ Sucrose
- ✔ Glucose

- ✔ Dextrose
- ✔ Corn syrup or corn sweetener
- ✔ Fructose
- ✔ Maltose

Balancing your body's yeast

Yeasts are single-cell organisms that live on the surfaces of all living things, such as fruits, vegetables, grains, and our bodies. They're one of many tiny organisms that contribute to the health of their host. One particular yeast, called *candida albicans,* lives in our digestive system and, along with the bacterias called *bifidobacteria bifidum* and *lactobaccillus acidophilus,* creates a healthy system that helps us digest our foods better.

Sometimes the delicate balance between the yeast in your body and the friendly bacteria is thrown off. The following things can trigger this to happen:

- ✔ **Taking antibiotics:** Antibiotics kill the bacteria in your body, including the good ones.
- ✔ **Taking birth control pills:** These pills often encourage yeast growth.
- ✔ **Eating sugar-laden foods:** Yeast feeds off of sugars and can grow out of control with too much sugar in our bodies.
- ✔ **Eating junk food:** Simple carbohydrates convert into sugars very quickly in our bodies. This sugar feeds the yeast.
- ✔ **Consuming alcohol:** Alcohol converts to sugar in our bodies, which feeds the yeast.

When you get an imbalance between the yeast and the friendly bacteria in your digestive system, this creates a condition called *dysbiosis,* which for some people seems to result in symptoms similar to those in AD/HD, including fuzzy/scattered thinking and inattention. This imbalance also tends to cause the following symptoms:

- ✔ Athlete's foot
- ✔ Allergies and food sensitivities
- ✔ Bloated stomach
- ✔ Constipation
- ✔ Diarrhea
- ✔ Fatigue
- ✔ Jock itch
- ✔ Vaginal or genital infections

To ensure that you keep a healthy balance of microorganisms in your digestive system, follow these guidelines:

- ✔ Eat a well-balanced diet like the one we recommend throughout this section.
- ✔ Avoid sugary foods.
- ✔ Avoid alcoholic beverages.
- ✔ Eat yogurt with live *lactobaccillus acidophilus* cultures in it.

If you get an imbalance, or if you suspect one, you may want to try one of the following treatments:

- ✔ **Take lactobaccillus acidophilus supplements.** These can be found in your local health food store.
- ✔ **Go on an anti-candida diet.** Several types of anti-candida diets exist; most of them restrict candida-friendly foods such as breads, simple carbohydrates, and alcohol. The length of time you need to follow this diet depends on your symptoms. If you want to go this route, we suggest consulting a good book on eating an anti-candida diet, such as the classic *The Yeast Connection: A Medical Breakthrough* (Random House) by William G. Crook or *Is This Your Child?: Discovering and Treating Unrecognized Allergies in Children and Adults* (William Morrow and Company) by Doris Rapp, MD.
- ✔ **Take candida remedies.** Many remedies — homeopathic and herbal — claim to kill the overabundance of candida yeast in your digestive tract. Check with your healthcare professional to find the best remedy for you.
- ✔ **Consult a healthcare provider who has experience with *systemic candidiasis.*** Be aware that this condition is not recognized by many doctors, so you need to talk to one who is familiar with its diagnosis and treatment. Ask your family practitioner if he knows anyone specializing in this area.

Figuring out the Feingold diet

In the 1970s, allergist and pediatrician Benjamin Feingold developed a special diet that he found to help children with hyperactivity. This diet sought to eliminate artificial ingredients that are made from petroleum (crude oil). Many studies have been conducted demonstrating the effectiveness of the Feingold program, but the diet is still considered out of the mainstream of AD/HD treatments. (By the way, many studies have also been conducted by food manufacturers showing that the chemicals targeted by this diet are safe to consume.)

Although we cover the basics here, if you're interested in trying the Feingold program or finding out about the research that's been done on the subject, check out the Feingold Association at `http://feingold.org/` or call 1-800-321-3287.

One theory about the efficacy of the Feingold program suggests that the chemical that Feingold tries to eliminate — called *salicylate* — has an effect on the enzyme phenol sulfotransferase (PST), which is needed to metabolize artificial colors and flavors. The level of this PST enzyme seems to be lower in people with AD/HD to begin with and is lowered even further by the presence of ingredients with salicylate.

Salicylates are contained in the following categories of petroleum-based food additives:

- Artificial food colorings, including Red #40, Yellow #5, and many others
- Artificial flavorings, which may be labeled as such or may simply be listed as "flavorings"
- Artificial sweeteners, such as Nutrasweet and Equal
- Synthetic preservatives, including BHA, BHT, and TBHQ
- Aspirin

This is a lot of stuff to try to cut from your diet. To make the task more complicated, you may have a tough time figuring out if the foods you buy contain some of these ingredients. The Feingold Association does research into which products available at your local grocery store *don't* contain any of the offending additives. If you want to try this diet, we recommend that you join the Feingold Association and get its list of approved foods. Doing so will make the diet much easier to follow and ensure that you don't accidentally eat the wrong foods.

Salicylates are also present in some foods, including the following:

- Almonds
- Apples and apple products, such as cider vinegar
- Apricots
- Berries, including blueberries, blackberries, strawberries, and raspberries
- Cherries
- Cloves
- Coffee
- Cucumbers and pickles

✔ Grapes, raisins, and grape products, such as wine and wine vinegars

✔ Nectarines

✔ Oranges

✔ Paprika

✔ Peaches

✔ Peppers, both sweet and hot

✔ Plums and prunes

✔ Tangerines

✔ Tomatoes

✔ Rose hips or acerola, which is often found in vitamins

According to the Feingold diet you may be able to eat some, if not all, of these foods after you've gotten the artificial forms of salicylate out of your body. The following sections explain further how the Feingold program works.

Starting the Feingold diet: Stage one

When you begin the Feingold diet, you need to stop eating anything that contains salicylate, including the foods we list in the previous section.

Many people also eliminate the following additives during this stage:

✔ Benzoates (SB). These are listed as *sodium benzoate* and *benzoic acid,* among others.

✔ Corn syrup or other corn sweetener. The Feingold diet doesn't restrict sugar in general, but corn sweeteners are often cut out during stage one because they contain hydrogen sulfide and other chemicals.

✔ Monosodium glutamate (MSG).

✔ Nitrites or nitrates (N).

✔ Sulfites. These may be used in restaurants to keep foods like potatoes and apples from turning brown, and they may be added to medication and wine. Sulfites come in many different forms and can be listed as

• Sulphur (sulfur) dioxide

• Sodium sulphite (or sulfite)

• Sodium bisulphite (or bisulfite)

• Sodium metabisulphite (or metabisulfite)

• Potassium metabisulphite (or metabisulfite)

• Potassium bisulphite (or bisulfite)

This stage of the Feingold diet lasts from four to six weeks, but most people start seeing some improvement in their symptoms in about week. If you try this program, we suggest sticking with it for at least four weeks, because not everyone sees improvement so quickly.

The main thing to remember about this program is that eating even a small amount of the restricted ingredient can prevent you from seeing any benefits from the diet. Keep in mind that many medications contain petroleum-based dyes, so if you're taking medication for your symptoms, you need to find out if it contains such a dye. If it does, ask your doctor about switching to another medication or possibly suspending your medication while trying the diet.

Living with the diet: Stage two

If you see some improvement in your symptoms after totally eliminating all salicylates, you can move to the second stage of the diet, which allows you to progressively add one salicylate-rich food at a time.

If a certain food causes a reaction or makes your symptoms reappear, you simply remove that food from your diet again. Most people are able to tolerate most of the foods that are high in salicylates after they've successfully removed the artificial petroleum-based additives and preservatives.

At no point do you add any of the artificial ingredients (the flavorings, dyes, or preservatives) back into your diet. They are off-limits as long as you want to stay on the Feingold diet.

Viewing Vitamin and Herb Supplements

Adding vitamins to your diet may be worth considering simply because most of us don't eat as well as we should. If you have concerns about the quality of your diet, a daily multivitamin can help make up for some vitamins you don't get from the foods you eat.

But aside from using a multivitamin, some people take specific vitamin supplements with the hope of reducing their AD/HD symptoms. In this section, we examine the most commonly used supplements and categorize them as either *supportive* or *specific*. Supportive supplements are those that support your overall health; specific supplements are more focused in their effects on your body's nervous system and neurotransmitter system.

Very little research has been conducted on the effectiveness of vitamins and herbs for treating symptoms of AD/HD. We strongly suggest that you discuss their use with your doctor and/or another professional, such as a nutritionist or herbalist, before starting to take any of them.

Some people react strongly (and negatively) to even the most common dietary supplements. If you start taking one or more of these substances and suspect you're experiencing problems as a result, stop the treatment immediately and consult your doctor. And while you want to be cautious about deciding to ingest any of these substances, you must be especially careful about giving them to your child.

With many of the herbs we discuss, results build up over time. You may need to take them consistently for a month before you see any real benefit. However, because the amount of active ingredients found in herbal remedies varies so widely, and because many of the ingredients in these herbs are not very well understood, you assume a risk (even if slight) in taking them for extended periods of time. We can't recommend strongly enough that you talk with your doctor or consult a qualified herbalist to help you find the herbs and dosages for you.

You can find the supplements we discuss in the following sections at most health food stores.

Singling out supportive supplements

Some supplements are used by people with AD/HD to help support their bodies and overall health. We list such supplements in this section.

Blue-green algae

Blue-green algae is a plant that grows naturally in water and is very high in a lot of nutrients, including amino acids (the building blocks of protein), minerals, vitamins, and essential fatty acids. Because of the concentration of nutrients in blue-green algae, some people take it to try to reduce the symptoms associated with AD/HD.

Several studies have indicated that blue-green algae may improve immune system response, increase concentration, and reduce anxiety. However, it's still too early to know if this substance can help people with AD/HD. We have heard some positive reports from some of our patients and clients.

Several species of blue-green algae exist, and each has slightly different components and characteristics. Certain types may have potentially harmful effects on some people; we strongly recommend reading about the experiences people have had with each type before deciding to take one.

Make sure you get your supplements from reliable sources. Not all companies go to the same lengths to assure their products are free from toxic contaminants. It's also useful to know that the products are consistent in their active ingredients. As with all supplements your best bet is to seek out a competent professional to help you find the best product.

Essential fatty acids

As we explain earlier in this chapter, essential fatty acids are, well, essential to life. And they aren't produced by your body, so you need to get them from the foods you eat. Because many people don't eat a diet with foods high in these nutrients, you may want to consider taking a supplemental form of Omega-3 and Omega-6. Many supplements are available that contain these fats, including the following:

- Flax seed oil
- Blue-green algae
- Evening primrose
- Fish oils
- Borage oil
- Grape seed extract

 Because Omega-3 and Omega-6 are inherently unstable (they break down easily in the presence of light and oxygen), you want to look for products that are stored in a refrigerator or freezer and are sold in opaque containers. Also, keep in mind that these oils don't keep very long even in a cool, dark place. If you don't ingest them within a few months of purchase, they may go rancid. If it smells bad, don't take it!

Calcium and magnesium

Calcium and magnesium are minerals that help your body absorb B vitamins. Some researchers have suggested that many people with AD/HD have a deficiency in these minerals. By adding calcium and magnesium to the diets of people with AD/HD, some researchers have reported an increased ability to focus and a decrease in hyperactivity.

Both minerals come in several different forms, not all of which can be effectively absorbed by your body. The types of calcium that are most easily tolerated are:

- Calcium bisglycinate
- Calcium citrate
- Calcium chelate

Avoid the calcium carbonate formulas.

The types of magnesium that are most easily tolerated are:

✔ Magnesium citrate

✔ Magnesium gluconate

✔ Magnesium sulfate

Avoid magnesium oxide.

Choline/lecithin

Choline is a substance that is essential for brain function. People with various cognitive problems often are found to have choline deficiencies. Choline is believed to have an effect on memory and concentration, mostly through its contribution to the synthesis of *acetylcholine,* one of the neurotransmitters.

You find choline in foods such as egg yolks, lean beef, fish, liver, oatmeal, soybeans, cauliflower, and kale, but many people take additional choline to give their brains a boost. Several forms of choline are available in supplements, but the form most often used is *phosphatidyl choline,* also known as *lecithin.*

Ginseng

Ginseng is often touted as an energy enhancer. This root has been used for ages to help reduce stress and improve physical performance. You can find ginseng in a variety of formulations, from dried powders to teas, from capsules to unprocessed roots.

Combinations of ginseng and gingko biloba are commonly used for people with AD/HD. You can find these at your local health food store.

Pycnogenol

Pycnogenol is an antioxidant made from extracts of the bark of a European coastal pine tree (Pinus Maritima, or maritime pine). Pycnogenal is a proprietary name for a concentration of the chemical proanthocyanidin.

Other antioxidants, such as grape seed extract, alpha lipoic acid, vitamin E, and vitamin C, are used in similar ways. Antioxidants are considered important in deactivating free radicals, and pycnogenol has 20 times the antioxidant properties of vitamin C and 50 times the antioxidant properties of vitamin E.

Some researchers have suggested that pycnogenol may support and improve the function of the neurotransmitters dopamine and norepinephrine (which we discuss in Chapter 2).

Pycnogenol has been used for decades in Europe. You can find this supplement sold as pycnogenol or oligomeric proanthocyanidins (OPC).

Surveying specific supplements

Some people with AD/HD use specific supplements to support and possibly enhance the function of the nervous system. We list the most commonly used supplements in this section.

Vinpocetine

Vinpocetine is a substance derived from the periwinkle plant. In Europe, it has been used to help protect people from having more extensive brain damage when they have strokes and other brain injuries. Vinpocetine is also being studied for use in slowing the progress of Alzheimer's disease.

This substance has two interesting properties that relate to AD/HD: It increases blood flow in the brain (especially in the frontal lobes), and it increases dopamine levels (which we discuss in Chapter 2). Your coauthor Mike predicts that people will become much more interested in using vinpocetine to treat AD/HD in the near future.

Melatonin

Melatonin is a hormone that helps regulate sleep. Some people find melatonin supplements useful if they have sleep problems along with AD/HD. People who have a hard time winding down at night and falling asleep, and those who wake up several times during the night, may be helped by melatonin.

If you choose to try melatonin, you may want to start with a small dose. Some people report that larger doses make them feel groggy and tired the next day, as if they have the type of "hangover" often associated with sleeping pills.

L-tyrosine

L-tyrosine is an amino acid and a building block for the neurotransmitter *dopamine*. (In Chapter 2, we discuss dopamine and its relationship to AD/HD.) L-tyrosine seems to increase the level of a brain stimulant called *phenylethylamine* (PEA).

This amino acid seems to improve attention and concentration for some people. Unfortunately, it can also contribute to health problems such as high blood pressure.

L-tyrosine can cause medical problems for some people, including if it's taken in combination with certain medications. Talk to your healthcare professional before you take this supplement.

5-HTP and tryptophan

5-HTP stands for *5-hydroxytryptophan.* (You can see why the name got shortened, right?) This substance is extracted from the seeds of a West African shrub called *griffonia simplicifolia.* 5-HTP is made by our bodies from L-tryptophan, an amino acid found in most protein-rich foods. Some research indicates that 5-HTP increases levels of the neurotransmitter serotonin, which is instrumental in regulating our sleep, our feelings of anxiety and aggression, and our ability to perceive pain, among other things.

Some people take 5-HTP to improve their sleep and overall mood and to decrease aggressiveness. According to some studies, 5-HTP is as effective for some people as prescription antidepressants. Because this substance can cause an upset stomach, and you're supposed to take it on an empty stomach, most people start with a small dose and increase the dosage over time.

Don't take 5-HTP in combination with any prescription antidepressants; they don't play well together and can cause serious side effects.

Gingko biloba

Gingko biloba is derived from the leaves of the Maidenhair tree and has been used for ages to improve memory, circulation, and digestion. The active ingredients in gingko biloba are ginkgo flavone glycoside and terpene lactone. These chemicals appear to have antioxidant qualities. In addition, good evidence exists that gingko can improve brain circulation, especially in the areas thought to be affected by AD/HD.

Because of the memory-improving effects associated with gingko biloba, many people with AD/HD have given it try. Some people report that it helps with their symptoms, while others don't notice much change.

Gotakola is another plant substance that acts in a similar way. Many people take gingko and gotakola together.

St. John's Wort

St. John's Wort is made from the flowers of the Hypericum plant. This herb is used most often for depression, insomnia, and anxiety because it increases serotonin levels in the brain. (As we explain in the "5-HTP and tryptophan" section earlier in the chapter, serotonin is a neurotransmitter with wide-reaching effects.) It also acts as a mild monoamine oxidase inhibitor, so it enhances the activity of dopamine and norepinephrine as well (see Chapter 2).

Some people with AD/HD find that St. John's Wort can help them feel more emotionally balanced, especially if they also suffer from depression or anxiety.

As with 5-HTP, don't take St. John's Wort with any prescription antidepressants without first checking with your friendly psychopharmacologist.

Valerian root

Valerian root is an herbal extract that has been used for a very long time to create a feeling of calm. Valerian is often used by people with AD/HD to help initiate sleep. Unlike melatonin, which is also used to help people get to sleep, valerian can sometimes be more effective for people who wake up early and can't get back to sleep. And it doesn't create grogginess in the morning.

Knowing about Nutraceuticals

Many vitamins and herbs are reported to help with some AD/HD symptoms. After reading this chapter, which presents just some of your options, you may not have any idea where to start using them in your life. To make things easier, many products are available that combine some of the vitamins and herbs we describe here with the specific goal of aiding people with AD/HD. These prefab combinations of vitamins and herbs are called *nutraceuticals*. (The term *nutraceuticals* refers to any food substance that is used to treat illnesses, but we limit our use of the term to these combination compounds.)

Nutraceuticals have become all the rage in a variety of areas, from people with AD/HD and autism to people with insomnia and depression. You can find these formulated combinations of vitamins and supplements for AD/HD by talking to your nutritionist or herbalist.

Little scientific research has been conducted to support the reported effects of many of the vitamins, minerals, and herbs that we discuss in this chapter. We want you to know they exist because each one seems to be effective for some people with AD/HD. But we don't have room in this book for an exhaustive treatment on each substance, so we strongly advise that you learn more, talk with healthcare professionals, and give these treatment options serious consideration before trying them.

Protecting Your Environment

When you have AD/HD, even your everyday environment can exacerbate your symptoms. (In fact, the environment can create AD/HD-like symptoms in people without AD/HD, as we discuss in Chapter 6.) Many environmental factors can make your symptoms worse. In the following sections, we discuss two categories of these factors: allergens and chemicals.

Allergens

Allergens are things in your environment that can cause you to have an allergic reaction if you are sensitive to them. Allergens come in many different forms, but the most common are dust, dust mites, mold, pollens, and animals. In this section, we offer advice for controlling allergens in your environment.

Your doctor can test your sensitivity to these allergens to help you understand if some of your AD/HD symptoms are being caused or exacerbated by these things. Many people feel that it's worth at least ruling out these allergens as a cause of symptoms. However, keep in mind that you may be sensitive to one or more of these allergens without showing a positive result on a test because these tests are not 100 percent accurate.

If your AD/HD symptoms get worse in the presence of any of the allergens we discuss in the following sections, talk to your doctor about ways to get your allergies or sensitivities under control. A variety of medications and natural remedies exist that seem to help a lot of people.

Dust

Dust is everywhere. No matter what you do, it's going to build up in your house. Unfortunately, regular household dust can be very toxic to sensitive people. This dust can contain everything from pieces of dead skin to residues from toxic chemicals. The best way to deal with dust is to eliminate it.

Here are some tips for getting dust and dust mites (which we discuss in the next section) under control:

- ✓ **Vacuum often — at least once a week.** Vacuuming your house can help, but you need a decent vacuum cleaner or else you'll just move the dust around rather than getting rid of it. Buy a vacuum with a good filter system, or use a whole-house vacuum system that exhausts outdoors.

- ✓ **Eliminate carpeting.** This step may not be practical for you, but if possible, get rid of your wall-to-wall carpeting and opt for wood floors instead. Carpeting tends to hold onto dust, and even the best vacuum cleaner may not get it entirely clean. Sweeping and mopping wood floors result in a cleaner house.

✔ **Clean regularly.** This is often easier said than done, especially when a family is dealing with the stress of AD/HD. But make it a priority so the dust doesn't accumulate.

✔ **Wash your bedding often.** We spend almost a third of our lives in bed, so if you only have time to make one room in your house dust-free (or at least dust-minimal), make it your bedroom. By washing your sheets and pillowcases often (at least every other week), you cut down on your exposure to dust.

✔ **Get an air cleaner.** A good air cleaner can catch the dust before it settles down on your stuff; we recommend a HEPA filtration system. If you use an air cleaner, make sure it's a high quality product and that you maintain it properly. A poorly working air cleaner is worse than no air cleaner at all.

✔ **Hang spider plants.** Spider plants absorb nasty *phenols* (toxic chemicals) from the air. Plant one in each of your rooms — maybe even two in your bedroom. These plants help clean your air, and they look nice too.

Dust mites

Dust mites are nasty little critters (from the same family as spiders and ticks) that eat the dust in your house (well, not just *your* house — everyone's). Dust mites themselves aren't so much a problem, but their droppings are. Some researchers have suggested that dust mite droppings are the leading cause of asthma around the world.

You can't tell the number of dust mites in your house by how clean it is; rather, your dust mite population depends on how moist your house is. People who live in warm, moist climates tend to have more dust mites than those who live in drier or cooler climates.

Here are some suggestions to help you get rid of dust mites (or at least minimize their impact):

✔ **Get rid of your carpeting.** We know, you already got this advice in the previous section, and your circumstances may not allow you to take this step. But if you can, removing carpeting is the single best way to reduce the mite population in your house. Replace the carpeting with wood or tile so that you can give a good cleaning often.

✔ **Use an allergen spray on carpeting.** If you can't replace your carpeting, at least treat it with an allergen spray made to kill dust mites, and vacuum often.

✔ **Use a good, sealed vacuum.** We're back to the vac again. To control dust mites, you must have a vacuum that doesn't spew dust everywhere. If you can afford it, look for a good HEPA filter system on a vacuum cleaner.

✔ **Use protective bed coverings.** Because dust mites tend to be a real problem in the bedroom, get protective coverings (called *dust mite covers*) for your mattress and pillows to seal the dust mites out. (Wash the covers in hot water before you put them on.) These covers come in many styles but usually consist of tightly woven fabric that dust mites can't penetrate.

✔ **Optimize the humidity in your house.** Mites grow best in environments that have 75 to 80 percent relative humidity, but they cannot live in areas with less than 50 percent humidity. You can achieve this lower level by using a dehumidifier when necessary.

✔ **If you have a forced-air heating system, install filters.** Filters prevent the mites from flying all over your house with the heat. You can also turn the heating vents off in your bedroom to reduce the chance that the dust and mites in your bedroom will blow around.

✔ **Wash your bedding often in hot water.** Water temperatures over 130°F will kill the mites on your bedding.

✔ **Keep your clothes in a closet, and keep the door closed.** This at least keeps any mites that get on your clothes away from you when you sleep.

Mold

Mold has received a lot of attention lately. More and more houses are being discovered to be breeding grounds for molds, especially in wetter climates. Molds are known not only to make asthma worse but to cause problems with cognition (your ability to think). People who have a mold allergy or sensitivity often have AD/HD symptoms, and people with AD/HD who have these sensitivities see their symptoms get worse in the presence of molds.

Mold is everywhere; about 100,000 types of mold exist. Most are relatively harmless, but a few (24 by some accounts) can cause some serious problems.

Mold needs moisture to grow, so to control mold in your house you need to make sure that you don't have any water leaks. If you do, fix them immediately. You can also install an air cleaner in your house — look for a HEPA or UV filter — to reduce the airborne mold spores.

Animal dander, fur, and feathers

Animal dander, fur, and feathers can cause allergic reactions in some people. If you are allergic to your furry (and feathered) friends, all you can really do to minimize the allergy's effects on your life is to not have a pet and to avoid homes that have them.

You may not even know that your AD/HD symptoms are made worse by a pet because you may not display the classic symptoms of a runny nose, sneezing, coughing, and so on. You may just feel tired or have scattered thinking.

If you suspect that your beloved pet is making your AD/HD symptoms worse, board him at a kennel or have a friend take him for a few days, and clean your house. If you symptoms improve and then get worse when your pet comes home, you may have a difficult decision to make.

Pollens

Pollens are a common cause of allergies. As springtime rolls around, some people are hit with such a bad reaction that they don't get to enjoy the outdoors in the good weather. If you have both seasonal allergies and AD/HD, your AD/HD symptoms may get worse at the same time that you're dealing with a runny or stuffed-up nose, labored breathing, headaches, and other allergy symptoms.

Even if there isn't a direct link between your pollen allergies and your AD/HD symptoms, you may find that your sleep is disrupted enough to make concentrating difficult. The solution is to safeguard your sleep by taking medication or a natural remedy to help with your allergy.

Chemicals

As if the typical allergens aren't enough to worry about, most of our home environments are riddled with chemicals that can make AD/HD symptoms worse for a person sensitive to them. Potential offenders include, but aren't limited to, the following:

- ✔ **Cleaning products:** Many cleaning products contain chemicals that are derived from petroleum. In the "Figuring out the Feingold diet" section earlier in this chapter, we explain that food additives that contain petroleum may impact your AD/HD symptoms. With cleaning products, just inhaling these chemicals may worsen your symptoms.

- ✔ **Fragrances:** If you look around your home, you'll probably notice a long list of products that contain fragrances, such as toilet paper, soaps, and deodorants.

- ✔ **Plastic toys, furniture, and appliances:** Certain plastics, such as polyvinylchloride (PVC), give off gases that are a problem for some people. Unfortunately, most hard plastic toys, furniture, and appliances are made at least in part from PVC.

    If you read labels, you may find some young children's plastic toys that aren't made with PVC; if PVC wasn't used, the product label usually says so. (If the label doesn't say, the toy is probably made from PVC.) Furniture and appliances aren't yet labeled so you may want to avoid plastic altogether if you're concerned about the gas given off by PVC.

✔ **Building materials:** Building materials, such as plywood and carpeting, are made with chemicals that can continue to give off gas for quite a while. (That's what creates the "new carpet smell.") These chemicals can be toxic; for example, formaldehyde is used in making plywood.

If you build a new house, consider all the materials that go into it. If you live in a fairly new house, be aware that it could be giving off chemicals that make your AD/HD worse. A good HEPA air filter system can help, but the only real solution is to remove either yourself or the offending materials from your house.

✔ **Synthetic fabrics:** Petroleum is a component of so many products that it can be hard to comprehend. Polyester fabric is one such product. People with sensitivities should wear only natural fiber clothing, such as cotton, wool, or silk.

✔ **Perfumes and colognes:** Personal fragrances are big business. Unfortunately, the smell of these products can make some people sick. As with other chemicals, some perfumes and colognes contain petroleum-based fragrances that can make AD/HD symptoms worse.

For most people, the chemicals we discuss in this section aren't a problem. But for people with sensitivities, even a little exposure can make their AD/HD symptoms much worse. If any of these products seem to make your symptoms worse, get rid of them.

Chapter 12

Examining Repatterning Therapies

. . . .

In This Chapter

▶ Understanding neurofeedback

▶ Exploring Rhythmic Entrainment Intervention

▶ Considering auditory training

▶ Viewing vision therapy

. . . .

As we explain in Chapter 8, the mainstream biological treatment for AD/HD is medication. While medication successfully provides symptom control for most people with AD/HD, it can also have serious side effects for some people. For this reason, some emerging therapies are being explored, which can offer benefits for people with AD/HD without the same level of side effects.

In this chapter, we explore therapies that are designed to repattern the brain. These therapies include neurofeedback, Rhythmic Entrainment Intervention (REI), the Tomatis Method and auditory integration training (AIT), and vision training. Neurofeedback uses computer-based activities to help you change your brain state, REI uses auditory rhythmic stimulation to activate the brain, AIT uses modulated frequency alterations to music to change the way you process sensory information, and vision therapies use eye training exercises to stimulate your brain. Although the approaches differ, each of these therapies creates overall changes in the way your brain functions.

These therapies are not often part of the more conventional AD/HD professional's therapy options and don't have the extensive research that pharmaceuticals have to back them up. As a result you'll have to look deeper for studies on these approaches and for professionals who may be able to offer them to you. To help you we include a section for each therapy on finding a provider. The resources we suggest can also provide information on the results of studies on the approach in question.

We say this many times in this book, but it bears repeating: The most effective way to treat AD/HD is to use a multimodal approach. Ideally, you want to use treatment approaches that cover the biological, psychological, and social aspects of the condition. The treatments in this chapter are biological in nature — they alter the way your brain functions. If you choose to try one of these treatments, you should combine it with psychological treatments, such as those described in Chapters 9 and 10, and social approaches, such as the ones we present in Chapters 14, 15, and 16.

Altering Brain Activity Through Neurofeedback

Neurofeedback (also called *neurotherapy* or *EEG biofeedback*) is a therapy that helps you change your brain activity by using specific exercises and watching how your brain wave states change as you do them. Neurofeedback is essentially an exercise program for your brain. As we discuss in Chapter 2, people with AD/HD experience lower activity in certain areas of the brain than people without AD/HD. With neurofeedback, you can increase this activity by actually seeing it and then using techniques to change your brain patterns.

Getting some background

Neurofeedback has been around since the 1960s and has been studied extensively for more than 30 years. This therapy relies on the idea that by changing the level of activity in the brain you can improve the symptoms associated with AD/HD.

In order to understand how neurofeedback works, you first need to understand the concept of brain waves. Brain activity can be measured as brain waves at different *frequencies* (speeds) and *amplitudes* (levels). The brain wave states indicate how active a particular part of the brain is, which relates to your overall level of awareness. There are four basic brain wave levels:

- ✔ **Delta:** Delta is the sleep state and exists at a frequency between 0 and 4 Hz (hertz, or cycles per second).

- ✔ **Theta:** Theta is the meditative state of consciousness, which consists of brain wave frequencies between 4 and 8 Hz. Many people with AD/HD have too much of this activity in their brains. This represents a lower than normal level of activity and, as we talk about in Chapter 2, may have something to do with the symptoms of AD/HD.

✔ **Alpha:** Alpha is a relaxed yet alert state. It encompasses frequencies between 8 and 12 Hz. Some people with AD/HD have too much of this rhythm in the wrong locations in their brains, which can interfere with the communication between different areas of the brain.

✔ **Beta:** Beta is a normal wakeful state of consciousness with frequencies above 12 Hz. The goal with neurofeedback is to try to increase the level of this activity in the brain areas that have too much theta. In many cases, the area in question is the frontal lobes.

The goal with neurofeedback is to train you to be able to change your brain wave patterns at will. This process involves doing learning exercises, which usually means playing specific video games on a computer (as we describe in the next section). By repeatedly achieving the desired balance of different types of brain activity, the brain learns to establish the conditions that support those new states, thus making a different way of functioning more likely. (In other words, your brain learns how to get what it needs.)

Although we don't have much direct evidence about the biological changes that take place in neurofeedback, quite a bit of evidence exists that the brain is changed by this procedure. For example, many people whose AD/HD is improved by neurofeedback are able to maintain their improvements over a period of years without further training.

Exploring the process

Neurofeedback usually starts with an intake process that may involve many of the psychological and neuropsychological tests that you went through when you were diagnosed with AD/HD. You're also hooked up to an EEG device (see Chapter 5), usually with 19 electrodes attached to your scalp, to have a baseline evaluation done. (Don't worry — it doesn't hurt.) This evaluation gives the practitioner a clear picture of what your brain activity looks like.

This data is compared to information about what "normal" brain activity looks like in a person your age. From this comparison, the practitioner selects appropriate exercises that can help you correct the areas where your brain functions differently than someone without AD/HD. These exercises usually involve a computer program that responds to the changes you make to your brain wave patterns. For example, one program uses a Pac-Man-like game where the movement of the Pac-Man figure depends on you producing certain brain waves. Another program uses an airplane, which flies based on your brain activity.

By using these programs, you discover how to consciously change your brain activity over time. Like any new activity, it can initially be frustrating. However, within a few sessions most people get the hang of it and can make the object move.

Generally speaking, the neurofeedback process involves between 25 and 50 sessions that last for about 40 minutes. These sessions are often done at least once a week, and assessments are made along the way to determine exactly how many sessions are needed.

Some computer-based programs are available that you can do at home, but they don't account for the way your brain works. In other words, with at-home treatment you don't get a baseline evaluation and have exercises tailored to you. Instead, you do standardized exercises that may or may not help you.

Knowing what to expect

Neurofeedback is being used for people with a lot of different conditions, including many that often occur along with AD/HD, such as depression and anxiety disorders (see Chapter 6). The AD/HD symptoms that are often improved by neurofeedback include the following:

- ✔ Impulsivity
- ✔ Hyperactivity
- ✔ Attention
- ✔ Sleep
- ✔ Mood regulation

A significant additional benefit for people with AD/HD is the improved self-esteem that comes from learning how to control your brain activity.

The effects of neurofeedback are generally long-term, assuming you go through enough sessions, and there don't appear to be any serious side effects. The side effects that can occur include the following:

- ✔ Irritability
- ✔ Trouble getting to sleep
- ✔ Anxiety
- ✔ Fatigue
- ✔ Feeling spacey

These side effects are often short-lived and disappear within a few weeks. Most of the time, negative side effects indicate a transition period, but they can be a sign that the training protocol needs to be modified.

Neurofeedback shows significant promise for people with AD/HD. The biggest drawback is its cost, which is often not covered by insurance, and the investment of time required for making up to 50 office visits.

Finding a provider

Generally, neurofeedback practitioners are mental health professionals, such as psychiatrists, psychologists, and counselors. However, you may find other healthcare providers who are qualified to administer neurofeedback. To find a qualified neurofeedback professional, check out one of these organizations:

- ✔ The International Society for Neuronal Regulation (www.isnr.org)
- ✔ The Association for Applied Psychophysiology & Biofeedback (www.aapb.org)

You can also ask your primary healthcare provider for a referral or look under "Biofeedback professionals" in your local phone book.

Using Rhythm to Stimulate the Nervous System

Rhythmic Entrainment Intervention (REI) is a therapy that uses auditory rhythm to stimulate the nervous system. Created by coauthor Jeff Strong, REI is based on the concept that our nervous systems are rhythmically organized and can be influenced by externally produced rhythms. REI has been around since 1993 and is used with people with AD/HD as well as with other developmental disabilities, such as autism.

Getting some background

REI is based on ancient therapeutic rhythm techniques that have been used around the world for thousands of years. These techniques use auditory rhythm to influence brain function and have been studied extensively since the 1960s. REI has been specifically studied since 1993, and the research has consistently shown that the use of auditory rhythm can have a positive impact on people with AD/HD. (You can see some of this research at www.reiinstitute.com.)

The theory behind REI is as follows:

✔ **Entrainment:** Not to be confused with entertainment, *entrainment* is simply the synchronization of two or more rhythmic cycles. This phenomenon was first discovered in the seventeenth century by mathematician Christian Huygens. When he was perfecting the design of the pendulum clock, he placed one clock upon the wall and started it; he then placed another clock next to it and started that one. He observed that the clocks would start by ticking in their own time and would eventually synchronize and begin to swing in unison: One clock would shift its cycle to match the rhythm of the clock next to it. You can find examples of entrainment throughout nature. (Use *entrainment* as your keyword in your favorite Internet search engine to see what we mean.)

Certain types of sound are able to influence brain wave activity; research has shown that external rhythmic stimulus can entrain the brain. A direct correlation exists between the speed of a rhythm and the ensuing entrained brain patterns. REI helps direct the listener's brain into the desired state of consciousness, which is usually the alpha state.

✔ **Stimulation:** Our brains like *novel* stimuli, meaning new or unrecognizable things. This is especially true for people with AD/HD. When you hear specific, complex rhythmic patterns, your brain is stimulated in ways that result in improvements in many of the symptoms of AD/HD.

As we note in Chapter 2, many people with AD/HD have lower activity in one or more parts of their brains than people without AD/HD. To increase the activity level, many treatments use some sort of stimulus. (As we explain in Chapter 8, many medications used for people with AD/HD are stimulants.) By using targeted rhythms and techniques, REI stimulates the brain.

Exploring the process

An REI therapy program involves the creation of a two-CD set that is custom-made for each person with AD/HD, based upon a questionnaire and interview process. Customization is crucial because each person has different symptoms, so the rhythms and techniques used for each person are slightly different. The right rhythms must be implemented properly to achieve optimal results.

The custom-made CDs serve the following purposes:

- ✔ **CD 1:** This CD is an introduction for your nervous system to the process of entrainment and the unusual nature of the CDs. (The auditory rhythm used in this therapy is presented in the form of hand drumming rhythms.) This CD is played once a day for the first two to three weeks and then used in conjunction with the second CD for an additional week or two.

- ✔ **CD 2:** This CD is the heart of the program and contains the rhythms that are designed to repattern your brain for the long-term. This CD is introduced at either week three or four and is played for at least the first week along with CD 1. After that, the second CD is played by itself once a day for six to eight more weeks.

One of the nice things about REI is that you can implement it in your home, and you (or your child) don't need to actively listen to it. You can go about your normal routine and let it play in the background, as long as you don't watch TV, play video games, or listen to other music while the CD plays. Because REI is implemented by you in your home, it's much less expensive than other repatterning treatments for AD/HD.

Knowing what to expect

Because the first CD in the set is designed to start the basic entrainment process, most people experience calming effects within the first few minutes of the first time playing the CD. At first, these effects last only for a short time after the CD stops. But after about a week of listening to the first CD, the calming effect can last for several hours after listening.

For most people, REI's most significant impact starts occurring after a few weeks of listening to the second CD (about six weeks into the entire program). At this point, you may see one or more of the following changes:

- ✔ Improved attention span
- ✔ Less distractibility
- ✔ Less impulsivity
- ✔ Less hyperactivity or restlessness
- ✔ Improved learning abilities
- ✔ Increased ability to regulate mood
- ✔ Improved social abilities
- ✔ Increased language abilities — both expressive and receptive

As long as you follow the directions for the program (starting with CD 1 and progressing to CD 2), you shouldn't experience any side effects. People who don't follow the program exactly — by playing the CDs more often than recommended or by skipping CD 1 — may experience agitation, irritability, or minor sleep problems. These effects can be eliminated by taking a few days off from the CDs and starting up again with CD 1. When the entraining period is over (in 8 to 12 weeks), you can stop using the CDs — although many people keep using them.

The gains don't stop when the entraining period is complete, and the gains are usually permanent. Only in rare cases have we seen any regression after the CDs were stopped, and in each instance reintroducing the second CD for a few weeks brought the improvements back.

Finding a provider

Until recently, REI was available only through the REI Institute, but there is now a network of authorized providers throughout North America. To find a provider in your area, or to find out how to have a set of CDs made for you if you don't have a provider close by, contact the REI Institute at 800-659-6644 or visit www.reiinstitute.com.

Changing the Way You Hear Sound

The Tomatis Method and auditory integration training (AIT) are sound-based therapies that are intended to change the way you hear sound. The Tomatis Method was created in France in the 1950s by Dr. Alfred Tomatis, while AIT was developed by Dr. Guy Berard — also a French physician — based upon his work with Dr. Tomatis. AIT became popular in the United States starting in 1992.

Both AIT and the Tomatis Method use specific types of frequency modulated and filtered music to try to correct problems with auditory processing. We cover both techniques in this section even though AIT has become much more popular and has been the subject of more research than the Tomatis Method.

Getting some background

In the 1950s, ear, nose, and throat physician Alfred Tomatis developed the theory that problems in hearing may lead to behavioral problems and learning difficulties. The basis for this theory is that if someone can't hear certain frequencies, they can't process certain sounds. This leads to communication problems, which can then lead to behavioral problems. The theory is more complex than this, but it's also a bit outdated, so we'll just stick with this brief overview.

AIT emerged from the Tomatis Method — Dr. Berard was originally a protégé of Tomatis. The application of AIT differs from the Tomatis Method, but the basic theory remains the same: Some people hear certain frequencies too softly or too loudly, which causes a problem in auditory perception and potentially leads to behavioral problems. Both doctors believed that people with auditory perception problems can experience improved learning and behavior if they listen to certain music that is modified to teach the person how to listen better and how to hear the missing frequencies or tolerate the ones that are being heard too loudly.

We have a bit of a problem with the basic theory behind these methods, and we aren't alone. Other researchers have come up with a slew of theories regarding these methods, but we won't bore you with them all. Here's the one we stand behind: The frequency modulation created by the Tomatis and AIT devices stimulates the brain, and this stimulation may have a positive effect for some people. This approach is better implemented if the modulation isn't random but is, instead, tied to the person's *audiogram* (an evaluation we describe in the next section). Unfortunately, not all practitioners of these approaches customize the stimulation used; many just use random stimulation, which provides random results.

Exploring the process

If you try AIT or the Tomatis Method, you'll probably start by getting an *audiogram* — a test to see how well you hear different frequencies. Using this audiogram, the practitioner should determine what types of music and modulation and filtering effects to use. (We say *should* because not all practitioners customize their treatments; some use a random sweeping of frequency modulation without any client-specific filtering based on the audiogram. In our opinion, this random approach isn't nearly as effective.)

When the audiogram is complete, the processes of AIT and the Tomatis Method diverge. The next sections lay out the process for each.

AIT

AIT consists of two 30-minute sessions each day for 10 days (a total of 20 sessions). Depending on the practitioner, this could be Monday through Friday for two weeks with the weekends off, or it could be ten days without any breaks. Regardless, you need to schedule a minimum of three hours between the two daily sessions, so you have to go to two separate appointments per day for those ten days.

During the sessions, you sit quietly and wear headphones while the modulated music plays. The music is played progressively louder over the course of the 20 sessions. The filtering and frequency modulation change over this time as well.

When the 20 sessions are completed, you're instructed to never use headphones again while listening to music.

The Tomatis Method

The Tomatis Method differs from AIT in that instead of going to 20 sessions over a period of 10 days, you attend many more sessions, the actual number of which depends on the results of your intake audiogram and a series of tests that are given along the way. Attending 75 sessions isn't uncommon for someone with AD/HD.

The Tomatis Method also differs from AIT in that the sessions are divided up into different types called *active* and *passive*. During passive sessions, you simply listen to the music as it plays in your headphones. During the active sessions, you are asked to repeat words or sentences as you listen to the music.

The Tomatis Method, like AIT, requires that you no longer listen to music through headphones when your sessions are completed.

Some CDs are available that use frequency modulation and random filtering in an effort to mimic the processes of AIT and the Tomatis Method. These CDs are used in the home, often without the guidance of a practitioner, and are not based upon the results of an audiogram. These CDs seem to have some random success, but don't confuse their use with AIT or the Tomatis Method, even though they may be based upon these methods.

Knowing what to expect

AIT and the Tomatis Method seem to produce similar results. Although most of the research on these approaches has focused on their impact on autism, people with AD/HD seem to experience one or more of the following improvements:

- Improved receptive and expressive language (understanding and expression)
- Decreased sensitivity to sounds (painfulness or discomfort)
- Reduction in noise or tinnitus in the ear

✔ Improved ability to talk at a normal volume

✔ Less hyperactivity

✔ Increased attention span

✔ Less distractibility

These results often appear within a few weeks of starting either program. Your coauthor Jeff's observation is that beyond improvements in sound sensitivity and language abilities, the effects are often subtle and vary considerably from person to person. (This may be due to the fact that many practitioners use random frequency modulation rather than tailoring the music to the client.) Generally, the results last for the long-term, but we've heard of instances where the results slowly disappear over several months.

Side effects are usually mild and temporary and can include anxiety, irritability, sleep disturbances, and aggressiveness.

AIT and the Tomatis Method don't specifically address the symptoms of AD/HD; instead, they try to improve your ability to hear properly and to process what you hear.

Finding a provider

A handful of AIT and Tomatis Method providers — often speech–language pathologists or psychologists — are in practice in North America. You can find one by checking out these Web sites:

✔ www.sait.org: This is the site for the Society for Auditory Integration Techniques, which focuses mainly on AIT but covers some other auditory treatments as well (including REI). The site contains a list of AIT providers.

✔ www.tomatis.com: This site offers fairly comprehensive information on the Tomatis Method, including a list of practitioners.

Many variations on AIT and the Tomatis Method are being used for people with AD/HD. Some practitioners use different types of music, and there are several different devices that create the frequency modulation effect that these approaches rely upon. The provider you choose may have his own way of doing things that differs from our description here. Providers also have different levels of effectiveness, so do your homework and choose the best provider for you (which may not be the person closest to you).

Exercising Your Eyes

Vision therapy is basically exercise for your eyes. This approach uses training exercises, vision aids, and stimulation techniques to help you process visual stimuli better. Several approaches to vision therapy exist. The two most common are behavioral optometry and the Irlen Method (which addresses what's called Scotopic Sensitivity Syndrome).

Getting some background

Vision therapies are regularly used for people with learning problems. The theory behind these techniques is that even though you may see clearly, you may not be able to process visual stimuli properly. Proponents of this type of therapy believe that some people with AD/HD have perception problems, which may include the following:

- **Not being able to get both eyes to focus on the same thing:** This is called *convergence insufficiency.* A recent study by Dr. David Granet at the University of California, San Diego School of Medicine suggests that people with this vision problem are three times as likely to have AD/HD as people without convergence insufficiency.

- **Not being able to track effectively:** This problem often manifests as not being able to follow the words on a page when you read.

- **Not being able to maintain focus on an object in space:** Focus may come in and out, which leads to the next vision problem . . .

- **Seeing objects moving on the page, or having your eyes fatigue easily:** These are symptoms of Scotopic Sensitivity Syndrome (SSS).

Researchers have suggested that these problems contribute to symptoms that are common in AD/HD, such as inattention and distractibility.

Vision therapies often employ techniques such as the following:

- **Compensatory lenses:** Many times, especially in the case of the Irlen Method, certain types of lenses are used to help either reduce the stress on your eyes or correct your vision imbalance. For example, to mitigate the effects of Scotopic Sensitivity Syndrome, the Irlen Method uses specially colored lenses that can either be worn all the time or only when you read. (Some people forego the lenses and simply use colored plastic sheets placed over their reading material to help them see the printed page better.)

- **Computer programs:** Some behavioral optometrists use computer-based vision exercises to help improve the areas that cause vision processing problems. These programs are like computer games that require specific visual processing tasks to help you strengthen your ability to process visual stimuli.

✔ **Vision exercises:** Behavioral optometrists often have you perform specific eye exercises to help you compensate for the areas that they determine are not functioning properly.

Most of these techniques are designed to address specific vision problems, which may or may not contribute to your AD/HD symptoms. Regardless, any visual stimulation is going to influence your brain. We believe that this stimulation is precisely the reason some of these techniques may work for people with AD/HD.

Exploring the process

Both behavioral optometry and the Irlen Method start with an evaluation. In the case of behavioral optometry, this evaluation (called a *developmental vision evaluation*) includes a series of tests to determine your aptitude with specific areas of visual skills. From these tests, the behavioral optometrist sees the areas where your vision may not function as well as it should. She then assigns exercises to help you develop these areas. A behavioral optometrist may also recommend certain types of visual stimulation to help your visual processing deficits. These can be in the form of office visits, take-home exercises, or devices that you purchase (such as computer software programs) that you can then use in your home.

For the Irlen Method, the evaluation consists of determining if you have Scotopic Sensitivity Syndrome and to what degree. This process also involves finding the specific colors or combinations of colors that you can use to alleviate the symptoms. You often choose between using colored lenses or contacts, or using colored overlays when you read.

Knowing what to expect

The results of behavioral optometry and the Irlen Method really depend on which perception problem you were determined to have — for example, not being able to get both eyes to focus on the same thing or not being able to track effectively. AD/HD-specific improvements from these approaches have been seen in the following areas:

✔ Increased attention

✔ Improved reading abilities

✔ Reduced hyperactivity

The side effects are minimal, if any, but keep in mind that the results of these approaches are wholly dependent on whether a vision problem is contributing to your AD/HD. If you don't have a vision problem, you obviously can't expect to see any changes in your AD/HD symptoms when doing one of these therapies.

Finding a provider

Providers of vision therapies include behavioral optometrists and sometimes psychologists and other therapists working with people with learning disabilities and AD/HD (see Chapter 4).

Many behavioral optometrists are in practice around the country; check your local phone book under "Optometrist." To locate a behavioral optometrist who specifically works with people with AD/HD, check out the Web site for the Optometrists Network at www.add-adhd.org.

To find a provider who specializes in the Irlen Method to deal with Scotopic Sensitivity Syndrome (or to learn more about SSS), check out www.irlen.com.

Chapter 13

Recognizing Rebalancing Therapies

As we explain in the previous chapter, many treatment options exist beyond the established approaches of medication and behavior management. The treatments we discuss in this chapter all have a similar goal: to help you create balance in your body. Some, such as sensory integration, focus on the nervous system itself; others, such as acupuncture, work on trying to create overall balance.

The treatments presented in this chapter aren't often the first line of defense against the symptoms of AD/HD; most haven't been studied specifically for their effectiveness for AD/HD. We include this chapter for two reasons. First, you'll probably hear about one or more of these treatment approaches while trying to find the best way to get your symptoms under control. Second, one of these techniques may make sense as part of your multimodal treatment strategy — an approach that covers the biological, psychological, and sociological aspects of AD/HD (see Chapter 7).

Balancing Energy Through Acupuncture

Acupuncture is an ancient Chinese system (several thousand years old) of balancing the flow of subtle energies through the body. In the last 30 years or so, it has been studied quite extensively and has grown in popularity in the Western world. In fact, according to the Food and Drug Administration, people in the United States made 12 million office visits for acupuncture in 1993. Acupuncture is used to support general health, but some people use it to reduce some of the symptoms of AD/HD, as well as many of the co-occurring conditions such as anxiety and depression.

Getting some background

Acupuncture is part of the Traditional Chinese Medicine (TCM) system, along with herbs, meditation, and a host of other techniques. Acupuncture (and the rest of TCM) is based on the concept that all parts of the body and mind are interconnected — every part influences the function of every other part.

The belief is that the various parts of your mind and body are connected by a vital energy called *Qi* (which is pronounced, and often spelled, *Chi* in the West). This Qi flows through the body, and any disruptions in this flow affect your health, resulting in illness. The goal of acupuncture is to keep this flow going smoothly, which keeps you healthy; or, if you're already sick, acupuncture frees the blockages that are causing your illness.

The Qi flows through channels called *meridians,* which connect your internal organs with the surface. In TCM, there are 12 primary meridians relating to each of your organ systems and 8 secondary meridians, for a total of 20 meridians. Acupuncture involves placing needles on certain localized points in the skin to direct the flow of Qi through each of these meridians.

Many theories are available on how this system works, but two stand out:

- The meridians lie along main nerve centers in the body, and each acupuncture point stimulates the nervous system in a specific way.
- The acupuncture points, when stimulated, stimulate the body to produce certain endorphins.

Regardless of the mechanism involved in acupuncture, its longevity alone suggests that it must help some people.

Exploring the process

As many as 2,000 acupuncture points exist, and an acupuncturist must figure out which point(s) to stimulate in order to offer you any benefit. Doing so involves a diagnostic process that usually includes the following:

- **Questions to determine your symptoms and history:** These questions may involve asking you about your tolerance to heat or cold, your eating habits, and your sleep patterns. Your answers provide a big-picture view of you and your condition.

✔ **Examination of your tongue:** According to TCM, a patient's tongue holds a lot of information, so your acupuncturist will likely want to take a look.

✔ **A check of your pulse:** Again, according to TCM, your pulse tells your provider a lot about your state of health. Unlike in Western medicine, an acupuncturist is interested in more than just the speed of your pulse; she looks for the strength and rhythm of it as well.

When the intake exam is complete, you're asked to lie down while your provider puts needles in different parts of your body. Before you get nervous, we assure you that these needles don't hurt if they're placed in properly. They are very small, and they go only a little way into your skin. Most people report only a mild prick when the needles are inserted. When the needles are in, most people don't notice them. (However, your coauthor Jeff often feels a very slight tingling sensation.)

If you feel any significant amount of pain from the needles, they aren't put in properly, and you may want to look around for a different acupuncturist. The most you should feel is a slight pricking sensation when the needle is inserted.

After the needles are in, you remain relatively still for up to 30 minutes, at which point the needles are removed and you're free to go.

Knowing what to expect

Your results from acupuncture are going to depend on your condition. Even though you have AD/HD, your acupuncturist may focus on other areas. Remember that the goal of acupuncture is to correct any disruptions in the flow of Qi in your body, so you should receive a very individualized treatment.

Generally speaking, it takes several sessions before you can expect to see any significant changes in your symptoms. Side effects, if any, are minimal. Most often, your acupuncturist is able to give you a clear idea after your initial examination as to the number of sessions you need (and their cost) and whether you'll need to return later for tune-ups.

Finding a provider

Many acupuncturists are in practice these days, but finding one who has experience working with people with AD/HD may be hard. As with any healthcare professional, your best bet is to get a referral from a family member, a friend, or another healthcare provider. If you can't find any referrals, start with your local phone book or check the bulletin board of your local natural foods market. If all else fails, do an Internet search for an acupuncturist in your area. Check the following Web sites, which also have quite a bit of information about acupuncture and TCM:

- ✔ www.acupuncture.com
- ✔ www.acupuncturetoday.com
- ✔ www.medicalacupuncture.org

Helping Your Body Heal Itself with Homeopathy

Homeopathy is intended to help your body heal itself using the concept that *like cures like*. Homeopathic remedies, which are designed to stimulate your body to eliminate your symptoms, are being used more and more for people with AD/HD. Homeopathy has been around for a couple hundred years and has gone through several periods of popularity, including now.

Getting some background

Developed by Samuel Hahneman in the late eighteenth century, homeopathy is based on the law of similars: Like heals like. In other words, homeopaths use very diluted doses (we're talking *minute* traces here) of substances that cause the exact symptoms you have. For example, in the instance of a sleep disturbance, a homeopathic remedy may have a minute trace of caffeine in it to help you get to sleep.

Homeopathic remedies are made from substances that, if taken in their undiluted form, are toxic. The key to homeopathics is in the preparation and dilution. The process of creating the remedy usually involves mixing alcohol and water with the active substance and diluting the solution substantially. According to Hahneman, the more diluted the solution, the stronger the effects.

Exploring the process

Effective homeopathy relies upon your homeopath getting a complete picture of your symptoms. Doing so involves a pretty extensive process of asking you about your symptoms, history, and lifestyle. Your provider then consults the homeopathic *materia medica* (the list of more than 3,000 remedies that have been tested) for the best remedy for you.

Your provider prescribes a certain remedy, or group of remedies, and asks you to take them according to a strict schedule (usually something like four pills twice a day) for a certain amount of time. These remedies generally come in the form of small pills that you dissolve under your tongue. You shouldn't eat or drink anything within about 20 minutes of taking the pills.

In most cases, you have occasional follow-up appointments to see how the remedy is working for you, and you're given different remedies if needed.

Knowing what to expect

REMEMBER

The effectiveness of homeopathy for the symptoms of AD/HD depends on which remedy you use. Determining the best remedy for an individual takes skill and practice, so your choice of provider has a huge impact on whether you end up seeing any significant benefits.

Both of us have seen homeopathy work well for people with AD/HD, but you should expect it to take some time to work — as much as several months. The good news is that side effects are often nonexistent. Some practitioners believe in a concept called *aggravations,* where your symptoms actually get a little worse before beginning to improve; other practitioners don't see this happening.

The cost of homeopathics is very low, but if you take a remedy for months at a time, the cost obviously adds up. How long you end up taking a remedy and how long the results last depend on many factors, including the severity of your symptoms and the appropriateness of the remedies taken.

Finding a provider

The best way to look for a local homeopath is the same way that you find any professional: Ask for referrals from people you trust. If you don't succeed at getting a referral, check your phone book or do an Internet search using "AD/HD homeopathy" as your search phrase. For starters, here are a few Web sites that we think provide solid information:

✔ www.homeopathyhome.com
✔ www.homeopathic.org
✔ www.homeopathic.com

If you're interested in learning more about homeopathy, check out these books:

- *Homeopathic Medicine for Children and Infants* (Penguin Putnam, Inc.) by Dana Ullman

- *Ritalin-Free Kids: Safe and Effective Homeopathic Medicine for ADHD and Other Behavioral and Learning Problems* (Prima Publishing) by Dr. Judyth Reichenberg-Ullman and Dr. Robert Ullman

Using Manipulation Therapies

Manipulation therapies — chiropractic, osteopathy, and CranioSacral Therapy — are concerned with the flow of cerebrospinal fluid and the alignment of the spine. Manipulation therapies are beginning to be used to assist those with AD/HD because some people believe that a disruption in the flow of the cerebrospinal fluid — caused by misalignment of the bone or soft tissues in the body — can affect nervous system function and may result in symptoms similar to AD/HD in some people.

Getting some background

The idea that manipulation of the body can help improve health goes back a long way. According to the American Chiropractic Association, people were writing about spinal manipulation almost 5,000 years ago in China. Ancient Greeks also used spinal manipulation. In fact, the Greek physician Hippocrates wrote extensively about the benefits of adjusting the spine, saying in one instance, "Get knowledge of the spine, for this is the requisite for many diseases." (The founder of osteopathy, Dr. Andrew Taylor Still, drew from Hippocrates's ideas when he developed the practice in the late nineteenth century.)

Following is a bit of background about each manipulation therapy:

- **Chiropractic care:** Chiropractic focuses on the alignment of the bones, but most chiropractors are also well-versed in preventive care, such as nutrition, and many are also trained in CranioSacral Therapy (which we discuss later in this list). There are also chiropractic neurologists who regularly work with people with AD/HD.

- **Osteopathy:** This field of medicine is also concerned with the alignment of the bones but goes a few steps further than chiropractic. Developed by Dr. Andrew Taylor Still in 1874, osteopathic medicine was the first Western form of healthcare to use the concept of *wellness* (preventive care). Osteopathic physicians often act as primary care physicians and are trained in osteopathic manipulative treatment (OMT), which focuses on your skeletal system and its relationship to your health.

✔ **CranioSacral Therapy (CST):** This therapy was developed by osteopathic physician John E. Upledger based on research he conducted starting in 1975. The original work on cranial rhythms was done about a century before by another osteopath, William Sutherland. CST uses very gentle pressure on the scalp to evaluate and improve the functioning of the craniosacral system. This system consists of the membranes and fluid that protect the spinal cord and brain.

The main idea behind these manipulation therapies is that neurological problems can develop due to misalignment of the bones in your body, and by realigning them neurological function can improve. Chiropractic focuses mainly on the spine, osteopathy covers the entire skeletal system, and CranioSacral Therapy concerns itself with the cranial rhythm (the specific flow of the cerebrospinal fluid) by adjusting the bones in your scalp.

Exploring the process

Each of the manipulation therapies begins with an intake process that evaluates the alignments of the particular area. For chiropractors, the exam focuses on the spine; the osteopathic physician evaluates the skeletal system; and craniosacral therapists look at the cranial rhythm. Most of these professionals also ask a lot of questions regarding your overall health, as well as your AD/HD symptoms.

When the evaluation is done, you get an adjustment. This usually isn't painful, and most people find it quite relaxing. (But, in fairness, your coauthor Jeff has had some uncomfortable chiropractic sessions in the past, which emphasizes the importance of finding the right practitioner.) After your adjustment, your professional will likely offer suggestions of things you can do at home to help the process, such as supplements or exercises.

The number of sessions required depends on your health and your professional. In some instances, one session is enough to make a dramatic change. For other people, three sessions a week for several weeks or even months may be required. After your evaluation and first adjustment, your professional should be able to give you a reasonable idea of how many sessions you may need.

Knowing what to expect

Many people describe a feeling of calm after receiving an adjustment. For conditions such as back pain, the effects of the manipulations can be significant and immediate. However, for the symptoms of AD/HD you may not see much improvement right away, and the results you do end up seeing may be subtle.

Finding a provider

Again, a referral is best, if you can get one. If not, check your phone book, or take a look at the Web sites for these organizations:

- **The American Chiropractic Association** (`www.amerchiro.org`): The ACA is the largest chiropractic organization in the world and offers a lot of information about chiropractic, as well as a listing of chiropractors.
- **The American Osteopathic Association** (`www.osteopathic.org`): The AOA is a professional association for osteopaths, and its Web site has a ton of great information.
- **The Upledger Institute** (`www.upledger.com`): CranioSacral Therapy was created by John Upledger, and this is his official site.

Helping Your Brain Process Sensory Information

The term *sensory integration* refers to the way your brain is able to process and organize all the sensory information that your body receives. Many people with developmental disabilities and learning problems have difficulties with sensory integration. Sensory integration therapy is designed to help these people better process and organize (neurologically) what their senses pick up.

Getting some background

Sensory integration therapy was developed by occupational therapist A. Jean Ayres, PhD, OTR, in the 1950s. Dr. Ayres studied the effects that sensory processing and motor planning have on learning and behavior. Her research suggested a link, and she spent many years developing ways to improve sensory processing. Since its inception, sensory integration therapy has become a common part of occupational therapists' treatment approaches, with almost 10,000 occupational therapists in the United States making it a part of their everyday work.

Sensory integration is the process of taking all the sensory input that you receive and making sense of it so that you can respond appropriately. A breakdown in this system can result in the following symptoms:

- Hypersensitivity to touch, movements, sights, or sounds
- Little or no response to sensory input

✔ Unusually high or low overall activity level

✔ Problems with coordination

✔ Developmental delays

✔ Poor motor planning, which can include problems with fine or gross motor skills

✔ Behavioral problems

✔ Learning difficulties

✔ Not knowing where your body is in space

The purpose of sensory integration therapy is to help your brain make sense of all the sensory information you receive so that you can respond better. By improving your ability to handle sensory stimuli, many of the symptoms listed above are reduced. Many people with AD/HD have some sort of sensory processing dysfunction.

Exploring the process

Just because you have AD/HD doesn't mean that you have a sensory integration dysfunction; however, sensory integration issues are often a co-occurring condition for people with AD/HD. So your first step is to find out if processing sensory information is a problem for you. This process usually involves certain standardized tests that evaluate your coordination, posture, balance, and response to stimuli, among other things.

If the occupational therapist determines that you have a sensory processing dysfunction, he suggests some exercises and other sensory stimulation techniques to try to improve your ability to process the sensory information that seems to be getting mixed up in your brain.

The exercises look like play and often involve balls, swings, trampolines, and other items that involve sensory stimulation. (Because most children with sensory processing dysfunction tend to seek out activities that stimulate them in the way that they need, many occupational therapists let children help choose what exercises to do. This lets them have some degree of control over the treatment and makes the process more dynamic for the therapist.)

In addition to exercises and activities performed with the occupational therapist, you're usually given exercises to do at home. Occupational therapy sessions usually occur at least once a week and can continue for several months.

Some schools have an occupational therapist on staff who can work a sensory integration therapy program into your child's school week. To access these services, you need to receive an official diagnosis by your child's school of a sensory processing dysfunction. You then have to go through the process for determining services under the special education laws, which we talk about in Chapter 15.

Knowing what to expect

As with the other therapies we discuss in this chapter, results of sensory integration therapy vary from person to person. Generally, you can expect to see some minor improvements within the first few sessions, with greater changes developing over time. Your occupational therapist will tailor your treatment according to the changes taking place and can give you a good idea of the type of progress to expect.

Finding a provider

Your best bet in finding a provider for sensory integration therapy is to look for an occupational therapist (OT) who specializes in this area near where you live. Your other healthcare providers may have a referral for you, but if they don't, you can check with the American Occupational Therapy Association (www.aota.org). This organization can give you a list of licensed OTs in your area who do sensory integration therapy.

You can also check out the Sensory Processing Disorder Network at www.sinetwork.org. This site has lots of information about the disorder, as well as links to help you find a professional.

Part IV
Living with AD/HD

The 5th Wave   By Rich Tennant

"I've tried Ayurveda, meditation, and aromatherapy, but nothing seems to work. I'm still feeling nauseous and disoriented all day."

In this part . . .

The chapters in this part help you develop strategies for effectively living with AD/HD. We begin with a chapter full of suggestions for making life at home as low-stress and rewarding as possible. Next, we tackle the school environment, discussing everything from knowing your legal rights and handling Individual Education Plan meetings to working with teachers and ensuring that your child does his homework. From school, we move to the workplace in Chapter 16, offering you ideas on how to handle the demands of work and determine the type of work that best suits your style. Chapter 17 is an ode to the positive aspects of AD/HD; this chapter helps you to find your strengths and accentuate them.

Chapter 14

Creating Harmony at Home

· ·

In This Chapter

▶ Developing strong family bonds

▶ Discovering ways to help your child

▶ Examining positive adult partnerships

▶ Exploring daily habits that minimize problems

· ·

*H*aving AD/HD in your home can be stressful. Many people with AD/HD don't realize the impact that their symptoms have on their family members and other loved ones. Symptoms like distractibility, impulsivity, hyperactivity, disorganization, and moodiness can create chaos and conflict in an otherwise controlled and loving household.

In this chapter, we get to the heart of relationships in an effort to help you create a stronger family bond and reduce conflict. We explore ways to make parenting a child with AD/HD less difficult, we suggest how you and your spouse can work together to make both your lives easier, and we present important things you can do daily to keep the symptoms (and disruption) of AD/HD to a minimum.

Laying the Foundation for Healthy Relationships

Regardless of whether you, your child, or your spouse has AD/HD, you can take steps to encourage family harmony by understanding some principles that help reduce conflict and create a more loving environment. These include having empathy, being able to communicate effectively, expressing emotions in a healthy way, and expressing appreciation. These are the cornerstones of loving relationships. We cover them all in detail in the following sections.

Exercising empathy

Empathy is the ability to identify with and understand what another person is feeling. Empathy is important in relationships because if you are able to put yourself in another person's place, you can see how your own actions impact that person. Also, by having empathy for a person with AD/HD, you realize that many of his behaviors are not intended to hurt you or anyone else.

When someone has AD/HD, his family often suffers because he may not be able to perform the seemingly simple task of empathizing. The problem isn't that he *chooses* not to empathize; it's that he doesn't know how. (Many people without AD/HD also have this problem.) So it's important for everyone in the family to actively learn how to have empathy toward everyone else.

To exercise empathy, you need to do the following:

- ✔ **Recognize that everyone feels things differently.** One of the most important prerequisites for empathy is to realize that other people — even those in your own family who have similar values and beliefs — don't necessarily feel the same way about things as you do.

- ✔ **Pay attention to the other person.** You must actively focus on other people's reactions and the messages they communicate, both verbally and nonverbally. This step may take practice.

- ✔ **Understand how you feel and think.** For this step, the famous AD/HD trait of being brutally honest is very useful; you just need to focus that honesty on yourself.

The key to empathy is to be aware of the people around you and how they're affected by your actions. Family members who don't have AD/HD must demonstrate compassion and understanding for the person with AD/HD, who may really struggle with demonstrating empathy. In other words, a person without AD/HD needs to have an extra dose of empathy for the person with it. And, if you're the one with AD/HD, you need to try to understand how your behavior affects the people in your life.

Here are some additional suggestions for developing empathy toward others:

- ✔ Identify the struggle that the other person is going through.

- ✔ Try to understand the person's feelings.

- ✔ Anticipate how what you're going to say or do is going to affect that other person.

- ✔ Reflect on how what you did made the other person feel.

- ✔ Ask the other person how she feels about a situation or interaction.

Expressing emotions

When you have AD/HD or live with someone who does, you may believe that you need to keep a stiff upper lip in the face of the stresses and challenges. But holding in your emotions is a surefire way to end up feeling unappreciated and angry.

Acknowledging your feelings and expressing them in healthy ways are vitally important. If you're the person with AD/HD, you may have to put out extra effort to figure out how to express your feelings verbally instead of acting them out. The effort is definitely worthwhile in terms of improving domestic harmony.

Following are some of the most common negative feelings that color family interactions when a family member has AD/HD, along with suggestions for how to deal with them effectively:

✔ **Frustration:** If you get frustrated or impatient when trying to complete a task (either because you don't know how to do it or can't ever seem to finish it), you may visit your frustration on the people around you (or on the object at hand). A healthy solution is to take a few minutes to talk about how thwarted you feel, then take some steps to make success more likely. For example, you can read more about what you are trying to do, acknowledge the amount of time the project may require, or ask (nicely) for help.

✔ **Anger:** Perhaps you often feel angry at your child or spouse for not doing what you want him to do, or maybe you get angry at yourself for letting other people down. Expressing anger is fine, as long as it's not accompanied by blame (even if someone is to blame). Acknowledge your anger, but don't let the anger control you and make you do or say something that you'll regret later.

✔ **Guilt:** Guilt has many shades. You may feel guilty for any number of reasons, such as for acting the way you did in a certain situation, for not finding help for your (or your family member's) AD/HD sooner, or for having angry thoughts and feelings about a loved one. A healthy way to deal with guilt is to express remorse — to recognize the pain that you and other people feel because of your actions or inaction, and to put that recognition into words.

✔ **Embarrassment:** It's normal to feel embarrassment when you or your loved one with AD/HD does something inappropriate. Resist the temptation to criticize or blame yourself (or your loved one) for the inappropriate behavior. Instead, focus on correcting the behavior and trying to make amends, if necessary. Also, try to employ a sense of humor in these situations (without making fun of a loved one's actions, of course).

The best way to deal with emotions such as these is to work at recognizing them and allow yourself time to reflect on them before taking action. While you're delaying acting, you can think about how to express your feelings in a way that doesn't judge or criticize yourself or others. Many times, strong unexpressed (or poorly expressed) emotions are the cause of further conflict in a relationship. When this is the case, it's often helpful to see a therapist or counselor to help you work through them (either individually or as a family).

Commanding communication

Miscommunication runs rampant in families that cope with AD/HD. First, many people (with or without AD/HD) tend to make assumptions about what others are thinking or doing. Second, many people with AD/HD start talking without listening first, or they have a tendency to speak without thinking. The end result is some serious miscommunication.

To prevent these communication issues from taking over your family's life, the entire family needs to learn how to listen and express themselves effectively. In many instances, clearing up communication problems among family members requires the help of a skilled counselor or therapist, but here are some ideas for getting started:

- **Actively listen as the other person talks.** Active listening involves reiterating the other person's point before responding with one of your own. For example, perhaps your partner says that she's angry because you didn't clean the garage like you said you would. Before making an excuse, first acknowledge the fact that she's angry.

- **If you're unsure what someone means, ask for clarification.** Don't just make an assumption.

- **Don't criticize.** Contrary to some people's beliefs, criticism is never constructive. Criticism serves only to prop up the person giving the criticism while belittling the person being criticized. We advocate the philosophy that mothers have advanced for generations: "If you don't have something nice to say, don't say anything at all." Removing criticism from your lexicon also removes a considerable amount of conflict.

- **Offer a positive before bringing up a negative.** When you discuss how you feel and what you'd like to have changed in your relationship, avoid jumping right into the things you don't like. Start by mentioning the things you appreciate about your current relationship, and then gently move into the things you'd like to change.

The key to effective communication is listening and making sure you understand the other person. Most conflict occurs when one person misunderstands or misinterprets what another person means.

Acknowledging appreciation

Nothing is more powerful in fostering a loving bond than expressing your appreciation for another person. Don't be shy about telling your loved ones when you appreciate something they've done. To get you started, here are some suggestions:

- ✔ **Say "thank you" after your child has completed a chore.** Do this even if you had to remind him to do his chore or if you had to help him do it.

- ✔ **Say "I love you."** Don't be afraid to tell the people you love that you love them. Everyone likes to hear this, and saying it can help break down feelings of anger and resentment.

- ✔ **Offer a smile or a hug.** You can do this anytime, but it's often especially appreciated after your loved one has done something for you.

When people feel appreciated, they're more willing to be helpful and appreciative back.

Canceling conflict

Some professionals believe that people with AD/HD have an almost compulsive need to create conflict. If that's the case, most people with AD/HD don't realize it (and few, if any, would acknowledge it if asked). One possibility is that conflict is stimulating for the person with AD/HD, and a stimulating situation may help his symptoms abate.

The problem is that creating conflict obviously makes life extremely frustrating for that person's loved ones and, therefore, it could end up being downright dangerous. Even if the theory of the stimulating effects of conflict isn't right, a lot of people practice conflict as a way of life. Conflict usually isn't the best way to get ahead.

So the big question is how to deal with this (possibly unconscious) need for conflict. If stimulation is what you crave, one suggestion is to engage in positive, productive activities, such as exercise or a hobby that really holds your interest. By doing so, you may be able to cancel the unconscious trigger to stir up tensions.

When conflict does happen, one of the most effective strategies for diffusing it is to take a time-out. Stop the conversation or activity that's causing the conflict, and come back to it at a later time. It also helps to think and talk about feelings and beliefs that may be contributing to your need to stir up trouble.

Healing the past

Many people harbor resentments over the past. These feelings of resentment often come up at the worst possible times — during arguments and stressful situations — and can cause considerable problems in the family. Before you can effectively live in the present and hope for the future, you need to let go of past hurts and resentment. This can be very difficult and almost always involves seeing a therapist who can help you work through your feelings. Many times, going to a therapist alone is the best option, but you may find that occasionally attending therapy sessions with your partner can help clear the air between you.

You may have lived a long time before finding out that you or your loved one has AD/HD. The legacies of your life before the diagnosis include many disappointments, failures, stresses, and frustrations. Your challenge now is to realize that you have an explanation to help make sense out of a lot of things that were probably mysterious sources of bad feelings and experiences in the past. You have enough work to do to make your present and future as positive as possible: Don't waste time trying to undo what's behind you.

You can't embrace the future if you're still holding on to the past. Take whatever steps necessary to let go of your resentment so that you can move forward with your life.

Being realistic

When you undertake a new AD/HD treatment plan, be pragmatic about the changes you'll see and be leery of treatments that claim to offer quick-fix "cures" for your symptoms. You don't want to set yourself up for disappointment and further feelings of failure.

Being unrealistic about the degree and rate of improvement to expect from AD/HD treatments is a common source of family conflict. The only way past this problem is to rein in unrealistic expectations. Recognize that progress is often slow, and it doesn't necessarily take a straight path. You'll have many gains and setbacks along the way. And in some areas, you may not see any change whatsoever.

Keep in mind that the more you discover about how AD/HD impacts you personally and your family as a whole, the more your perspective will change. What you now see as a difficult problem may later look like a gift. And what you now consider to be a "cute quirk" may seem like a much more serious issue down the road.

Improving Your Life with AD/HD

As we stress many times in this book, having AD/HD presents many challenges, especially when you interact with people who don't have the condition. In this section, we tackle some of the more important issues that people with AD/HD have when they live with people who don't have it.

Managing moods

One of the main characteristics of AD/HD for most people is extreme, frequent changes in mood. One minute you may feel happy and hopeful, and a minute later you feel angry and frustrated without anything outside of you causing the change. This phenomenon is a product of several different factors, the most important of which are:

- ✔ **A biological disposition to react more strongly than other people to the ups and downs of life:** This tendency is usually helped to some degree by the biological treatments we discuss in Chapter 8. Other biological causes, such as depression, anxiety, or bipolar disorder, can also contribute.

- ✔ **Past experiences:** Most people with AD/HD have come up short on meeting their (and others') expectations, so they tend to have an internal dialogue that is demeaning and negative. That tendency to have a low opinion of oneself can be formed, worsened, or reinforced by . . .

- ✔ **Others' words:** How many times can a person hear "I'm disappointed in you" or "You could do so much better if only you tried harder" before turning that criticism inward (and often making it even stronger)? We submit, very few. Most people with AD/HD bear deep scars from criticism directed at them over and over again.

- ✔ **A tendency to jump to conclusions:** As we say earlier in this chapter, in the section "Commanding communication," people with AD/HD have a talent for jumping to conclusions ahead of the evidence. (This talent can also be called "being intuitive.") After you've jumped to a conclusion, an attitude isn't far behind. If you have an attitude about every conclusion you jump to, you're probably going to come across as moody.

- ✔ **Medication wearing off:** If you take medication for your AD/HD, as it wears off you may experience changes in mood. If you notice a mood pattern that seems to coincide with your medication schedule, talk to your physician about adjusting your medication, dosage, or schedule.

Here are some suggestions to deal with negative thoughts that can lead to negative moods:

- ✔ **Stop the thought and ask yourself if it is based on what's happening at the moment.** Most of the time, negative thoughts are simply popping up without relating to your life at the moment.

- ✔ **Breathe through it.** When you have negative thoughts, your body tenses up, and your breath becomes shallower. Take a few deep breaths, and you'll begin to relax.

- ✔ **Cancel that thought.** After you acknowledge that the thought isn't based on what's happening and you've had a chance to take a breath, you can let it go.

- ✔ **Reframe that thought.** Even if you think a negative thought *is* based on what's really happening, you don't have to let it lead you to a negative feeling. Try to reframe negative perceptions, thoughts, or words into positive ones. If you can see the humor or the benefit in a difficult situation, you can probably feel better about it.

- ✔ **Don't take things personally.** All of us have internal pressures, reasons, or ideas that make us do the things we do. When someone directs a negative comment or action your way, try to realize that it's not necessarily about you. If you can do so, you may not feel the need to have such a strong reaction. Work on understanding the causes and consequences of your own and other people's actions and reactions. If you succeed, you may be able to let us all off the hooks of blame, resentment, and general bad temper.

Extreme moodiness may be a sign of depression or bipolar disorder (see Chapter 6). Because both of these conditions are common among people with AD/HD, have a professional screen you for these conditions (see Chapter 4).

Taking responsibility

We've said this before and we'll say it again: AD/HD is an explanation, not an excuse. You must take responsibility for your actions regardless of the fact that AD/HD has a biological cause. If your behavior is causing problems in your life, you need to seek the best possible help in getting it under control.

If you hurt someone, create a problem, or make situations more difficult — even unintentionally — don't use your diagnosis of AD/HD as an excuse. You and everyone else will benefit if you can focus on understanding how your actions caused the hurt or contributed to the problem. If you can find a way to express that understanding to the other people involved, all the better; they can then realize that you have not ignored their feelings and rights. (They also won't think you're an absolute idiot [*viz.* another publisher].)

The most important thing you can do is to learn from situations in which your AD/HD plays a part in creating bad feelings or less-than-optimal outcomes. That way, you can take responsibility and continue on the road to self-improvement.

Parenting a Child with AD/HD

We could easily write an entire book on the best ways to parent a child with AD/HD. Some excellent books are available on this subject, such as:

- *Helping Your ADD Child: Hundreds of Practical Solutions for Parents and Teachers of ADD Children and Teens (with or without Hyperactivity)* (Prima Health) by John F. Taylor, PhD
- *Taking Charge of ADHD: The Complete, Authoritative Guide for Parents* (The Guilford Press) by Russell A. Barkley, PhD

In this section, we discuss the most pressing concerns that parents have about improving life at home with a child with AD/HD. We focus on ways that you can prevent problem behaviors from happening, work with those behaviors when they do show up, and deal with your AD/HD child if you have more than one child at home.

If you have a child with AD/HD, the chances are pretty high that you or your child's other parent may have it, too (see Chapter 2). If you do have AD/HD, treating your own symptoms can go a long way toward making parenting easier for both you and your child.

Preventing problems

The best way to improve life at home with a child with AD/HD is to minimize the possibility of behavior problems rather than deal with them after the fact. This section offers some ideas for reducing behavioral problems by using treatment effectively, establishing a clear set of rules and expectations, creating an environment that leaves little room for misbehavior, and focusing on positive behaviors rather than negative ones.

Treating your child's AD/HD effectively

Years of experience and research by a large number of clinicians and parents has shown that coping with a child's AD/HD is much easier when you start out by addressing both biological and psychological issues:

- ✔ Because undesirable behaviors are based on problematic functioning, the most important place to start is to choose one or more of the biological treatment options that we describe in Chapters 8, 11, 12, and 13. You need to allow enough time for them to start working.

- ✔ You can address psychological factors by implementing some of the approaches we discuss in Chapters 9 and 10, such as various forms of psychotherapy and behavior modification. Doing so can help you to avoid dealing with the obstacles of ongoing conflicts while you are trying to develop better living strategies.

Taking these two steps will likely lead to a significant reduction in the symptoms and behavioral problems in your child. After doing so, you'll be better able to assess what behaviors need to be addressed using the tips and techniques we describe in this chapter and in Chapter 15. Also, your child will have a much easier time cooperating with your efforts and making use of the skills you want to help her learn.

Understanding characteristics of AD/HD behavior

Many behavioral characteristics accompany AD/HD. Understanding these characteristics can help you better address the behaviors that cause problems in your life. These characteristics can include:

- ✔ **Having difficulty following rules:** Your child with AD/HD needs to learn how to comply with rules that are necessary for his safety and for the smooth operation of the household, school, and society.

- ✔ **Looking for loopholes:** People with AD/HD often have a talent for finding the loopholes in any system or set of rules.

- ✔ **Questioning authority:** Most likely you have already discovered that your child has a knack for questioning authority and for questioning any rules that she is asked to follow.

- ✔ **Creating distractions:** Because kids with AD/HD are subject to distractibility, they are also often masters of distracting other people, especially if the distraction helps them avoid being punished or controlled.

- ✔ **Demanding fairness:** Fairness is a major issue for many people with AD/HD. This is true even if the person doesn't make any particular effort to treat other people with fairness or respect.

✔ **Sticking up for a cause:** People with AD/HD are more likely than others to take the side of the underdog. As a result, they sometimes fight for a cause with all their might when you think they are just trying to cause trouble. It also often means that your child is more involved in other people's business than his own.

✔ **Picking up skills at a slower pace:** Children with AD/HD often take longer than others to learn new skills, especially if the new skill involves changing things they already do some other way. As we discuss in Chapter 15, they also often learn in slightly different ways than other people.

✔ **Struggling with repetitive tasks:** AD/HD children have more difficulty learning and doing repetitive and tedious tasks, such as memorizing multiplication tables, doing chores every week, or even brushing their teeth every day.

✔ **Bending the truth:** Many parents find that their children with AD/HD are more flexible with the truth than they would like. This can take the form of telling tall tales more or less for entertainment, or it can be outright lying. Kids with AD/HD (like other children) may lie for a variety of reasons, but they are often better at it than others. In many cases, they are so good at it that they believe their own lies. That's why we say they are flexible with the truth.

✔ **Struggling to connect cause and effect:** Children with AD/HD often have trouble connecting cause and effect if the cause is too far removed in time from the effect. That means your AD/HD child needs immediate feedback: discussion, rewards, and punishments close to the time of the behaviors (see Chapter 10).

✔ **Having difficulty with tasks that require planning:** Kids with AD/HD may have difficulty learning how to work on — and finish — tasks that require planning and meeting intermediate goals. This is a good place to practice spending some quality time with your child, helping her to learn these skills.

✔ **Having trouble getting started:** People with AD/HD often have a hard time getting started on a project or switching from one activity to another. You may have to work with your child to get him over the hurdle of getting started by breaking down the task into manageable chunks and maybe even assisting in the first step. After he's going, he'll likely need no more guidance.

How you deal with these characteristics depends on the age of your child. For young AD/HD children (under 8 or 10), behavioral modification techniques usually work better than explanations and discussion. As your child gets older, you can enjoy the wonders of rational discussion and intellectual fencing. At all ages, you need a blend of love, patience, and clever luck to manage the challenges of AD/HD parenting.

Unlike some other children, those with AD/HD rarely learn best by being told how to do something. They are much more likely than others to do what you do and not what you say. You and your child are going to be a lot happier if you practice the principle of setting a good example as the first rule of teaching good behavior.

Setting rules and expectations

Children with AD/HD have a great need for structure and clarity. Without establishing clear guidelines for proper behavior, you can't expect your child to conform.

Therefore, one of your first steps in getting the types of behaviors you desire is to create a clear set of expectations based on a realistic assessment of your child's abilities. With these expectations in mind, establish a set of rules and specify clear, appropriate consequences for disobeying them. Following is a breakdown of this process:

- ✔ **Make assessments.** Wait until your child's AD/HD treatment is well underway, so you'll be able to see what areas still pose a problem and what areas don't.

- ✔ **Set expectations and rules.** When you know what areas you need to work on, you can create a set of rules and expectations. Here are some commonly used rules to get you started:

  - Treat each family member with respect by not hitting, teasing, or arguing.

  - Follow mom or dad's instructions without complaining.

    Make sure your child understands you before determining that he didn't follow your instructions. For example, ask him to repeat back what you said, using his own words. Or ask him to look you in the eye when you speak, so you can feel certain he's paying attention. Neither technique is foolproof, but both should help.

  - Finish your homework before playing any video games or watching TV.

  - Tell the truth.

  - Clean up after yourself. Put your toys and clothes away when you're finished with them.

  The best rules are both clear and positive. Instead of saying "Don't take your brother's things," say "Respect your brother by asking first (and getting his okay) before you take something that belongs to him."

- ✔ **Explain the rules clearly.** Before you put the rules into effect, make sure that everyone in the family understands them, as well as the rewards and consequences associated with each of them.

✔ **Reward positive behaviors.** When your child does something right, reward him. This can take the form of simply acknowledging the good deed (saying "thanks" and giving a hug), or it can be more formal, such as offering special treats or trips to someplace your child wants to go or letting him stay up a little later than usual.

✔ **Provide appropriate consequences.** The consequences for breaking the rules need to be appropriate for the situation. They also need to be enacted without emotion; don't take these actions when you're angry. Providing consequences is a complex subject that we cover in detail in the upcoming section "Dealing with discipline."

Write your rules down. If your child is too young to read, you can make a pictograph that explains the rules. If they aren't written down, you or your child can easily forget them. Post the rules someplace prominent in the house so that your child is reminded of them throughout the day.

Creating a structured environment

Kids, especially kids with AD/HD, do best in a structured environment. By providing a structured place in which to live, you minimize the possibilities for misbehavior and improve the opportunities for success.

Structure isn't about hovering over your kid and correcting her after she makes mistakes; structure is about creating an environment that makes it easy for her to do the right things. Here are some suggestions for creating a positive structure for your child:

✔ **Chart it out.** Create charts for chores and your child's daily schedule. Many people with AD/HD relate better to pictures than words, so having a graphic display of what you expect and how the day is structured can help your child better understand and follow it. Have a place in this chart for notes and stickers that show that a chore was completed. Place this chart in a prominent place where your child can easily see it.

✔ **Prevent boredom.** How many parents have heard their kids chanting the mantra "I'm bored"? All kids experience boredom, but for children with AD/HD who need stimulation in order to function, boredom is often a major problem. You can prevent boredom several ways:

• Think about and discuss with your child the idea that people perceive boredom in situations where they are craving external stimulation that is lacking or that is available in a form they cannot appreciate. One good way not to get bored is to develop personal resourcefulness.

• Keep a busy schedule. Set up your child's day so that she has little time to get bored (and into trouble). This can also help keep negative behaviors at bay. However, don't make your schedule so hectic that you and your child don't have any spare time just to relax and enjoy life.

- Have an activities board in your house with a list of fun things your child can do. This will help her find ways to combat boredom.

- Keep plenty of art supplies and other hands-on activities on hand and accessible. The key here is to make these supplies accessible so that your child can dig in whenever she wants.

- Create a safe outdoor space with plenty of things to do. Physical activity — especially outdoors — can dramatically improve AD/HD symptoms. If possible, set up a play area outside, such as a fenced backyard with a playground set, where your child can go even if you aren't available to join her.

✔ **Provide supervision.** By closely supervising your child, you can keep her from making decisions without thinking — one of the hallmarks of children with impulsive-type AD/HD. One difficulty that some parents have is in making the transition from constant, one-on-one supervision to the situation of the child being responsible for her own actions. This is usually a process that takes 18 years or so to complete, but with AD/HD children it can take even longer. It's best to start early and keep at the development of self-awareness, self-discipline, and responsibility.

Most of our learning from birth onward comes in the form of thousands of little, subtle messages from the people around us every moment of every day. A smile or laugh, a frown, a little comment like "Good little girls don't . . ." — all are ways that we learn how to behave and how not to behave. Even others' acts of responding (or not responding) to us teach us about how to behave. These methods also teach us how to think about ourselves, so they have a direct impact on our self-image and self-esteem. Keeping these truths in mind, along with remembering to set a good example, will help you when you're trying to figure out the finer points of managing your child's (and your) emotions and behavior.

Perpetuating positive behavior

The best way to increase positive behaviors is to acknowledge them when you see them and accentuate them over the negative behaviors. Here are some ideas for reinforcing positive behaviors in your child:

✔ **Don't dwell on the negative.** Many parents spend most of their time looking for their child to make a mistake, only to pounce on him when he does. One of the best pieces of advice your coauthor Jeff was ever given about parenting was "Try not to notice so much." This is also called *selective ignoring*. If the behavior doesn't pose a threat to the health and safety of anyone, and it doesn't inflict emotional stress on someone, ignore it. You have plenty of other things to focus on.

✔ **Point out the positive.** Want to know the best way to encourage positive behavior? Point it out when you see it. Everyone likes praise, especially children who feel as though they can't do anything right. Make it your goal to point out positive behaviors ten times more often than you point out negative behaviors.

✔ **Offer support.** When your child tries to do something, offer your help and support. Sometimes just knowing that someone is there to help can give him the confidence to try a little harder and actually do it. Just make sure that if your child doesn't get it right you don't come down hard on him.

Also, don't be too quick to do the job for your child — a common mistake many parents make. Your child needs to figure out how to do tasks himself, and he also needs to feel the accomplishment that comes with completing a project. Your job in offering support is to help him get over the hurdles while helping him learn. Then you and your child can both take pride in your accomplishments.

✔ **Provide incentives.** Many people do better when they have some extra incentive beyond the intrinsic satisfaction of a job well done. For example, you probably prefer getting paid for your work rather than simply having the satisfaction of knowing that you did it. Likewise, your child with AD/HD will likely take more interest in doing what he needs to do if he has some incentives.

Here are some examples:

- Pay your child an allowance for accomplishing his weekly tasks.

- On the chart that lists your child's chores (which we discuss in the previous section), place a sticker next to each chore when he finishes it.

- Say "thanks" and give a hug for a job well done (or even just attempted).

- For big accomplishments, like finishing a project for school, offer a special treat, such as a trip to the movies or a meal at his favorite restaurant.

- If your child finishes his homework early, let him play video games or watch TV a little longer than usual.

✔ **Spend time together.** Nothing provides a better opportunity to shape your children's behavior than actually spending time with them. Get to know your kids. Talk to them about what they like and dislike, what they think and feel. Doing so helps you develop a bond so you not only gain a better understanding of what makes your children tick but also let them feel as though you care about them and understand who they are. This is especially important with teenagers.

Dealing with discipline

The purpose of discipline is not to punish your child for misbehaving; it's to teach her how to act responsibly. We believe the best way to understand this is to think of the concept of *self-discipline*. Your task as a parent is to help your child learn self-discipline by the time she grows up. You may have already guessed that we don't think this means learning how to punish oneself. Rather, we see self-discipline as being able to act in a responsible manner through the choices you make. In this section, we offer some suggestions for disciplining your child with this goal in mind.

Doling out discipline

One of your jobs as a parent is to provide the environment in which your child can safely learn the principles and techniques that create self-discipline. This means you have to be aware of the necessary steps and watchful of the potential pitfalls. In effect, you start out providing the direction and controls for your child's behavior, then you gradually — through a process of creative partnership over a number of years — hand over the reins.

The big question that many parents have when dealing with a child with AD/HD is how to discipline her when she makes mistakes or acts out. First, you need to keep in mind some basic principles:

- **Safety is very important.** You should consider whether your child or someone else is endangered by your child's actions. Basically, the principle behind this is, "If someone is dead or seriously injured, it's really hard for them to have a lot of fun ever again." The idea that goes along with this is, "If we are the cause of someone not being able to have fun, we can't really have fun either."

  The best way to head off dangerous situations is by anticipating the possibility and making arrangements to avoid negative outcomes. Violations of safety may require immediate, physical restraint. If this does become necessary, you probably want to discuss the situation with your child after the dust settles.

- **Image isn't everything.** Just because your child does something unusual or out of the ordinary, that doesn't mean the attention she attracts deserves punishment. Stop and think about whether your child did something wrong or whether you are just embarrassed by what she did.

- **Life is a process of successive approximation.** Nothing is ever perfect, especially people's behavior. You are not going to make your life or your child's life better by trying to create a rule for everything that may enter her little mind to try out. If you can teach her the values of a good life and give her a chance to try, stumble, and try again, she'll gradually get closer and closer to what you're striving for.

✔ **Steer, don't direct.** You're probably never going to be able to ram your ideas of what your child ought to be doing down her throat, especially if she has AD/HD. Besides, you're trying to teach your child how to choose wisely, not how to follow directions. Offer guidance instead of directing your child's every move: You'll be happier, and your child will be more responsive to your desires.

If, after considering the points above, you think you need to put the brakes on your child's behavior, here are five simple steps to follow:

1. **While making eye contact with your child, calmly but firmly explain — in simple terms — that her behavior is not acceptable.**

2. **State what you expect from her.** Again, maintain eye contact and speak clearly and firmly.

3. **Ask her to repeat your expectations back to you.** You don't need her to quote you verbatim. In fact, if she uses her own words, she's more likely to understand and remember what you said.

   This step is very helpful for a younger child but may cause resentment with an older child. You don't want to risk causing further problems, so determine the necessity of this step based on who your child is.

4. **Explain the consequences for not obeying you.** Make the consequences logical to the situation, and make sure she understands them. (See the next section for a detailed discussion of consequences.)

5. **If you're sure your child understood your instructions and didn't follow them, employ the consequences.** Do so without getting angry or belittling her.

Keep the following tips in mind as you follow this five-step plan:

✔ **Don't act out of anger.** Doing so just creates anger and resentment on your child's end and guilt and remorse on your end. Always wait to enforce discipline until you have your own emotions under control. Tell your child that you're angry at her for her behavior and that you'll deal with the consequences of her action after you've had a chance to cool off. This time will give you a chance to let go of the anger and your child a chance to think about her behavior.

✔ **Use few words.** Avoid nagging or rambling on about how what your child did was wrong. Talking too much is the surest way to get her to tune you out. Explain yourself in a few carefully chosen words.

✔ **Stay calm and speak softy but firmly.** Yelling only escalates the feelings of frustration and anger for both of you; speaking calmly is much more likely to get her attention.

✔ **Don't withhold love or affection.** Withholding love or affection as punishment only creates more problems, such as lowered self-esteem and increased anger and resentment.

Use discipline to teach your child appropriate behavior, not to punish her for acting inappropriately. Maintain love and empathy for your child as you discipline her.

Considering consequences

As much as possible, consequences for your child's misbehavior need to be logical and natural. That is, they need to fit with what would generally happen anyway. For example:

- ✔ If your child doesn't do his homework, he goes to school without it.
- ✔ If he doesn't get dressed in time to catch the bus to school, he can ride his bike (in his pajamas, if necessary!).
- ✔ If he uses more than his share of minutes on the cell phone, he pays for the extra time out of his own money.
- ✔ If he breaks his big brother's models, he has to stand by and watch his brother tear up his Yu-Gi-Oh! cards.

This list could go on and on, but we're sure you get the idea.

For behaviors that don't have natural consequences, or whose natural consequences are not desirable (such as getting hit by a car for riding a bicycle on a busy street), you need to set some specific consequences that he knows about ahead of time.

The purpose of consequences is to discourage or stop undesirable behavior. Enforcing consequences for behaving undesirably or not behaving desirably is a lot more work for everyone than arranging for the appropriate choices and actions to be taken in the first place.

Dealing with defiance

Children with AD/HD are often perceived to be defiant. However, we believe that in many cases the defiance that parents and other people in authority experience is really, as the warden in *Cool Hand Luke* says, "a failure to communicate." In many cases, a child with AD/HD either doesn't appreciate that his style of communication is offensive, or he doesn't understand that the person talking to him has certain expectations about how he will respond to that communication.

In other words, children with AD/HD don't quite get the concept, "I'm the adult — you do what I say, and you don't talk back to me." Lots of times, the child with AD/HD is just going on his own self-directed way, not differentiating between people of different ages or ranks that he meets, and the authority figure stumbles into his path. When this happens, the child with AD/HD is likely to say something like what he has heard all his life — something he would say to any of his friends — such as, "Hey, stupid, watch where you're going. Get out of my way."

Of course, at times children with AD/HD are intentionally insolent and defiant. Our guess is that many children learn that sort of behavior from watching how others in their lives cope with conflict. Here again, it's easier to head this sort of behavior off than to stop it after it's started.

Defiant behavior may also be a way for children with AD/HD to get their daily dose of stimulation (see the "Canceling conflict" section earlier in the chapter). If that seems to be the issue, work with your child to find alternative forms of stimulation, including physical exercise.

If your child's antisocial behaviors affect people outside the family, you may need to enlist the aid of a mediator. This doesn't necessarily mean a formal sort of mediation, but it may help to have an objective, nonpartisan participant involved in the discussion of how to deal with a conflict. Mostly, you want to avoid involving the police and the legal system. Occasionally, parents of a child with AD/HD find it necessary to involve juvenile justice or a psychiatric hospital in order to take control of a very bad situation.

As we explain in Chapter 6, many people with AD/HD also have oppositional defiant disorder (ODD), the main symptom of which is breaking rules. This defiance can range from breaking family rules to perpetrating violence and getting in trouble with the law. If ODD is the reason for your child's defiance, your approach needs to be firm, and you likely need to wait until your child calms down before taking any steps to discipline him. If you experience these levels of defiance, you most likely need the skills of a professional counselor to help you deal with the behaviors. (You also need to undertake biological treatments for the disorder, such as medication. In this case talk to your prescribing physician.)

Raising more than one child

The more children in your household, the more complicated raising them becomes. When you add one or more children with AD/HD to the mix, you get a very complicated, stressful situation. You'll find yourself frequently needing to deal with how your kids interact. In this section, we explore some of the most common areas of concern for families with more than one child.

Creating cooperation

We've all been told that "it's a dog-eat-dog world out there" and we must compete in order to survive, right? Well, we disagree with this sentiment. Most people misunderstand competition and think that it's the way to get ahead in the world. That may be true in sports, but it doesn't always work in the rest of the world, especially in interpersonal relationships (one-on-one interactions). Any parent with more than one child will tell you that cooperation is much more pleasant than competition.

With this in mind, here are some ideas for fostering cooperation among your children:

- **Play cooperative games instead of competitive ones.** Lots of games allow you and your children (you may as well play with them) to work toward a common goal instead of being pitted against each other. One great source for noncompetitive games is www.familypastimes.com, or do an Internet search using "cooperative games" as your keyword.

- **Set up the household chores so that they are a team effort.** For example, if toys need to be picked up in the family room, have everyone work together to get it done instead of assigning one person to do it. Or when doing dishes, have one person empty the dishwasher while the other one fills it. (Or, if you do dishes by hand, have one wash and the other dry.) When cleaning the floor, have one person sweep and the other mop.

- **Create a family project that involves everyone.** Plant a garden, for example. Select a project that allows people of different abilities to work together. In the case of planting a garden, the younger kids can help plant the plants or pull the weeds, and the bigger kids can dig the holes.

If you use your imagination, you can identify many ways to create cooperation among your children (and the entire family) and remove competition from your life.

Settling sibling rivalry

If you have more than one child and not all of them have AD/HD, you have a challenging situation. We're sure you've already discovered that you can't possibly treat your children exactly the same way; a child with AD/HD needs more supervision and attention than a child without the condition.

The result is often jealousy and anger on the part of the child who doesn't have AD/HD; she may feel it necessary to compete for your attention. Also, as she sees her sibling being treated differently and seemingly being allowed to get away with things she can't, she may get resentful and feel as though she's being treated unfairly.

Although no one has yet found a cure for sibling rivalry, here are some ideas for defusing a tense situation:

- **Treat each child according to his abilities.** Concern yourself with being fair to each child. If your non-AD/HD child is better at following the rules and acting appropriately, give him more responsibility and more freedom to do things that your less responsible child is not allowed to do.

- **Provide each child with the same opportunities.** As you offer more freedom to the more responsible child, let the less responsible one know that he can earn the same freedoms as he shows more responsibility.

✔ **Talk openly about your situation.** Tell your non-AD/HD child that you have higher expectations for her because you believe that she can meet them. And let her know that the extra attention and "freedom" that your child with AD/HD receives is a result of his misbehavior and his difficulties rather than a reward. This attention and perceived freedoms come at a cost that your non-AD/HD child doesn't have to pay.

✔ **Arrange for special time with each child alone.** Plan dates to play with each of your children one-on-one. Spending time together playing and talking will create a bond that won't be broken by having to parent each child according to his abilities. The non-AD/HD child will get the attention he desires without having to resort to misbehavior, and the child with AD/HD will be reassured that you love him in spite of the difficulties you go through together. You benefit by being able to know your kids better.

Enhancing self-esteem

Self-esteem is fragile for a person with AD/HD. The symptoms that accompany AD/HD — inattention, distractibility, impulsivity, and hyperactivity — often make the person feel like a failure because he can't control certain behaviors. We see very young kids suffer from eroding self-esteem. Your coauthor Jeff recently worked with a 5-year-old who already has low self-esteem. He's lost all belief in his abilities and has little, if any, interest in trying to do anything because he's so afraid of failing.

The single most important thing you can do for your child is to help him improve his self-esteem. With a strong belief in oneself, all the challenges that come up when dealing with the symptoms of AD/HD are much easier to handle. Here are some suggestions that we've found to help children enhance their self-esteem:

✔ **Offer encouragement.** Be a cheerleader for your child's cause. Spur him on with encouraging words when he's trying to do something challenging.

✔ **Have faith.** Your child needs to sense that you have faith in his abilities. This goes beyond offering encouragement when he's doing something — it means believing in him and letting him know that you do even when he's not involved in any particular task.

✔ **Point out positives.** Acknowledge the things he does right.

✔ **Offer assistance.** Helping your child with tough tasks is a tricky venture. You want to offer assistance, but you don't want to do too much. Be available to your child and make it clear that you'll help when he asks, but only after he has honestly tried to do it himself.

✔ **Acknowledge improvement.** Just as you point out the positive things that your child does, also be sure to acknowledge the progress that he's making. Don't be afraid to praise your child. You won't spoil him, and you won't make him not want to keep improving (both common misconceptions about praise). Instead, you'll give him the confidence and desire to keep striving to do better.

✔ **Minimize mistakes.** This doesn't mean that you don't let your child make mistakes; it means that you help put mistakes he makes into perspective. Let him know that making mistakes is a natural part of life and that he can learn from them. Keep in mind that children with AD/HD often make the same mistake over and over; you need to be patient in dealing with the same mistake more than once.

✔ **Focus on the process instead of the product.** Don't be overly concerned with how well something is done. Instead, revel in that fact that it was done at all.

✔ **Empathize.** We cover this subject earlier in the chapter, but it bears repeating. Empathize with the difficulty your child is having. Let him know that you realize things are difficult for him.

✔ **Identify your child's strengths.** Help your child find something he is really good at, and encourage him to practice that activity to get even better. Such "islands of competence" are very important, especially to people who have a hard time getting approval for many of the things they try to do.

Parenting as a team

As parents of a child with AD/HD, you'll often have disagreements about how to best deal with your child's behaviors. Add to this the fact that many children with AD/HD are masters at manipulating by pitting each parent against the other, and you end up with a situation where chaos can easily reign. Furthermore, divorce is common in families with a child with AD/HD, so you often have to contend with the stresses of having two separate households as well as up to four different parents.

The most effective strategy for parenting a child with AD/HD is to practice what's called *co-parenting*. This means that both (or all) parents work together on every aspect of raising their child(ren). Obviously, this is an ideal to strive for, and it may not work for everyone, but here are some basic tenets of co-parenting:

> ✔ Agree to discipline only according to a pre-established list of conse-
> quences or by conferring before issuing a consequence for improper
> behavior.
>
> ✔ Make all household decisions together, especially the ones regarding
> raising your child.
>
> ✔ Let your child know that all decisions require both parents' consent, not
> just one.

By eliminating your child's ability to act as a wedge between you, you are
able to more effectively address your child's behavior.

Living with an Adult with AD/HD

Having an adult with AD/HD in the house has its own issues that need to
be understood. Whether you or your partner is the person with AD/HD,
the following sections offer suggestions to help both of you improve your
relationship.

Getting informed

Your best strategy for learning to live with an AD/HD adult is to learn everything you can about AD/HD. Understand its symptoms and causes. Keep up-to-
date on the various treatment options available. Find coping strategies to help
you deal with the behaviors that come with AD/HD. Obviously, you've already
started this process by reading this book — good for you! Chapter 20 offers
suggestions for other resources that offer even more information on AD/HD.

The more you know about AD/HD, the better you'll be able to understand and
respond to the challenges that this condition creates.

Working together

Healthy relationships involve give and take. Determine each of your strengths
and weaknesses, and try to work them into your relationship. If you're the
organized one, for example, support your partner by teaching him how to
get organized and helping him stay organized.

Be careful not to fall into the trap of being codependent. If your partner has AD/HD, don't do everything for him, and don't allow him to treat you or anyone else poorly or to rely too much on you to do things for him. (Allowing this type of behavior is called *enabling*.) This issue is particularly important in families where more than one adult has AD/HD. In this case, take everything we say and square it, then multiply by four.

Working together means just that: working *together*. Be supportive without enabling. Be a partner, not a servant. Demand responsibility, but be available to help out in areas where your partner with AD/HD has difficulties.

Staying close

One of the healthiest things you can do for your relationship is to schedule time for dates. This isn't a time to talk about your differences; this is a time to let down your guard and get to know your partner. Some couples go out to the movies or dinner, while others simply carve out a couple of hours once a week to check in with each other. Do what you can to schedule time each week to just hang out and have some fun.

Taking time for yourself

In addition to scheduling weekly dates with your partner, make sure that you regularly schedule time for yourself — time to just be alone doing something that you enjoy. Read a book, take a bath, go to the gym, take a walk. Living 24/7 with anyone — whether AD/HD is a factor or not — takes its toll on your ability to know yourself, and knowing yourself is key to being able to have a successful relationship with another person.

Getting Into Good Habits

You can do several things to make the day-to-day struggles of AD/HD fewer. These things can all help reduce the level or impact of your AD/HD symptoms. Our suggestions include getting organized, doing aerobic exercise, limiting TV and video games, ensuring that you get enough sleep, and having some fun.

Becoming organized

Disorganization is a hallmark of people with AD/HD. Distractibility leads to scattered thinking, which leads to a disorganized environment. One of the best things you can do to improve life at home is to get organized. We offer a bunch of organizational strategies in Chapter 18, but here are the basics:

- ✔ **Keep track of your schedule.** Use whatever technology you need (computer, PDA, calendar) to keep track of where you need to be, when, and (if necessary) why you need to be there. Put all your appointments in this tool, and use it. Doing so means you don't need to keep all this information in your head.

- ✔ **Plan your projects ahead of time, and follow the plan.** With a plan in hand, you're more likely to get through your project because you won't forget what it involves and what else remains to be done.

- ✔ **Get rid of the clutter in your house.** Create a place for everything in your house, and use color-coding (see Chapter 18) to make it easy to find what you need.

Lots of great books are available on organizing your home and life. If you don't know where to start organizing, one of these books may help you develop some skills:

- ✔ *Organizing For Dummies* (Wiley) by Eileen Roth and Elizabeth Miles

- ✔ *Organizing Plain and Simple: A Ready Reference Guide with Hundreds of Solutions to Your Everyday Clutter Challenges* (Storey Books) by Donna Smallin

- ✔ *How to Be Organized in Spite of Yourself: Time and Space Management That Works With Your Personal Style* (Signet) by Sunny Schlenger

Disorganization doesn't need to be a problem if you understand where you tend to have trouble and develop strategies to overcome these tendencies. For example, if you often get lost, create maps for yourself before you leave the house. If you tend to lose your keys, wallet, or purse, designate one place in your house for these items to be stored, and make a habit of always putting them there. (This is something your coauthor Jeff has to do. If I don't put my wallet, car keys, or sunglasses in their designated place, it takes me hours to find them.)

Exercising regularly

As we say many times throughout this book, the best way to reduce your AD/HD symptoms is to get adequate physical activity. For kids this can mean simply playing outside with other kids; for adults, this means getting some form of aerobic exercise.

Intense exercise increases blood flow and levels of endorphin and acetylcholine in the brain, which seems to help with the symptoms of AD/HD. Many people report being able to focus better after intense exercise, including your coauthor Jeff. When I was younger, I relied heavily on exercise to cope with my symptoms. In fact, I had a boss once tell me that unless I exercised before going to work, I shouldn't even bother to show up at all. Without the exercise I was irritable, edgy, and unfocused, but with it I was calm and able to concentrate and get my job done.

Exercise offers many benefits, including the following:

- ✔ Lifting your mood
- ✔ Developing coordination
- ✔ Improving self-esteem
- ✔ Releasing pent-up energy

Exercise increases endorphins in the brain. This creates a feeling of euphoria and can reduce the feelings of depression that many (most) people with AD/HD experience. For restless or hyperactive people, regular intense exercise can make sitting for any length of time much easier.

As far as the best exercise for people with AD/HD, here are some suggestions:

- ✔ **Make it last.** It takes time for exercise to trigger a release of endorphins, and you really want this release to happen, so plan on at least 30 minutes of intense exercise to get the most benefit. We know of many people who regularly exercise for an hour at a time in order to have the most reduction in their symptoms.

- ✔ **Make it intense.** You need aerobic exercise in order to get the blood flowing. If you go for a walk, make it a fast walk. If you do yoga, make it astanga or kundalini yoga instead of one of the more passive types.

- ✔ **Keep it interesting.** Running on a treadmill or mounting a stair-climber machine can be agonizing for people with AD/HD (or anyone) because these activities are so boring. If you want to run, run outside. The scenery will help keep you from getting bored.

✔ **Make it flexible.** Many people with AD/HD don't do so well in team sports. This is partly because social interaction can be troublesome but mainly because they don't get to control the length or intensity of the exercise. Choose an activity that allows you to keep control of both the intensity and the time that you do it. This increases the chances that you'll enjoy what you're doing and allows you the flexibility to follow your desires for the day. If you like team sports, though, don't let us talk you out of participating in them.

✔ **Make it convenient.** If you have to drive across town or go through some elaborate ritual in order to get your exercise, we guarantee that you won't keep it up for very long. Find an exercise program that's easy to get to and get started with. This increases the chances that you'll keep it up.

✔ **Keep it simple.** Avoid exercise that takes too much mental energy to figure out or that can be frustrating if done incorrectly. For adults, this means staying away from golf (just kidding!). For children, this means choosing exercises that match their level of ability. For example, if you enroll your child into a martial arts program, make sure it isn't too advanced for your child. Choose activities that allow room for error so that you can focus on getting your heart rate up rather than having to focus on making sure you do everything right.

Limiting TV and video games

TV and video games can be a lot fun, but they can also cause problems for people with AD/HD. (For that matter, they can cause problems for everyone if not used properly.) Aside from the obvious consideration that when you're watching TV or playing video games you're not engaged in a more fulfilling activity, such as interacting with the people you love or doing something physically active, TV and video games have an impact on your nervous system.

We won't go so far as to claim that TV and video games can cause AD/HD (check out the sidebar "Can TV cause AD/HD?" in this chapter), but we've seen that it can make life at home worse. For the most part TV and video games promote solitary activity, immediate gratification, and passivity.

 We suggest that you monitor your or your child's TV viewing and look for signs that indicate the worsening of symptoms after watching. Take a break from the TV for a week and see how your symptoms change. If your symptoms improve, consider cutting TV out of your life. (This is something your coauthor Jeff did five years ago, and it's made life a lot easier.)

Can TV cause AD/HD?

A study published in the journal *Pediatrics* in April 2004 looked at how watching TV impacts very young kids. In this study, 1- and 3-year-olds were assessed for their ability to maintain their attention, and their parents were surveyed regarding how much TV they watch each day.

This study showed that for every hour of TV a child watches each day — regardless of the content — the risk of having attention problems by age 7 goes up 10 percent. Though this study doesn't prove that TV causes AD/HD, it does suggest that TV may increase inattention in some people.

Another fact that came out of this study is that only 37 percent of the 1-year-olds and 7 percent of the 3-year-olds didn't watch any TV. The American Academy of Pediatrics recommends that children under age 2 watch no TV at all.

If you're going to watch TV or play video games, try to balance these passive activities with physical activity to ensure that you don't become too sedentary. Also, playing video games that involve other people can at least help you develop social connections.

Ensuring the best sleep possible

One very difficult aspect of AD/HD is that your sleep is generally disturbed. And if you're the partner or parent of someone with AD/HD, chances are her sleep problems sometimes keep you awake.

The key to getting a good night's sleep is following what's called good *sleep hygiene*. Here are some tips for improving your own sleep hygiene:

- ✔ **Use sugar and caffeine wisely.** For many people, avoiding sugar and caffeine for at least two hours before bedtime can help them wind down to go to sleep. But this isn't always the case. Some people with AD/HD find that, far from keeping them awake, caffeine can actually help them go to sleep. And if you happen to drink a glass of warm milk to help you go to sleep, putting some sugar or honey in it will actually help the tryptophan get absorbed into the brain where it can promote sleep.

- ✔ **Get enough exercise during the day.** There is no better way to ensure good sleep than to be physically tired. Be aware that exercising late in the day may cause sleeplessness.

✔ **Eat a protein-rich snack before bed.** Nighttime hunger is one of the more common reasons a person can't get to sleep. This can be more of a problem if you experience a loss of appetite due to the medication you're taking for your AD/HD. Eating a protein-rich snack can fill you up and calm you down.

✔ **Make your room a quiet and dark sanctuary.** Eliminating light and noise can do wonders for your sleep. (Of course, exceptions do exist — you may be the sort of person who can't sleep without a radio or TV on.) For younger children who need a light on, try using a nightlight or a slightly opened door to create a subdued light.

✔ **Set a consistent bedtime.** Most people function best with a consistent routine, and bedtime is no exception. Set a bedtime and try to stick to it. You'll find that your body gets into the groove, and the transition becomes easier. This is especially important for kids, who thrive on consistency and need their sleep.

✔ **Create a bedtime transition ritual.** This can involve reading a book, taking a bath, or doing any low-key activity that helps you transition from the activity of the day and allows you to calm down.

✔ **Listen to calming music.** Find some music that calms you down, or use music specifically designed to help calm your nervous system. (Shameless plug time: Check out coauthor Jeff Strong's Web site, www.reiinstitute.com, for some options.)

Providing play and fun

If "All work and no play makes Jack a dull boy," and "The family that plays together stays together," somebody must think that playtime is important. We agree.

Life can get hectic (how's that for understatement?), and it's easy to put having fun way down on your list of things to do. We hear ya. But we strongly suggest that you move it up the list a bit. Try to set aside at least part of one day a week to do something fun together as a family. Go to the park or a museum. Play a game at home or in the yard. Do something together, and do it regularly. Putting an emphasis on fun makes everyone less stressed and brings you together as a family.

Chapter 15

Creating Success at School

· ·

· ·

*F*or a child with AD/HD, school can seem like an endless source of confusion and frustration. In fact, failure in school is often the first indication of AD/HD.

Helping your child succeed in school requires that you understand the challenges that kids of different ages experience, know your legal rights and how to assert them, work with your child's teachers, and help your child study at home. In this chapter, we discuss each of these topics, plus a few more, so you can be prepared to help your child get the most out of his educational opportunities.

Overcoming Challenges at Any Age

Students with AD/HD face several challenges that get in the way of being able to learn in a traditional school environment. We don't mean that all people with AD/HD have learning disabilities, although many do. What we mean is that the symptoms of inattention, distractibility, impulsivity, and hyperactivity result in specific difficulties in a classroom. The following sections explore how these difficulties manifest at different ages, as well as how to overcome them.

As a parent you can do only so much for your child's education. You also need the help of teachers and other school professionals. We encourage you to share this chapter with your child's teachers and work with them to implement some of the ideas we suggest.

Addressing elementary school issues

Elementary-age children face a host of challenges that can make learning difficult. These challenges include:

- ✔ **Understanding instructions:** Misunderstanding is a common problem for people with AD/HD. Some people struggle mostly with written instructions, while for others verbal instructions are more difficult. To minimize misunderstandings, you (or your child's teacher) can provide instructions in both verbal and written forms. Also, you can break down instructions into single steps instead of expecting your child to remember a sequence of steps. For younger children who can't yet read, use simple language or pictographs and ask him to repeat back what you want him to do.

- ✔ **Reading:** AD/HD and reading problems are closely related. Many people with AD/HD also have specific reading problems, such as dyslexia. If your child has trouble reading, we suggest that you have an evaluation done to determine whether a reading disorder exists. This evaluation usually isn't performed until second grade because many 7-year-olds have some delay in reading that corrects itself naturally.

  Other problems that may be related are difficulties with spelling and arithmetic. By identifying these problems early, you can minimize the damage and work with your child's school to develop strategies for coping with them.

- ✔ **Handwriting:** Try as they might, many people with AD/HD have difficulty with handwriting. The mechanics of writing — especially in cursive — take a tremendous amount of effort. Some AD/HD adults still print because they can't read their own cursive handwriting.

- ✔ **Maintaining attention:** Obviously, inattention is one of the central aspects of AD/HD. For children with AD/HD, maintaining attention in school is the most difficult task they are asked to do. The best way to get and keep an AD/HD child's attention is to create a stimulating environment. If you make something interesting, most people with AD/HD can focus very well. Of course, this is easier said than done in a classroom with 20 or 25 students, because they won't all find the same things interesting.

- ✔ **Sitting still:** This one almost goes without saying, but sitting still for children with the hyperactive/impulsive type of AD/HD is next to impossible. The best ways around this issue are to make sure that whatever biological treatments you're using (such as medications or supplements) are working as well as possible, and to try to allow your child the freedom to move in the classroom occasionally. This movement may mean taking periodic breaks or having tools to fidget with. (Check out the sidebar "A few tips for teachers" later in this chapter for more details.)

✔ **Following rules:** Many youngsters with AD/HD don't remember rules. Encourage your child's teacher to post the rules for the classroom on the wall at the front of the class and to frequently repeat them.

✔ **Understanding boundaries:** Young students with AD/HD often invade other children's space, take their things, and just generally annoy them. If this describes your child, you need to work hard to help him realize the impact he has on the people (and the environment) around him. You can use repeated reminders or behavioral interventions, such as those we discuss in Chapter 10.

✔ **Getting started:** Getting a young student with AD/HD started on an activity can be difficult. Two strategies seem particularly helpful: Provide a specific motivation for doing the activity, and show the child how to get past the obstacles that prevent her from starting.

✔ **Changing activities:** After you manage to get your child started on a project, you may have a hard time getting him to change to something else. The most effective way to deal with this situation is to prepare him for the change by telling him what's coming up next and reminding him of the change until it happens. Then when the time comes, redirect him to the new activity.

✔ **Being organized:** One of the earliest and most persistent problems that a person with AD/HD has is getting and staying organized. The sooner you start teaching your child methods for organization, and the more you practice them, the better off you all will be. Your child will probably struggle to keep track of her personal possessions, to remember school papers and assignments, and to maintain order in her work and play spaces. We cover organization in more detail later in this chapter and in Chapter 18.

Managing middle school difficulties

Middle school (junior high) has its own challenges that arise out of both the age of the student and the vastly different structure of upper-level schools compared to elementary schools. The schools themselves have less structure, more transitions throughout the day (often a child goes from having just one teacher all day to having five or six), and more social pressure. Here are some common challenges that the middle school student with AD/HD encounters:

✔ **Being organized:** We don't mean to sound like a broken record, but disorganization really is a constant issue. As a student with AD/HD reaches middle school, the problems of disorganization expand. Because of this fact, we cover this important subject in detail in the final section of this chapter and offer ways that you can help your child become (and stay) more organized.

✔ **Managing conflict:** The combination of a more chaotic atmosphere, less supervision, and added importance on peer relationships means that many middle school students with AD/HD have problems getting along with other students. Couple this fact with the tendency of people with AD/HD to have less-than-ideal judgment, and the result may be fights and other adverse social interaction, including ridicule and bullying. For tips on reducing opportunities for conflict to arise, see the section "Dealing with Difficult Times in School" later in the chapter.

✔ **Completing homework:** Moving from elementary school to middle school usually results in an increase in the amount of homework assigned each day. Your child may struggle with forgetting assignments, getting distracted while doing the work, misunderstanding assignments, procrastinating, and (perhaps most frustrating) doing assignments and not turning them in! Homework is such an important issue that we cover ways to improve performance in detail in the section "Helping with homework" later in the chapter.

✔ **Relating to peers:** Many people with AD/HD have troubles in peer relationships, and these relationships become more important in adolescence. Several problems may be at work:

  • A person with AD/HD can be very self-involved, thus not really paying attention to other people's needs.

  • Many children with AD/HD feel that they have to go out of their way to please other people (a result of low self-esteem).

  • Some children with AD/HD just don't have very good social skills in terms of meeting and getting along with others.

  We hasten to add that some children and adolescents with AD/HD have better-than-average social skills. We cover this topic more in the section "Opportunities for socialization" later in this chapter, and in Chapters 14 and 19.

✔ **Composing essays or research papers:** Many people with AD/HD struggle to understand the structure of what they are trying to write. Perhaps they can't see the main ideas and how to link them, or they have too many ideas, or they don't have a clear grasp of the mechanics of composition. It can help tremendously to have a good teacher who can analyze the particular difficulties a child is having and devise methods for overcoming them.

  Another common problem with composition is that many students with AD/HD struggle to put their thoughts onto paper. Many times the person's mind goes completely blank as she tries to write. Using a computer to write can sometimes help. In addition, software programs are available that can change speech into written text.

✔ **Remembering:** Forgetfulness is a big problem for people with AD/HD. Your child can deal with this problem in many ways, from using a PDA (personal digital assistant) to having a beeper, from keeping good notes to using a *traveler* (see the section "Helping with homework") to record all school-related information. This is another big subject, so we cover ways to keep from forgetting in the section "Working with Your Child at Home," later in the chapter.

Aside from these added challenges, middle school students also struggle with many of the same challenges that elementary students face. However, the way these challenges manifest is slightly differently due to the environment and age differences. For example, the lack of ability to honor personal boundaries in elementary-age children can result in a verbal fight over a toy, whereas in middle school it can turn into a major brawl.

Handling high school challenges

Most of the challenges that exist among younger children also exist for teenagers with AD/HD. Again, these challenges change over time. For example, a child who had a tough time sitting still (or at all) in elementary school may be able to do so in high school, but he now needs to fidget and feels restless while he's sitting. Additional issues that high school students face include:

✔ **Taking notes:** A student with AD/HD may struggle to separate important facts from unimportant ones, which makes taking notes tricky. You may find that your child records unimportant information or fails to make important connections. The other problem with note-taking relates to the following bullet: Many people with AD/HD have difficulty listening and writing at the same time. Talk with your child's teachers about allowing him to use a tape recorder in the classroom to alleviate this struggle.

✔ **Following lectures:** Listening to a lecture requires the ability to stay focused on the speaker and the content of the speech. People with AD/HD struggle with wandering attention, so they miss pieces of information in this situation. In addition, often neither the teacher nor the student is aware that information has been missed. Again, requesting the teacher's permission to use a tape recorder during the lecture may be the solution.

Even if a student can muster the attention to focus and follow what's said, she may have an auditory processing problem, which is common among people with AD/HD (see Chapter 6). The result is that she won't be able to discern the meaning. This problem can result from extraneous sounds masking the important stimulus, or it can result from being unable to decode what's actually heard (this is called a *central auditory processing disorder*). Using visual aids and limiting background noises can help reduce this problem.

✔ **Getting lost academically:** Because of the added number of kids in the school and the added demands that are placed on them, many high school students with AD/HD get lost and aren't helped or, in some cases, even identified. This situation can lead to all sorts of problems, including poor academic performance, dropping out, violence, and drug use. Being an active participant in your child's education and being her advocate when dealing with school staff and teachers are the best defenses against this downward spiral.

✔ **Using drugs:** Drug use among high school kids rises sharply as students get older, and research shows that untreated teens with AD/HD are especially prone to this problem. You must keep a close eye on any possible drug use and shut it down before it becomes a problem. Fortunately, several studies show that adolescents with AD/HD who are treated for their condition are less likely than their peers to abuse illicit drugs.

✔ **Facing an increased workload:** The added workload placed upon high school students often pushes the person with AD/HD further behind. This can lead to feeling overwhelmed, failing, or even dropping out. You must closely supervise your child's performance, help him stay on top of his homework, and help him overcome issues of time management. You may find it necessary to provide a private tutor to help him get through the tough areas.

✔ **Lacking motivation:** Lack of motivation is common throughout the life of a person with AD/HD, and keeping a high school student with AD/HD on track requires ingenuity. In high school, conflicts between academic and social demands on the student's time and energy increase substantially. One of the best ways to ensure academic performance is to tie it to something your child is already motivated to do. For example, most schools have a minimum grade point necessary to play sports, and many children with AD/HD like sports — perhaps this is the tie you need to motivate your child to pay attention to academics.

Cluing into college challenges

By the time a student with AD/HD hits college, he has likely developed a variety of strategies to compensate for his condition. However, he still faces some challenges. Many of the high school issues we discuss in the previous section are still relevant in college, and some — such as getting lost academically — become more serious with the additional level of responsibility and academic stress that can accompany college life.

Additional challenges that are specific to the adult education years include the following:

- ✔ **Managing time:** Without parents looking over their shoulders and the structure of high school to keep them in line, many students have difficulty managing their time efficiently and effectively. For example, they may sleep through their alarm in the morning or stay up all night talking or partying.

- ✔ **Maintaining self-discipline:** Many college students start a semester with great enthusiasm only to drop classes by midterm because they don't keep track of their class assignments and they fall behind.

- ✔ **Getting lost academically:** Often college students with AD/HD don't recognize when they're having academic difficulties and don't seek out help in time to avoid catastrophe.

One of the best ways to avoid these potential problems is to enlist the services of an AD/HD coach (see Chapter 9) to help you develop some systems for managing your time and set (and follow through on) realistic goals. A coach also checks in with you to make sure that you're not getting lost academically and to keep you on track toward your goals. If hiring a coach is not a possibility, be sure you meet regularly with your academic advisor at school and work closely with your teachers to keep tabs on your progress in your classes.

Getting to Know Your Legal Rights

Three laws, which apply to people with a variety of conditions, may support your efforts to get the best education you can for your child. These laws are:

- ✔ The Individuals with Disabilities Education Act (IDEA)
- ✔ Section 504 of the 1973 Rehabilitation Act
- ✔ The Americans with Disabilities Act (ADA)

IDEA and Section 504 are the most used of the three acts for people with AD/HD (and any conditions that may occur with AD/HD). Although the ADA may come into play for some children, it's not the first place to look for help for your child, so we don't cover it in this chapter. (Chapter 16 has more information on the role of the ADA for people with AD/HD.) This section gives you a glimpse into the often-misunderstood IDEA and Section 504 laws and offers some suggestions for using them to help your child.

For more detailed information about IDEA and Section 504, check out the Web site www.wrightslaw.com. This site contains comprehensive information about the legal aspects of special education and childhood disabilities.

Having realistic expectations

We don't want to sugarcoat the situation: Figuring out if your child is eligible for services under one of these laws is tough, and, although many schools try hard to follow the law, getting your child's school to provide these services may require some effort.

To receive any special services from your child's school, your child must be evaluated. Schools require that the evaluation be conducted by the school district's educational diagnostician (see Chapter 4), but some school districts also accept a diagnosis from a private psychiatrist or psychologist for inclusion in this process. Be sure to talk with your school to find out what criteria exist within your district.

Also, just because your child is officially diagnosed with AD/HD — and acknowledged to have it by the school district — doesn't mean that he is eligible for accommodations or special services. The current interpretation of these laws tends to be that in order to receive accommodations for a disability, the person must be shown both to have a potentially disabling condition and to be suffering from this condition to a degree that it significantly impacts his abilities.

Regardless of your child's legal status, remember that your goal is to help your child get the best education he can. The best way to do this is to develop a positive relationship with your child's school and not an antagonistic one. (We discuss this topic in the section "Working with your child's teacher" later in this chapter.) Work on communicating well with the staff at your child's school, guidance counselors, and teachers, and avoid trying to strong-arm them with the law (unless doing so becomes necessary).

Examining IDEA

The Individuals with Disabilities Education Act (IDEA) is designed to make sure that children with disabilities receive "free appropriate public education." This education is determined through an Individual Education Plan (IEP), which we discuss in the "Accessing an Educational Plan" section later in this chapter.

IDEA is a great idea, but figuring out whether the law applies to your child is not easy. Some children with AD/HD qualify for services under this law, while others don't. Qualification is largely based on a school district's interpretation of the IDEA statutes — not on your child's diagnosis or level of symptoms.

Because the criteria for qualification under IDEA are left up to the school's interpretation, we recommend that you read the IDEA statutes yourself. This way, you can understand how the law is being interpreted and challenge the school's interpretation if necessary.

If your child's school performance suggests that there is a problem with his ability to learn, your child's school is obligated to evaluate him to determine if he is eligible for services under IDEA. Unfortunately, just having a diagnosis of AD/HD doesn't ensure that your child will be evaluated; the school must decide whether to do so.

If your child's school refuses to evaluate your child for protection under IDEA, it has to give you notice of your due-process rights to contest this decision. Likewise, if the school does evaluate him and decides that your child doesn't qualify for IDEA, you have an opportunity to appeal that decision.

If your child does qualify for services under IDEA, you can expect to be involved in an IEP process where your child is given services to try to deal with his impairments. These services can (but may not) include:

- ✔ Special education classes
- ✔ One-on-one tutoring
- ✔ A classroom aide
- ✔ Speech/language therapy
- ✔ Occupational therapy
- ✔ Other services offered under Section 504, which we discuss in the next section

Many times a school will refuse services under IDEA and allow accommodations under Section 504 instead. This may sound fine, but (as we explain in the next section) under Section 504 your school isn't obligated to offer the same level of services for your child.

Securing IDEA status for your child doesn't guarantee that his education will improve. It only means that your child receives special education services. Your job is to make sure that these services are right for him and that they actually result in a better education. We cover this topic in the "Accessing an Educational Plan" section later in this chapter.

Utilizing Section 504

Many people refer to Section 504 as a consolation prize for children who are disabled but don't fit the more stringent criteria for special education services under IDEA. Section 504 is a more general law that ensures that children with disabilities have access to the same education as children without disabilities.

To qualify for Section 504, your child must have "an impairment that substantially limits a major life activity," such as learning. Compare this wording to the diagnostic criteria for AD/HD in Chapter 3, and you can see a pattern emerging. (Take a minute to think about it; we'll wait here.)

Yep. It's not a black-and-white issue. The subjective nature of both the AD/HD diagnosis and the Section 504 protections leaves a lot of room for interpretation (just like with IDEA). Guess who does the interpreting? Right again: your child's school. This is why, as with the IDEA statutes, we suggest that you educate yourself about Section 504 and be prepared to fight for your rights if you need to.

If your child has AD/HD and demonstrates that she has difficulties with learning, your child's school must evaluate her for qualification under Section 504 after you have put the formal request in writing. If the school does not recommend an evaluation, you'll be notified of due process and be able to contest this decision. Likewise, if the school does evaluate and decides that your child doesn't qualify for Section 504 designation, you can appeal that decision.

If the school determines that your child is eligible for services under Section 504, you'll have access to certain accommodations in her regular classroom. These may (or may not) include:

- ✔ A more structured learning environment
- ✔ Modified tests and/or homework assignments
- ✔ Additional learning aids, such as audiovisual equipment or computer-assisted lessons
- ✔ The ability to use a tape recorder for lectures and instructions
- ✔ Simplified or repeated instructions
- ✔ Visual study aids
- ✔ Modified class schedules and increased time on tests

Your child may also be able to attend special education classes, but this is not common under Section 504.

Some schools create an educational plan for your child to determine what accommodations she needs, while other schools just offer certain adjustments as a matter of course. Both IDEA and Section 504 require that a student be placed in the "least restrictive environment" consistent with her educational needs.

Accessing an Educational Plan

If your child qualifies for services under IDEA or, in some instances, Section 504, the school creates an educational plan designed to address his unique needs. (A word about our conventions: Section 504 calls it an Educational Plan. IDEA calls it an Individual Education Plan [IEP]. If we use the term *educational plan,* that means we're referring to both.)

The process of developing an educational plan involves evaluating your child's educational needs and developing a plan to meet them. To get the best education for your child, you need to be a key player, along with the teachers, in both the development and implementation of this plan. In this section, we offer advice for getting the right plan created and for making sure that it's followed up on properly.

Just because your child has an educational plan doesn't mean that he'll learn any more than he would without it. Like it or not, you have to get into the mud with everyone else if you want to ensure that your child gets the education he's entitled to.

Understanding what an educational plan is

An educational plan is simply a method for educators to determine the best way to teach your child and help him with his difficult areas. While each plan is slightly different, they all cover the same basic issues:

- ✔ Your child's present skill/knowledge level
- ✔ The ways the student learns best
- ✔ Goals and objectives
- ✔ The means to accomplish these goals and objectives
- ✔ A way to determine progress (or lack thereof)

We cover each of these issues in detail in the upcoming section "Developing an accurate plan."

Your child's educational plan should spell out exactly where your child is lagging behind and provide detailed strategies for getting him up to speed. Of course, this is an ideal scenario. You must work with the school to make sure that the areas addressed in the plan are indeed the areas your child struggles with and that the plan provides clear objectives and steps for implementation.

Getting involved

If your child qualifies for services under IDEA, your school will schedule an IEP meeting, which you'll be invited to attend. If your child receives services under Section 504, he may or may not get an educational plan — talk with the school staff to find out.

Make sure you attend the meeting(s) scheduled to set up your child's educational plan. You can play a big role in the process and serve as your child's advocate. Some schools may say that you don't need to attend, or they may even discourage you from coming. We strongly recommend that you don't bow to that pressure — insist on being there, and be ready to fight for your child's rights if you need to.

Developing an accurate plan

When you go to the educational plan meeting (you *are* going, right?), one of the most important things you can do is to make sure that the meeting covers the areas of concern for your child and that these areas are adequately addressed.

We certainly hope that your experience with developing an educational plan is positive, but we want you to prepare yourself for the possibility that it won't be. Educate yourself on IDEA and Section 504 before you go into the meeting. Also, bring all the records you've kept for your child (see the "Documenting Your School Experiences" section later in this chapter).

Following are the areas you and the school representatives will address as you develop the educational plan:

> ✔ **Your child's present skill/knowledge level:** To know where you're going, you have to first know where you are. Therefore, you must first assess where your child is lacking — in which areas he lags behind other kids his age. The plan should contain scores from tests that were used to determine the areas in which your child is having trouble. The school should use objective measures, such as tests, along with observations to determine your child's skill level.

✔ **Goals and objectives:** A good educational plan has clear, realistic goals for improving your child's performance in problem areas. The goals and objectives should be specific, and they should relate to each of your child's problem areas.

✔ **The means to accomplish these goals and objectives:** Without a plan for accomplishing them, goals are useless. Your child's plan should list clear, detailed steps for meeting each goal. For example, if one of the goals is to improve reading skills by one grade level, make sure that specific reading programs are listed in the plan.

✔ **A way to determine progress (or lack thereof):** During the meeting you should ask, "How will you determine if my child is making progress?" The plan should include specific steps for measuring its success. These steps should include tests and other objective evaluations, as well as homework and in-class exams.

While you're at the educational plan meeting, make sure that you understand who's accountable for implementing your child's plan. Get that person's contact information so you can follow up over the course of the plan.

Keeping tabs on the progress

Call or meet with your child's teacher(s) regularly, and ask for progress reports. Make sure that these reports use objective measures to determine if your child is making progress.

If your child is not making progress using the educational plan, you have the right to request that the plan be revised. IDEA requires that each student who has an IEP be reevaluated every three years. Overworked school staff may miss that deadline, so you need to keep track of when the reevaluation is due.

Getting the Most from Your Child's Teachers

The teacher who your child learns from each day has a huge impact on whether he succeeds or not. (Okay, teachers, how's that for some added pressure?) Finding a good teacher (if you have options) and working with her to develop the best learning environment for your child is in your best interest, and your child's. We discuss both topics in this section, as well as ideas for teachers to help create an AD/HD-friendly learning environment.

A few tips for teachers

Following are a few tips for teaching children with AD/HD:

- **Involve as many senses as possible.** Use visual aids, such as charts and diagrams. Employ as many interactive teaching tools as possible, such as lab work, role-playing, group discussions, and multimedia presentations. Use your imagination to get as many senses involved in the learning process as possible.

- **Be clear about your expectations.** When you ask the student to do something, be clear about what you want. You may have to get in the habit of checking to make sure the student hears and understands you. (For example, ask him for immediate feedback.)

- **Help develop study skills.** Pacing and planning — the heart of good study skills — are harder to develop for people with AD/HD. By helping students with AD/HD develop these skills, you provide them solid abilities that carry over to many other aspects of their lives. Supervise and direct your students in being able to plan for the long-term and to create (and implement) intermediate goals. Chapter 16 discusses planning and creating goals as it relates to adults and careers; the same principles apply to students.

- **Create structure.** People with AD/HD usually work better when they have an external structure to follow. This structure doesn't need to be rigid, but it does need to be clear (see Chapter 14).

- **Encourage organization.** Help your student with AD/HD organize his work and time so that he can complete an assignment or project. Lay out a schedule or a list of steps for him to follow, and check to see that he's actually following it. Use frequent communication and reinforcement to keep motivation high.

- **Make it interesting.** People with AD/HD need stimulus in order to focus. By making lessons interesting (as we're sure you always do!), you provide a stimulus that encourages a person with AD/HD to be able to maintain his attention.

- **Avoid the phrase "if you'd only try harder."** Anyone who knows a person with AD/HD understands that a lack of desire or effort isn't causing the academic problems associated with AD/HD. In fact, by trying harder, she may actually make the biological mechanism responsible for AD/HD worse (see Chapter 2).

- **Encourage self-esteem.** Or at least try to preserve it. One way to do this is to avoid singling out the child with AD/HD or putting him down in front of the class. Try to find areas where the student shines, and emphasize them.

- **Eliminate distractions.** Most students with AD/HD benefit from sitting in the front of the class and away from the windows. However, sometimes a student needs different accommodations for her distractibility. For instance, some people are more distracted by noise behind them than by things going on in front of them; they would benefit from not having any other students sitting behind them. Use your observations and judgment and work with your student to find the best place for her in the classroom.

- **Give instructions slowly and clearly.** Also be prepared to repeat instructions if necessary. This takes patience. It helps if you can remember that the student isn't willfully misunderstanding; she may be trying as hard as you are. It is helpful to provide input in both a verbal as well as written format.

Also, many students with AD/HD benefit from receiving instructions in the same format and at the same time each day. This consistency helps the student develop the ability to pay attention and comply reliably without having to be monitored constantly.

✔ **Respect parents' wishes.** A student with AD/HD may be engaged in a treatment program that requires adherence to a schedule (such as taking medications or herbal remedies) or certain restrictions (such as being on a special diet). Be as consistent as possible. Whenever you have information that indicates the treatments are ineffective or need adjustment, let the parents know so they can do something about it.

✔ **Allow breaks.** If you can, allow students a few minutes to move around once in a while. This activity can stimulate the student with AD/HD and help him stay on task longer.

✔ **Encourage participation.** The more you get the student involved in the learning process, the better he'll be able to understand and retain the information. (This goes for all students but is especially key for students with AD/HD.) Design your lesson plans around

participation, even if it's as simple as asking questions. If you do ask questions to encourage participation, let the class know you're going to do so. Otherwise, the AD/HD student may freeze up when you call on him.

These suggestions are just a few of the ways you can help your students with AD/HD. Many resources are available to help teachers and parents deal with the AD/HD student's problems, such as:

✔ *Teaching Teens with ADD and ADHD: A Quick Reference Guide for Teachers and Parents* (Woodbine House) by Chris A. Zeigler Dendy

✔ *How to Reach and Teach ADD/ADHD Children: Practical Techniques, Strategies, and Interventions for Helping Children with Attention Problems and Hyperactivity* (Jossey-Bass) by Sandra F. Rief

Teaching a student with AD/HD uses the same basic skills as teaching any other student, but it definitely takes more time, energy, and patience than teaching the average child. If you approach this as a challenge and get to know the student, the experience will be rewarding for both of you.

Looking for the right teacher

You may not be able to choose your child's teacher, in which case the information in this section doesn't apply. But in case you have some say in the matter, here are some characteristics to look for in a teacher who can handle the challenges of a student with AD/HD:

✔ **Acknowledges that AD/HD is real:** A few teachers and other education professionals still don't believe that AD/HD is real. A teacher who takes his stand in the face of evidence to the contrary shouldn't be teaching your child. If your child's teacher falls into this small category, do whatever is in your power to get a new teacher for her.

✓ **Is educated or is willing to be educated about AD/HD:** With the level of press that AD/HD has received in recent years, it's a pretty safe bet that your child's teacher will know quite a bit about AD/HD or at least know enough to be interested in finding out more.

✓ **Is patient:** Teaching is a tough job, and the best teachers are very patient people. Look for a teacher with deep reserves of this attribute — students with AD/HD need patient people around them.

✓ **Employs multisensory learning strategies:** Find a teacher who creates a lively classroom and uses teaching aids that encompass more than simply lecturing in front of the class.

✓ **Understands how much effort students with AD/HD exert:** As you probably know, your child with AD/HD has to work very hard to do things that are fairly easy for people without AD/HD. Unless a teacher has worked with a student with AD/HD, she may not know this simple fact. If she doesn't, let her know. If she accepts this fact, she's a good candidate for teaching your child.

✓ **Adapts assignments as needed:** Teachers who have experience working with students with AD/HD almost always make minor adjustments to assignments to accommodate them. These accommodations can be as simple as letting the student print rather than write in cursive, or giving a little more time to finish an assignment.

✓ **Supports your treatment efforts:** Many treatment approaches need to be adhered to while your child is in school, and everyone seems to have strong opinions about different approaches. Your child's teacher needs to be able to honor your wishes as a parent, as well as assert his professional point of view.

This list could go on, but the most important thing to look for in a teacher is someone who is able to treat your child as a unique person and who is willing to work with you to ensure that your child gets the best education he can.

Working with your child's teacher

One way to improve your child's success in school is to develop a positive relationship with his teacher(s). Your child is in the presence of his teacher all day long, so you need to have an open line of communication with this person. Here are some suggestions for developing a positive relationship with your child's teacher:

- ✔ **Meet with the teacher.** Use this opportunity to explain your child's specific situation.

- ✔ **Offer insight and education.** Provide insights into your child's specific challenges, as well as strategies that you've developed to deal with them. If the teacher isn't well-versed in AD/HD, offer to help her learn about it. (For example, lend her this book.)

- ✔ **Develop a plan together.** Help the teacher develop a plan to work with your child. Because you understand your child better than anyone, you can offer valuable ideas and feedback. You can do so when your child's educational plan is developed, but even if your child doesn't have one, you can still work with the teacher to figure out a less formal plan. Most teachers welcome the input and involvement from a concerned parent.

- ✔ **Keep in contact.** Talk to your child's teacher on a regular basis to keep in touch about progress and areas that are causing problems in the classroom.

- ✔ **Respond to concerns.** If the teacher presents a concern to you, take it seriously and work with him to try to address it. This show of good will can go a long way to developing trust between the two of you.

- ✔ **Offer support.** Let the teacher know that he has an ally when working with your child. The suggestions in this list are good starting points, and you can also consider volunteering in the classroom or helping with difficult times in school, such as transitions. (See the section "Dealing with Difficult Times in School" later in this chapter.)

Trusting relationships between parents and teachers diffuse many of the problems students (and their parents) have in school. If, for some reason, your child's teacher isn't interested in working together, you may need to talk to the school administrators and arrange a meeting with the teacher to work out problems. Or you may need to lobby the school for a different teacher for your child.

Documenting Your School Experiences

We're willing to bet that you're going to have quite a bit of interaction with your child's school over the course of his education. We're also willing to bet that not all of this interaction is going to go smoothly. So, in order to ensure that your child gets the most appropriate education possible and that you have the information you need to make this happen, we strongly recommend that you keep detailed records of your child's school experiences. Doing so can help you keep your child's education on track. These records should include the following:

- ✔ **Report cards:** These records offer a big picture view of your child's progress.

- ✔ **Educational evaluations:** In particular, make sure you get (and file) copies of any evaluations conducted by the school or other professionals that you hired privately.

- ✔ **Schoolwork samples:** A sampling of schoolwork, including tests, reports, and papers, can provide an overview of your child's progress.

- ✔ **Correspondence between you and the school:** Keep all letters, memos, and notes from telephone messages that you receive from the school, along with your responses to them.

- ✔ **Notes from meetings and telephone conversations:** Try to take notes as you interact with anyone from the school. This may help you ensure accountability later if you need to.

- ✔ **Medical records:** These records should include not only a health history but also documentation of all the AD/HD medications you've tried for your child, what dosages you've used, and their results.

- ✔ **Treatments and results:** List all the treatments you've tried for your child, when they took place, how long they lasted, and how effective they were.

- ✔ **School personnel contact information:** This list should include all of your child's teachers and counselors, as well as the nurse, the principal, and any other administrators you've talked to or dealt with.

- ✔ **Healthcare professional contact information:** All the professionals you work with should be on this list, along with their mailing addresses and phone numbers.

- ✔ **Diagnostic records:** These records include results of any neuropsychological, medical, and psychiatric exams, along with any other information you gathered when trying to determine a diagnosis.

- ✔ **IDEA and Section 504 statutes:** You can find these statutes at www.wrightslaw.com.

- ✔ **Educational plan data:** This information should include notes from the meetings, the educational plan itself, and any data regarding the outcome of the plan.

How does your child learn?

Understanding how your child learns can help you make sure that he gets the best possible education. Many people with AD/HD don't do well in traditional classrooms because they have a difficult time learning through verbal instruction.

People learn in different ways and fall into at least one of these learning categories:

✔ **Auditory:** Auditory learners absorb information best through verbal instruction. They may have problems with reading or writing and often miss subtle body language cues. Some students with AD/HD, though not most, fall into this category.

✔ **Visual:** Visual learners learn best through visual teaching methods, such as images, color, graphs, diagrams, and charts. These people may have a hard time with verbal instructions and need to have assignments written down for them. More people with AD/HD seem to be visual learners than auditory learners.

✔ **Kinesthetic:** Kinesthetic learners do best when they can get their hands and bodies involved in the process, such as by doing lab work, building models, or role-playing. Kinesthetic learners often struggle in traditional classrooms because of the lack of movement; they may have a hard time sitting still. The majority of people with AD/HD seem to learn best this way.

If your child is a kinesthetic learner, a regular classroom setting is probably difficult for him (even without the AD/HD symptoms interfering with learning) because the modern public school relies for the most part on auditory and visual approaches. If you have the option, look for a school environment that employs teaching methods that incorporate multisensory activities, interactive computer learning, and hands-on projects.

The purpose of these records is to track and evaluate the progress, or lack thereof, of your child in school. This monitoring is very helpful for making future decisions regarding his education. These records are especially important if you're seeking (or have already received) accommodations for your child under either IDEA or Section 504.

Exploring Schooling Alternatives

Even with an effective treatment plan and solid life strategies, some children with AD/HD just don't fit very well into the modern-day school system because of their different learning styles (see the sidebar "How does your child learn?"). A standard classroom with a teacher lecturing most of the day is often the worst possible environment from which to acquire information and knowledge.

Your child may not have to be stuck in this type of classroom. Other types of school environments offer a variety of teaching styles that may be more effective for your child with AD/HD. Depending on where you live and your lifestyle, you may have alternative options for schooling your child. These options include:

- ✔ **Charter schools:** Most school districts have at least one school that uses alternative methods of teaching or that focuses its curriculum on a specific area of study. These schools are called *charter* or *magnet schools*. Check with your district to see if a charter school exists, and if it has a program that relies less on classroom lectures and more on interactive or hands-on approaches.

- ✔ **Private schools:** Most large towns and cities have a variety of private schools, and some offer a more varied learning environment than the traditional public school. Even if the teaching style is traditional, private schools often offer smaller classes, so each child is more likely to get individual attention. If a private school is a possibility for you financially (you may find a school that offers scholarships or other financial aid), you may find a program that meets your child's needs.

  Residential private schools also exist, some of which offer help for specific learning problems. Your child may be a long way from home, but he may also get a super education.

- ✔ **Homeschooling:** Homeschooling is a viable option for families that have a parent at home during the day. Once relegated to the lunatic fringe (we mean this in the nicest way possible — your coauthor Jeff is raising a homeschooled child), homeschooling has become a legitimate form of education and can offer much more flexibility for a child who has difficulty in a traditional schoolroom setting.

  Homeschooling takes many forms, from *unschooling* (unstructured, natural learning) to curriculum-based programs, and each state has different requirements for monitoring homeschool education. If you're interested in exploring this approach, check out these Web sites:

  - *Homeschool World* magazine: www.home-school.com

  - Homeschool.com: www.homeschool.com

  - Homeschool Central: http://homeschoolcentral.com

If your child's school isn't cutting it for you (or him), don't be afraid to look into alternatives. You may end up finding (or creating) a better schooling situation for him — one where he can learn the way he learns best.

Dealing with Difficult Times in School

Certain times of the day, and certain situations, cause more problems than others for a student with AD/HD. The culprits are often the less structured times of the day, such as lunchtime and recess. Other problem situations include transitioning from one activity to another, interacting with fellow students or teachers, and dealing with people who don't understand AD/HD.

Lunchtime and recess

Even though lunchtime and recess can allow great opportunities for your child to burn off some energy, they are also two of the most difficult time periods for students with AD/HD for several reasons:

- **The noise and chaos can be overwhelming.** Overstimulation in a noisy or busy environment can cause behaviors that are difficult to control, such as tantrums (for younger kids), frustration, and aggression. Try to keep the student out of the main thrust of activity, and offer a calm, quiet place for her to retreat to.

- **Other kids can pick on them.** Without the structure of a classroom and the close oversight of the teacher, lunchtime and recess often provide an opportunity for other kids to pick on a student who is "different."

- **They can get into trouble.** Again, because of the lower level of supervision during lunchtime and recess, many students with the hyperactive/impulsive type of AD/HD can get into trouble. They may impulsively do things they shouldn't or act out in inappropriate ways.

- **Getting back to work is tough.** Going from the high-stimulation lunchroom or play yard to the (supposed) quiet of a classroom takes time for someone with AD/HD. It's important to build this time into the student's day in order for any work to get done after lunch.

Because lunchtime can be overwhelming for students with AD/HD, it may be beneficial to offer younger students a quiet place to eat so they don't become overstimulated and difficult to calm down when it's time to get back to work. Another option is to schedule their mealtime at a different time of the day. Naturally, this type of accommodation needs to be weighed against students' need for socialization and the need to avoid being stigmatized. If separating a student from his peers doesn't seem like the best option, the suggestions in the next two sections can help mitigate the problems that lunchtime can pose.

Transitions

Changing activities (moving from one class, assignment, or activity to the next), environments (such as coming inside after recess), and schools are all hard on children with AD/HD. These transitions can cause frustration, depression, tantrums, and other reactions. Many children with AD/HD tend to get stuck and not want to change activities.

The best way to deal with transitions is to prepare the student for them. You can do this by trying these ideas:

- ✔ **Tell him what's coming next.** Repeatedly let the student know what activity or change is coming and what you expect from him during the transition. By knowing what's ahead, many people with AD/HD can more easily break from one thing and move on to another.

- ✔ **Make the change gradual.** You can soften some transitions by creating a gradual change, such as by adding an interim activity that allows for a change in mindset and makes a ritual event out of the transition itself.

- ✔ **Create a set routine.** When you do things in a routine way, everyone involved gets in the groove, and you all know automatically what comes next and when. This kind of routine is self-reinforcing, too.

Opportunities for socialization

Many children with AD/HD have problems socially. Some kids with AD/HD are socially isolated or say and do inappropriate things; others are overly social. These problems often stem from the person with AD/HD having difficulty understanding boundaries (figuring out where her own space ends and someone else's begins). Also, many children with AD/HD have difficulty recognizing how other people feel. (We discuss empathy in Chapter 14.) Other social problems stem from the child's difficulty with regulating her own emotions or attention. Sometimes problems arise from a simple lack of training in the necessary skills.

Some of the most common social problems that AD/HD children have are:

- ✔ **Being self-centered:** Sometimes it seems that children (and adults) with AD/HD don't understand that other people have their own interests and needs. This may stem from a lack of self-awareness or from the child's difficulty understanding himself in the context of the groups he belongs to. This trait often causes problems with peers, parents, and teachers.

- ✔ **Taking over:** Many children with AD/HD dominate their peers through bullying or being bossy. This can cause them to have trouble making and keeping friends, especially in their own age group.

✔ **Being a poor sport:** Some children with AD/HD have a serious problem with losing. They may cheat to win at games, or they may throw tantrums if they lose.

✔ **Commanding all the attention:** In a classroom, a student with AD/HD may try to take all of the teacher's attention. (Often the class clown is a person with AD/HD; making her peers laugh may give her self-esteem a needed boost.) Sometimes the child has difficulty modulating the intensity of her communications, so she speaks too loudly, talks too much, or intrudes physically into ongoing activities. At other times, the child may simply require a lot of the teacher's attention in order to stay on task and behave appropriately.

✔ **Invading another person's space:** Children (and adults) with AD/HD often have a hard time recognizing other people's personal space. They may also have a poor concept of their own presence in space. As a result, they often invade the space of others.

✔ **Butting into conversations:** AD/HD makes it hard for children to keep a thought in mind for long, especially if they have to wait for someone else to finish speaking. Because of this, and because of the difficulty people with AD/HD have picking up on subtle body language, they often miss the rhythm of a conversation and choose the wrong time to add to it.

✔ **Being unable to follow a conversation:** Many times, children with AD/HD misunderstand what's being said in a conversation. As a result, they may say something that doesn't relate to what's been said.

✔ **Taking over a conversation:** Again, because someone with AD/HD may not pick up on cues relating to other people's needs, he may command the conversation and not let other people have their say.

✔ **Not understanding why others get upset at them:** Because people with AD/HD often miss social cues and have difficulty understanding another person's viewpoint, your child may not understand why someone is upset with him.

✔ **Misinterpreting what others say or do:** This is a cause of much conflict in the lives of people with AD/HD. Because they often misinterpret what others say or do, they tend to get upset for what may appear to be no reason — or the wrong reason.

Improving social skills is crucial to improving the educational success of a child with AD/HD. The best way for her to learn better social skills is in a group context. Some schools offer social skills classes given by a teacher, school guidance counselor, psychologist, or social worker. Church groups that focus on social interactions are another possibility. And modeling is the best teacher, so be sure you schedule family practice and discussion times.

One of the best ways you can improve your child's ability to get along with other people — and to understand social cues — is to get him involved in a mediation training program (if your school has one). Mediation training involves learning about interpersonal social interactions, learning to see another person's view, and understanding the nature of conflict and how to defuse it.

Interactions with some teachers and administrators

Unfortunately, some teachers and administrators don't yet understand AD/HD. Even though AD/HD gets a good deal of media attention these days, and professional training on the condition is available, your child is bound to encounter a teacher or school administrator who is uneducated about AD/HD.

Most likely, your child will encounter a well-meaning educator who thinks she knows about AD/HD but holds false impressions or personal biases about the condition and its treatments. Some teachers and administrators still apply methods of teaching or behavior management that are counterproductive for the AD/HD student.

Obviously, you don't want to tolerate actions such as a teacher humiliating your child in front of peers to attempt behavior control. Nor should you tolerate a principal refusing to provide accommodations on the grounds that they are not necessary for "troublemakers." As we discuss in the section "Getting to Know Your Legal Rights," you may have to be firm (perhaps even forceful) when intervening in these situations.

Sometimes you will deal with educators who have strong opinions about your choice of AD/HD treatment(s). Usually the central issue is whether or not you choose to give your child medication. You may be lucky enough to have a rational discussion with the educator in question, or you may find yourself in a power struggle with the school.

In this type of situation, you may have to defend your actions and beliefs to your child's teacher or the school administration. The best way to do so is to remain unemotional (easier said than done, we know) and arm yourself with as much scientific data regarding the validity of your position as you can find. Obviously, you will benefit from having close contact with professional resources, such as your child's doctor, so you can get outside support.

Working with Your Child at Home

To help your child succeed at school, you need to deal with many aspects of her education at home.

Children with AD/HD take longer than others to learn self-discipline, and they need a much more structured environment (though not a *rigid* one) in which to learn this skill. Part of your job as a parent is to help your child learn this skill so that she can take care of herself. This often means letting her experience the consequences of bad choices (not doing her homework, for example) or inappropriate behaviors.

Helping with homework

You'll almost certainly need to offer more help with homework to your child with AD/HD than you would to a child without AD/HD. Here are some suggestions for helping your child with his homework:

- **Provide a quiet, distraction-free place to study.** The fewer distractions — such as other people, TV, or radio — the better the chance your child will be able to concentrate. Help your child find a quiet place to work, or help him screen out noise by providing aids such as earplugs, a white noise generator, or his favorite music (as long as the music actually helps him focus).

- **Take breaks.** Allowing for a break every 20 minutes or so can help tremendously. Many families use a timer and set it for 20 to 25 minutes. When it dings, your child takes a 5-minute break, which should include some physical activity.

- **Work in small chunks.** Set a time limit on a particular piece of homework. During one 20-minute work period, for example, have your child work on one thing. Then, even if that project isn't complete, switch to another activity during the next work period, and come back to the first project later. By varying the activity, he'll have a better chance of getting something done rather than staring at the same thing over and over again.

- **When it's beneficial, let your child work for as long as he is on track.** The previous two bullets are true for many students with AD/HD, but if your child has difficulty getting started on a project, it may be best to let him work undisturbed after he gets going.

- **Set a schedule.** Having a set time of the day to do homework can help your child remember to do it and be more prepared to focus on it.

✔ **Keep track of assignments.** One of the main problems that students with AD/HD face is not remembering the homework assignment or forgetting to bring the proper materials (such as books) home in order to do it. Develop a system to keep track of homework. One common solution is what's called a *homework tracker* or *traveler.* This is a journal that goes back and forth between school and home and documents whether homework assignments are received, completed, and turned in. Having a homework tracker makes keeping track of schoolwork much easier and helps you understand where the breakdown in follow-through occurs. Talk to your child's teacher about setting one up.

✔ **Help get the homework back to the teacher.** A good method is to have one folder where finished homework is placed as soon as it is complete. Nothing but ungraded, finished homework goes in the folder, and the folder is permanently bonded to your child's skin so she can't forget it (just kidding). Develop the habit of making sure the folder is in your child's possession (in her backpack or notebook) as she leaves for school.

✔ **Manage time.** Most students with AD/HD have no idea how to manage their time. They may look at an assignment and not know how long to expect it to take, or they may doodle on something for hours, not getting anything done. Help your child manage his time by looking over his assignments and helping him devise a schedule to follow when doing the work. This is especially important with long-term projects that are easily pushed off until the last minute. Teach your child to pace himself so he can get a bit of work done on a long-term assignment every day. A big, monthly calendar with enough space to write out assignments and work plans can be very helpful.

You walk a fine line between helping your child do his homework and actually doing it for him. Resist the temptation to help too much. You want to help keep him on task and help him over any hurdles that stop him while he works. But make sure that you don't fall into the trap of having to ride your child in order for any work to get done. This is called *negative reinforcement,* and it is a hard pattern for everyone to break. (We cover this important point in more detail in Chapter 10.)

Arranging for a private tutor

In spite of your best efforts, and the school's, you may not be able to get your child to learn what he needs to know. In this case, you may find that a private tutor can help break ground that you or the school can't on your own. With a private tutor, your child gets one-on-one instruction from someone who (we hope) is an expert at helping kids with learning difficulties.

Sometimes a child just needs some tips and motivation from someone who has done the work before. In that case, an older student who did well in the subject may be the ticket. The tutoring won't cost you as much, and it may be easier to find a willing student than a professional tutor.

If you decide to seek a professional tutor for your child, here are some things to look for:

- ✔ **Experience with children with AD/HD:** Look for a tutor who has worked with children with AD/HD before and understands the special needs that they have. For example, most experienced tutors know that a student with AD/HD can't sit for long periods of time and learns best when he is actively engaged in the learning process. Look for a tutor who uses a lot of multisensory teaching aids.

- ✔ **An evaluation that identifies problem areas:** Many tutors look at schoolwork samples and report cards, and they talk with parents at length about the areas that need addressing.

- ✔ **A clear, specific plan for your child:** After an evaluation, most tutors develop a clear plan — much like a school's educational plan — to show you what they're going to work on with your child.

- ✔ **Communication and follow-up:** Because the tutor works only for you, you can expect direct communication and follow-up regarding your child's progress.

Private tutors can do wonders for helping your child get over some learning hurdles. You can generally find good ones in your area by asking your child's teachers or by asking your AD/HD professional.

Supporting self-esteem

The biggest hit to self-esteem that a child with AD/HD takes is from school. Between peers, teachers, and failed schoolwork, a student with AD/HD struggles to keep a positive view of herself. Add to this the fact that many people with AD/HD are barraged by negative thought patterns, and you end up with a recipe for low self-esteem.

According to psychologist Robert Brooks, the most important keys to self-esteem are the approval and attention of a respected elder and the development of *islands of competence* — areas of activity that the child is good at already and that she is encouraged to develop further.

Check out Chapter 14 for ways to keep school from eroding self-esteem, as well as ideas to help build it back up again.

Helping your child stay organized

Organization and planning are two of the most difficult areas for people of any age with AD/HD to handle, but for children these areas can be exceptionally problematic. We offer suggestions for getting organized in Chapter 18. But this is such an important issue that we want to provide some specific suggestions for things that you can do with your child to help him be organized at school:

- ✔ **Use a calendar.** Write down your child's schedule on the calendar and post it where he can easily see it.

- ✔ **Get your child a watch.** By having your child wear a watch you not only reinforce the idea that time means something; you also increase his chances of keeping on schedule throughout the day. Many people with AD/HD find alarm watches helpful because they can set the alarm for important events. Some watches vibrate quietly instead of making noise, which prevents the alarm from distracting others.

- ✔ **Use a PDA.** As we discuss in Chapter 18, a PDA is a great tool for a person with AD/HD. The key, however, is not losing the PDA. The solution for any child (or adult) with AD/HD who tends to lose things is obvious: Superglue!

- ✔ **Color-code.** Using visual reinforcement for the placement of your child's things can go a long way to helping him keep his stuff organized. Chapter 18 has more on color-coding.

- ✔ **Use organizing systems.** Develop simple systems that improve organization: Provide cubby holes for different items in his room; list chores or the day's schedule on a bulletin board or white board; keep a series of well-marked notebooks to assist with homework assignments; and so on.

- ✔ **Set aside time to keep organized.** Have a set time each day to go over what has happened and what needs to happen, and to help return order to spaces that have gotten out of control. This can also serve as family time together because you don't want to do all the work yourself, and your child probably won't want to do it without some congenial company to help her keep on task.

Chapter 16

Winning at Work

• •

In This Chapter

▶ Considering your legal rights at work

▶ Examining positive adult partnerships

▶ Exploring daily habits that minimize problems

• •

*T*he symptoms of AD/HD obviously affect your ability to perform a job. For example, distractibility often makes it hard to keep on task and do the job at hand. Inattention often leads to misunderstanding what other people say and can cause problems with work relationships or assignments. Impulsivity in the form of saying the wrong thing without thinking first can result in problems with coworkers or your boss. Hyperactivity or restlessness makes sitting at a desk for long periods of time uncomfortable, if not impossible.

In this chapter, we explore many of the challenges that people with AD/HD face in the workplace. We let you know what your legal rights are and discuss whether you should let your boss or coworkers know about your condition. We also explore ways that you can more effectively manage yourself, as well as ways to improve work relationships. The chapter ends with ideas to help you be successful both on a daily basis and in creating a career that is rewarding and enjoyable.

 Many of the challenges that present themselves at work are the same as those you have to deal with at home or your child confronts at school. Check out Chapters 14 and 15 for ideas about daily life skills that may help you in your professional life as well.

Understanding the Challenges at Work

For people with AD/HD, work presents a variety of challenges. Many of these challenges mirror difficulties that exist in any other relationships, but some are unique to a job or career. This section offers a glimpse into some of the struggles that may be present in your daily work environment, which we discuss in more detail throughout the chapter. These include:

- ✔ **Creating balance:** People with AD/HD have a real tendency to go to extremes. You may tend either to avoid work or be totally absorbed in it (a workaholic). As a person with AD/HD you need to work harder than other people at the job of creating and maintaining balance in your life.

- ✔ **Getting along with others:** Relationships are often tough for people with AD/HD, and the various relationships at work present specific challenges. Depending on your position, you need to ensure that your relationships with coworkers, your boss, and/or your employees (if you're the boss) are as strong as possible.

- ✔ **Maintaining perspective:** Seeing the big picture while also dealing with the day-to-day aspects of a job can be especially tricky for someone with AD/HD. You can easily get lost in the project at hand and forget that other work needs to be done as well. On the flip side, you may have trouble focusing on the task at hand because you're so fascinated with the grand scheme of things.

- ✔ **Being organized:** Organization (as we say many times in this book) is a major life challenge for people with AD/HD. Being organized at work is not as impossible as you may imagine, though. The tips we offer in this chapter can make it fairly painless.

- ✔ **Managing yourself:** To be an effective employee or boss, you must be able to control your emotions, take responsibility for your actions, and just generally have a handle on yourself.

- ✔ **Planning ahead:** One of the areas where people with AD/HD struggle is in being able to make a plan to achieve a specific end, whether that end is related to a single task or your entire career. The ability to plan, execute, and completely follow through takes some skill, which we help you develop in this chapter.

- ✔ **Sticking with it:** Being able to stay on task — both on small and big projects — is difficult for many people with AD/HD. You need to be able to follow through on a project, and you need to not quit your job impulsively.

To Tell or Not to Tell

Should you inform your coworkers and boss about your AD/HD? The answer is not clear-cut. In this section, we explore some legal aspects of making this decision, as well as the practical ones.

Legally speaking: Understanding your rights

If you have AD/HD, the Americans with Disabilities Act (ADA) may offer you some legal protection at your job. The ADA was designed to protect workers against discrimination based upon their disabilities and to allow for some accommodations on the job or in the work environment.

Just because you're officially diagnosed with AD/HD doesn't mean that you are eligible for accommodations under the ADA. The current interpretation of the law is that in order to receive accommodations for a disability, you must demonstrate both that you have a disabling condition and that you are disabled by the condition to a significant degree. The way eligibility is determined varies depending on where you work, such as if you have a government job or work in private industry, and whether you work for a big or small business. You'll need to check with your human resources office to find out what the procedures are for determining your eligibility.

For people with AD/HD, the ADA may offer accommodations such as the following:

- ✔ **Altering your work environment:** This may include such things as letting you use a white noise generator or music to block out the sounds around you, or allowing you to work in a private office instead of in a large room with other people.

- ✔ **Trading for a different job:** Sometimes a person covered under the ADA can trade jobs with another employee and end up in a more suitable position.

- ✔ **Moving to a vacant position:** If another job exists that you could do better than the one you're in, and that position is vacant, you may be able to change jobs.

The ADA is not designed to help you find or keep a job: It's intended only to protect you from discrimination due to your disability. What this means in the real world is that you still need to be qualified for the job and able to perform the job offered to you.

Even if you do receive accommodations at work, you're still required to perform your job according to the job description at the level required by your employer. Accommodations under the ADA don't entitle you to slack off or protect you from being let go if you don't meet your employer's expectations.

The ADA offers some protection, but an employer can fire you — or not hire you in the first place — for many reasons. For this reason, it is extremely difficult to sue an employer and win on the grounds of discrimination under the ADA. For more information about the ADA, check out `www.usdoj.gov/crt/ada/adahom1.htm`.

Practically speaking: Making your decision

Now that you know a little something about the limitations of the ADA, you're probably still asking, "Should I disclose my AD/HD at work or not?" Well, in some cases you must disclose your AD/HD. These instances include:

✔ **If you're on medication and your employer uses drug tests to enforce a *zero tolerance* policy.** The AD/HD medication you take may cause you to test positive for amphetamines. You must let your employer know ahead of time that you're taking medication for your AD/HD so you avoid being fired as a result of a positive test.

✔ **If your employer requires that you disclose your health as a condition for employment.** You may face this requirement if you need a security clearance, for instance. Not telling your employer about something like having AD/HD may be grounds for not hiring you or for dismissal.

✔ **If your employer requires a medical history for health insurance coverage.** When you apply for the job, you may not be required to tell your employer that you have AD/HD. But if you have to declare your past medical history for coverage under your employer's health insurance, you may have to disclose your AD/HD or else risk having your insurance cancelled when the company discovers that you didn't disclose your condition.

If these scenarios don't apply to you, and if your symptoms don't deter you from doing your job, you may not need to let your employer know about your AD/HD. Only you can make the final decision, based on figuring out who your employer is and how she treats people who require some accommodations.

Even if you decide not to disclose your AD/HD at first, you may need to rethink your decision later, so keep your options open by not misleading the boss or your supervisor. Being private is not dishonest, but some people with AD/HD can't resist embellishing the truth. If you tell a tall tale about yourself to cover up the fact that you have AD/HD, don't be surprised when the boss gets upset about finding out the truth.

Managing Yourself

No matter how you slice it, *you* are the person responsible for conducting yourself in a professional manner at work. Some of the issues you need to work on include:

- ✔ **Improving your self-esteem:** People with AD/HD often have fragile self-esteem, if they have any at all. Low self-esteem in the workplace can manifest in a variety of ways, but a key thing to beware of is relying too much on other people's perceptions of you and your abilities. If you put too much weight on what other people think, you risk feeling defensive or trying too hard to please them. As a result, you may feel angry and underappreciated.

- ✔ **Coping with emotions:** The biggest emotional struggles that people with AD/HD have are not acknowledging their emotions and/or externalizing them. If you don't acknowledge your emotions, you may react strongly (externalize) without knowing why. Acting out your feelings could result in various difficulties with your coworkers. You must work on recognizing what you really feel. When you know what your feelings are, you can more easily communicate them to other people and get what you need.

- ✔ **Getting to know yourself:** AD/HD can inhibit self-awareness; as a result, you may not even know where your strengths and weaknesses lie. Such knowledge is crucial for success both on the job and in personal relationships. Knowing how you think and react can help you develop skills for handling situations better. In Chapter 9, we discuss many forms of counseling and therapy that can help increase your self-knowledge.

Part of knowing yourself is understanding your values. It is easier to be honest and consistent when you know what is really important to you. Developing an awareness of your value system helps improve your self-esteem, too.

- ✔ **Taking responsibility:** Many people with AD/HD aren't able to see the role that their own actions play in their lives. For example, perhaps you struggle to understand that pointing out where your boss is wrong may not be a good career move. (After all, you're right, and that's the point, right?) So if you get fired for being insubordinate, you may think your boss is at fault, not you. To be successful in any aspect of life, you must be able to own up to your responsibilities and understand your role in the situation you're in.

- ✔ **Sticking with it:** If you're impulsive and easily distracted, you're going to have to work hard at sticking with projects, jobs, relationships . . . anything that requires long-term commitment. For example, you may need to pay close attention to your periodic desire to bail from your job. See the sections "Doing Day-to-Day Tasks" and "Creating Overall Success" later in the chapter for tips on developing skills to help you stay focused for the long haul.

Working on Work Relationships

Success at work depends on being able to get along with other people, which isn't always easy whether you have AD/HD or not. When AD/HD is part of the mix, you may struggle to understand subtle nonverbal cues that make up a good portion of everyday communication.

Also, distractibility impedes communication. For example, you may be talking to someone but not paying close attention to what you're saying, or you may not be listening because you're thinking of what to say next. Or you may jump from one topic to another. We discuss communication in Chapter 14, and we delve into work-specific topics in the following sections.

Having a hand on the pulse of office politics

To be in tune with what's happening at your workplace, you must develop skills for understanding subtle nonverbal messages, which play a large role in interpersonal relationships. Here are some suggestions:

- ✔ **Ask for clarification.** If you tend to misunderstand what other people say, take this as a cue to ask for clarification. Sometimes the real intent of what someone says isn't very clear, so even if you clearly understand the explicit message, you may miss the point.

- ✔ **Find allies.** It can be helpful to talk to your coworkers and get their take on what is happening. It's always nice to make friends where you work anyway.

- ✔ **Study.** Even though people with AD/HD don't come by the skill of interpreting nonverbal messages naturally, you can learn how to do it with practice. For example, try watching TV with the sound off or going to a public place and watching people communicate without being able to hear what they say. You can also find books on body language, some of which have a greater scientific basis than others.

Another aspect of politics in the office is understanding how the workplace works. In other words, you need to know where everyone fits in, especially you! You will be much happier if you know whose toes you can step on without getting your block knocked off and who you need to keep your toes away from. It is usually easier to get things done if you know how your job fits with everyone else's, too.

There is usually an *official* structure in an organization and an *unofficial* one. Finding the official structure should be easy; it's usually published as an organizational chart or written down as a description of the relationships between various job titles (the organizational hierarchy). Finding the unofficial structure requires some sleuthing or experience. This involves watching carefully or talking to old-timers in the workplace to see how things actually get done.

Dealing with authority

It's no secret that many people with AD/HD have a problem with authority. Some feel that they can do a better job than their bosses or that their bosses lack vision. Others just don't want anyone to tell them what to do or how to do it. If either description fits you, you need to work on dealing with your feelings about authority without getting fired.

Perhaps you've already developed mechanisms for controlling the impulse to tell your boss exactly what you think every time you think it. If you haven't, we're willing to bet that you've been fired at least once for saying a little too much. You may be asking, "What can I do about my propensity to want to tell my boss off?" We're glad you asked. Here are some suggestions:

- **Consider the possibility that you're not correct.** Most people tend to believe they're right most of the time, and AD/HD can inflate this belief. If you stop to consider that maybe, just maybe, you're wrong and your boss is right, you can often stop yourself from saying something that wouldn't be good for your career.

- **Consider that being correct isn't really the point.** As hard as this may be to accept, in the workplace the important issue isn't always who's right, but who's in charge. You may have the greatest idea in the world or be absolutely correct about something, but if your boss doesn't agree, you're outta luck. This is Office Politics 101 and a hard thing for many people with AD/HD to accept. But before you open your mouth, you must take a moment to decide if being right is the best thing for your career. If you can resist the impulse to be right and wait for a better time to offer your insight, you may get to keep your job and get a positive response to your ideas.

- **Take a breath.** By taking a deep breath before you blurt out what you want to say, the impulse has a chance to abate a bit. Taking a deep breath can also help diffuse the feelings of anger or frustration you may feel, which contribute to your impulse to speak.

✔ **Bite your tongue.** The idea here is to develop a personal cue that helps you stop from saying anything that you may regret later (or that may be bad for your career). This cue can take many forms, from biting your tongue (you thought we were kidding, didn't you?) to squeezing your wrist with your opposite hand. Choose a discreet physical cue that gets your attention.

✔ **Tell your boss.** If your boss knows about your AD/HD, you may find it helpful to let her know that one of your symptoms is to say things without thinking them through. This may buy you some leeway and get you out of trouble when your mouth runs off on you.

Getting along with coworkers

To be fair, we can't make a blanket statement about how all people with AD/HD relate to their coworkers, but we're going to try. People with AD/HD generally fall into one of two broad categories: Those who are socially adept and those who aren't. (Of course, some people are socially competent in some situations and incompetent in others.)

Many people with AD/HD are very social, gregarious, and fun-loving. They're great to have around, at least until everyone (specifically your boss) realizes that no work is getting done. If you're this type of person, your main challenge is to resist the temptation to drop your work and talk to your coworkers.

Other people with AD/HD may be very uncomfortable in social situations and often come across as being unfriendly or odd. These impressions may arise because these people often misunderstand or misinterpret what others say. Or the problem may be distractibility, an inability to pick up on nonverbal cues, or the tendency to misread the emotions of other people. These people may also struggle to communicate how they feel.

If you fall into this general category, you may need to improve your social skills with the help of a counselor or therapist. Or, if you're confident that you can't or don't want to develop your social skills, you may need to find a job that requires minimal social contact so you're not forced to interact with others.

Being the boss

Being the boss has many advantages for the person with AD/HD. One of the biggest is the ability to have other people do the work that you're not so good at doing, such as tending to the little details of a project. Unfortunately, this advantage also opens a can of worms because in order to have someone else do something, you need to communicate what you expect. This management task isn't always simple.

As the boss, you have several challenges when working with your employees. Here are some of the most common challenges and ways to overcome them, or at least minimize their impact:

- ✔ **Speaking too fast:** People with AD/HD tend to talk fast. If you speak too quickly when handing out assignments or running a meeting, both you and your employees may become frustrated, and you may need to repeat yourself frequently. Make a conscious effort to slow your speech down. Sure, it'll take longer to get your point across, but you'll ultimately spend less time explaining yourself or dealing with misunderstandings.

- ✔ **Not completing your thoughts:** Scattered thinking — a common symptom of AD/HD — often manifests outwardly as incomplete thoughts when talking to other people. If you tend to lose track of what you're saying, you may need to use an outline when you're talking with employees, or consult a list of points you want to make. This requires preparation, but it's time well spent.

- ✔ **Being unclear:** Because of scattered or fast thinking, many people with AD/HD aren't able to express themselves clearly. If this is one of your challenges, make a conscious effort to be clear when communicating with your employees. Often, it helps to provide written as well as verbal instructions and check to make sure you are understood.

- ✔ **Not following through:** If you agree to do something for an employee, write it down and follow through on it.

- ✔ **Being impatient:** People with AD/HD are notoriously impatient. If this is your tendency, work on developing patience skills. Taking deep breaths in times of stress can help, but your situation may be severe enough to warrant a trip to a therapist (see Chapter 9).

- ✔ **Expecting too much:** Along with the tendency to expect too much of themselves, many people with AD/HD also expect too much from others. Be realistic about what your employees can accomplish, and don't pile so much work on them that they burn out.

When you're the boss, you can tailor your work environment to accentuate your strengths and minimize your weaknesses. Unfortunately, many people with AD/HD don't stick around their jobs long enough to get a chance to move up the ladder into a leadership position. We talk about this problem in more detail in the "Creating Overall Success" section later in the chapter.

Doing Day-to-Day Tasks

In the following sections, we offer tips for getting your work done as efficiently and painlessly as possible.

Getting organized

In Chapters 14, 15, and 18, we devote a lot of attention to organization — obviously, this is a real problem for someone with AD/HD. Following are ideas for creating an organized workspace:

- ✔ **Use a calendar.** Write down every aspect of your schedule on a calendar, and use it! If you're electronically adept, use your computer or a PDA to accomplish the same thing. Or purchase an organizer that has a calendar, pages to create to-do lists, and a planning section.

- ✔ **Color code.** Using visual reinforcement for the placement of your things can go a long way to helping you keep your stuff organized. See Chapter 18 for specifics about using this system.

- ✔ **Use systems.** Develop simple systems that you can use. These include file cabinets, In and Out boxes, white boards, or other things that can help you keep track of both your time and things. For example, keep an In Box and an Out Box on your desk, and set aside time each day — even if it's only five minutes — to review what's in each.

- ✔ **Make time to organize.** Set aside a few minutes during the day to get organized. But be careful: It's easy to let a ten-minute "put stuff away" period turn into a day-long "gut it and start over" affair. Limit yourself to a set amount of time. And as logical as it may seem to set aside a few minutes at the end of the day to straighten your desk, this time of day is often the worst for organizing. By the end of the day, you may be so far behind schedule that performing this seemingly simple task could keep you at work all night. You're better off starting your day with some organizing time. If you need, bring an egg timer to the office and set it for ten minutes (or whatever length you determine is necessary). When the timer goes off, move on to the next project.

If being organized is especially difficult for you, you can hire a professional organizer to help develop a system that works for you. You can find a professional by checking with the National Association of Professional Organizers (NAPO). For information, see the Web site at www.napo.net.

Managing your time

When you have AD/HD, you can easily spend an entire work day doing inconsequential things (although they seem important at the time), such as watering plants and making copies. The day may come and go without you getting any significant work done.

To avoid this problem, create structure for yourself and to stick with it. (We talk more about the importance of structure in Chapter 15.) Here are some suggestions for structuring your day:

- ✔ **Plan your time.** Set a schedule for yourself. Many people with AD/HD find day calendars or computer appointment programs indispensable.

- ✔ **Make priorities.** If you have a list of things to do that don't have to occur at a certain time, such as researching facts for a report, organize your list in order of importance. For example, cleaning off your desk would be a lower priority task than returning phone calls from yesterday (unless your desk hasn't been cleared off for three months, and you know there are some papers on it that need your attention).

    Prioritizing takes practice, because when you have AD/HD, cleaning your desk and watering the plants may seem as important as writing a report. In fact, your thinking may go like this: I can't write a report on a messy desk, and I can't focus properly if I'm worried about my plants withering up! We hear ya, and we understand that perception may be a problem. But as you make prioritized lists (perhaps with the help of your boss or a coworker at first), and as you see the results of following them, you'll discover which tasks are more important than others. (Of course, it doesn't help that the same activity may be important to one person in your office and unimportant to another. You won't always please everyone, but with practice the task of prioritizing gets easier.)

- ✔ **Set manageable goals.** People with AD/HD tend to think they can do more than is humanly possible in a day. Don't put so much on your list for a given day that you set yourself up to fail. Choose a few important things to focus on, and leave others for tomorrow. If you get to the end of your list and have time left in the day, you can always start working on tomorrow's tasks. This is another area where a professional, such as an AD/HD coach (see Chapter 9), can help you to get started.

- ✔ **Stay on task.** When you have your list set, follow it. Resist the temptation to veer from the list, even if you notice how desperately your file cabinet needs to be reorganized.

✓ **Avoid missing appointments.** If your job requires that you meet with people, and you have a tendency to get distracted, develop a method of keeping your appointments. For example, consider using a PDA with an alarm, or get a pager and ask an assistant or coworker to beep you before the meeting begins. Whatever method you use, allow yourself ample time to travel to the meeting site and get yourself focused before the meeting begins.

✓ **Ask for help.** If you're lucky enough to have an assistant or someone else you work with to manage your schedule, this person can help to provide the structure you need. (College students are often great assistants.) Take advantage of the assistance by asking this person to remind you about returning important phone calls, attending meetings, following up on details of a project, and so on.

Handling projects

Compared with tasks that can be completed in a single work day, long-term projects are exponentially more difficult. In Chapter 18, we offer ideas for successfully handling any type of project. If you combine that information with the tips we offer here, you can tackle every project that lands on your desk:

✓ **Create an overview.** Start by taking a look at the big picture. Write down the goal of the project and its major components, such as who is involved, what interim deadlines need to be met, and what resources (financial and human) are required to get it done.

✓ **Break it down and set a schedule.** Create manageable steps to follow and determine when they need to occur. Depending on the size of the project, this may mean creating a daily schedule for yourself, or it may mean establishing milestones that you must meet each week or each month. Build some flexibility into the schedule, because it takes practice to become accurate at gauging how long certain tasks will take.

✓ **Take it one step at a time.** With a solid plan in hand, your job is simple: Follow the steps and the schedule you've created. (Sounds easy, right?) Don't forget to give yourself some reinforcement for getting steps done. If you have opportunities in staff meetings to report on your progress, do so. And consider giving yourself incentives for reaching significant milestones, such as "If I complete the database on Thursday, like I've planned, then on Friday I'll go out to lunch instead of eating at my desk."

✓ **Reassess when you get stuck.** Until you have lots of practice breaking down and scheduling a project, you may find yourself getting stuck either because you didn't allow enough time for a step or you missed an important part of the process. As you work on your project, take time once in a while to reassess whether you're on the right track. Make adjustments as you need to. This reassessment helps you avoid the pitfall of just giving up when you hit a snag.

REMEMBER

Whatever you do, don't wait until the last minute to start a big project. Procrastination is a common problem for people with AD/HD. Some people may need to have the stress of a deadline to motivate them; others may not know where to start on a project; still others may simply forget to keep working because of other things taking up all their time. Regardless of the reason, you must do a little bit each day to move your project forward rather than waiting until the last minute to get started.

If you're the boss and you have other people to help with your project, you also need to learn how to delegate. Yes, for those of you reading this who love to maintain control, we said *de-le-gate.* If you don't know what this means or you have a physical aversion to it (which many people with AD/HD have), we're talking about letting someone else do some of the work. For tips on working successfully with employees, see the "Being the boss" section earlier in this chapter.

Staying focused

With all the distractions inherent in the workplace — coworkers talking, phones ringing — it can be hard for anyone, let alone someone with AD/HD, to stay focused and get work done. Try employing these strategies to help you stay focused:

- **Don't forget treatment.** If you're on medication or doing other treatments to improve your attention, follow your treatment plan.

- **Manage distractions.** Learn to recognize things that easily distract you, and develop techniques for getting back on task. For example, if you have a window in your office, you may need to keep the blinds down or curtains closed whenever you need to concentrate. If pictures on the walls or your desk frequently attract your attention, get rid of them. However, some people find it easier to concentrate when surrounded by chaos; figure out what works best for you before putting yourself in solitary confinement.

- **Take breaks.** Taking a break every half-hour or so to walk around or stretch can help you focus. While a little physical activity is ideal, you can also just take an occasional daydream break. After all, you're the most creative person in the office *because* you daydream, right?

- **Use music and sound wisely.** Some people find that certain music or background sound can help mask the sound of other people talking. Depending on your work environment, you may need to ask your boss for permission to play music or sound, or you may need to use headphones.

Dealing with details

Everyone, even the boss, has to deal with some details on the job — minor tasks such as returning phone calls. Unfortunately, many people with AD/HD aren't good at taking care of details. Here are some things you can do to make sure that you get even the uninteresting parts of your job done:

- ✔ **Write each job down.** Write down even the little tasks so you'll remember them.

- ✔ **Put the list where you can see it.** If your desk is a complete mess, don't put your list on your desk — you'll never find it. Post your list on a wall or door or wherever you will be sure to see it frequently.

- ✔ **Consult your list regularly.** Having a list does no good unless you use it.

- ✔ **Set a schedule.** Determine which tasks you're going to accomplish in a given day. But be careful: Many people with AD/HD have an unrealistic view of what they can accomplish. Every task takes time, and with practice on the job you'll get better at figuring out how much.

- ✔ **Check the steps off when you're done.** Doing so reminds you that you finished the task and also gives you a sense of accomplishment.

If you're comfortable, use technology to help you keep track of the details of your job. For example, computer calendars with alarms can be very useful, especially if your job requires you to be at a computer during the day.

Creating Overall Success

With all the challenges that AD/HD creates in the workplace, you may be wondering if it's even possible to have a successful career. This section assures you that it is possible. We can't guarantee that you'll earn millions (although that would be nice), but we can help you figure out how to be happy and satisfied with your life on the job.

Finding the best career for you

If you have AD/HD, identifying a career or job that suits you is even more important than if you don't have it. Your symptoms may make certain types of jobs (or certain duties at many jobs) impossible, or at least very difficult, to accomplish.

To find the best career or job, you must have a clear picture of your strengths and weaknesses. Chances are that you have a pretty solid idea of where you tend to struggle, and you've probably learned some skills and techniques for minimizing these areas. Finding your strengths may be more difficult. If you don't know where to start, check out Chapter 17. You may also find that therapy can help you discover your strengths (see Chapter 9).

After you identify your strengths and weaknesses, you can then start looking for a job that fits them. This may involve seeing a career counselor and finding a good book on the subject. You can locate a career counselor in the Yellow Pages or on the Internet. Also, colleges and universities have career counseling offices, and government agencies such as the Division of Vocational Rehabilitation may be useful. (Check the government pages of your phone book.)

A wide variety of books are published that deal with the issue of finding a career. Here are two that we recommend:

- *Zen and the Art of Making a Living: A Practical Guide to Creative Career Design* (Penguin) by Laurence G. Boldt
- *I Could Do Anything If I Only Knew What It Was: How to Discover What You Really Want and How to Get It* (Dell Publishing) by Barbara Sher with Barbara Smith

Looking at long-term plans

How do you want your career to progress? Where do you want to be five years from now? How can you get there? These are all questions that many people with AD/HD don't know how to answer (or perhaps even recognize to ask). Even if they do know how to answer them, the answers may be vastly different from one day to the next. Your coauthor Mike is a good example: I always found that when I tried to imagine what I wanted to do, I could picture it in detail, but the next day the picture changed. To have a career that advances, you need to know where you want to go and how to get there.

As we note in the previous section, some great books and other resources, such as career counselors, are available to help you manage your career, and we suggest that you take advantage of these resources. When you have a plan, follow it consistently and reassess it periodically to ensure that you're going where you want to go.

You'll spend a *lot* of time working in your life. You should absolutely strive to do something that you enjoy and that is rewarding. Having a plan can help you make this happen.

Making do at your current job

Job-hopping is a common problem for people with AD/HD. For some people, it results from being impulsive; they quit because something doesn't go their way. Others take the wrong job in the first place and become disillusioned. Still others struggle with repeatedly making mistakes and being fired for not performing the job properly.

One of the problems with job-hopping, regardless of the reason, is that it makes finding another job more difficult; employers want employees who are going to stay around for a while. If you're constantly starting over, your chances of moving up the ladder at work are slim as well. If you want a career that has forward momentum, you need to learn how to stick with a job long enough to move up from an entry-level position.

If you're currently in the wrong job, make sure that you stay with it long enough to find a job better suited for you so you can keep a roof over your head and food on your table. Resist the temptation to quit without having another job to move into. Also, sometimes "the wrong job" may really be the wrong way of thinking about what you're doing. If you suspect this is the case, have a friendly chat with yourself, and make sure your mental mirror didn't come from a funhouse.

Sticking it out when you're in an unpleasant situation can be hard. Here are some ideas to help cope with the situation:

- ✔ **Talk to yourself positively.** Remind yourself why you're working at this and the reasons why you need to stick with it.

- ✔ **Take breaks.** When the stress starts getting to you, take a break if you can. Go to the restroom, step outside, or take a walk if that's an option. Most jobs allow you some ability to take a short break.

- ✔ **Make a plan and follow it.** Create a plan for finding a job that fits you better and follow it. Having a goal can help keep you motivated enough not to do something impulsive like quitting before you can afford to.

Understanding your value

Every employee needs to recognize her economic and practical value to other people. As a person with AD/HD, you must work on developing a realistic understanding of your value in the workplace (which relates to your skills and education level) and how it relates to the current job market. (For example, there may not be jobs available that pay you what you think you're worth.)

People with AD/HD often have an unrealistic view of their value in the work-force. Some people, often because of low self-esteem, undervalue themselves and end up in jobs that don't pay enough or don't tap into their skills and abilities. This can lead to many problems, including the person quitting even if it isn't in her best interest to do so.

Other people with AD/HD have the opposite problem: They overvalue themselves and have an unrealistic view of their worth. They may believe that they're indispensable and end up wondering why they were fired or passed over for a promotion.

Sometimes, too, people take jobs that they are totally unsuited for out of perceived necessity. Before long, they are forced to recognize that they hate the job or can't do it properly. They quit the job, only to be forced to repeat the cycle. Understanding your economic value, as well as your personal values, can help avoid this frustration.

Striking a balance

Workaholism is rampant among the AD/HD population. People with AD/HD who find work that suits them generally do very well and get a feeling of success from it. And because many people with AD/HD tend to be hyperfocused and have trouble changing activities, everything but work may get pushed aside.

If this description fits you, you must make a conscious effort to create and maintain a healthy balance in your life. Consider these steps:

- **Honestly evaluate your schedule.** Take a hard look at what you spend your time doing. If your days are completely filled with work, and you don't spend time with your family or pursuing other interests, your life is not balanced.

- **Adjust.** After you've evaluated how you spend your time and energy, make adjustments in order to create more balance. Talk with your boss or (if you're the boss) your employees about the fact that you need to reduce your work schedule.

- **Schedule family or other activities.** Initially, you may feel like you're forcing yourself to spend time with your family or to do other activities. With practice, the effort of doing so will decrease, and your enjoyment will increase. The time away from work may also enhance your abilities at work, and it will certainly make you a more well-rounded person.

Going It Alone: Being Self-Employed

Many people with AD/HD dream of being self-employed. Self-employment means not having to answer to a boss who doesn't have a clue, being able to work the way you want to, and being able to take your great ideas all the way to the top. Sounds good, right?

Yeah, but — and it's a big *but* — self-employment also means having to be self-motivated (through large doses of self-discipline), having to plan projects and follow through on them, and needing to figure out what your clients want and delivering it to them in a timely manner. Do you see a pattern emerging?

Yep, the skills you need to be successful running your own business are precisely the skills many AD/HD people struggle with. Does this mean that you can't or shouldn't work for yourself? Absolutely not. It just means that you need to understand what you're getting into and figure out how to overcome your weaknesses.

Here are some suggestions for succeeding at self-employment:

- ✔ **Know your strengths and weaknesses.** This is the same advice we offer earlier in the chapter for finding the right career. By knowing where you excel and where you have difficulty, you can create a situation that emphasizes your strengths and find ways to compensate for your weaknesses.

  For example, your creativity is probably one of your best strengths. You can use it to help you find a place for yourself in the work world, and you can use it to help you find a way to make the world work for you, too. See Chapter 17 if you need help identifying other strengths.

- ✔ **Get organized.** Here we go again! See the section "Doing Day-to-Day Tasks" earlier in the chapter for a variety of suggestions on this topic, and check out Chapter 18.

- ✔ **Be realistic.** Grandiose thinking is common among people with AD/HD. Couple this tendency with wanting to start a business, and you may end up with an unrealistic expectation of your ability to succeed. On the other hand, your boundless enthusiasm (if you happen to be blessed with that) can give your business a tremendous leg up.

- ✔ **Get help.** Being self-employed doesn't have to mean working alone. You can get the help you need in many ways:

- **Hire an employee.** If you can afford it, hire someone to help you in areas that you don't have the time or the skills to deal with yourself.

- **Subcontract.** If you don't want to (or can't afford to) hire someone to work for you consistently, hire out aspects of your business on a per-project basis.

- **Hire a professional.** If you're not a detail-oriented person, you can hire a variety of professionals to help you with some annoying tasks. For example, a bookkeeper or accountant can help you keep your finances straight and pay your taxes on time, an attorney can review contracts, and a secretarial service can provide key support when stacks of unanswered requests are piling up.

If you want to go the self-employment route, read about starting and running a business, attend business seminars, meet with people who've been successful doing what you want to do, create a business plan, and save enough money for start-up costs before you quit your day job. In other words, look before you leap.

The Small Business Administration (SBA) can be a big help with all these steps. You can reach this organization at www.sba.gov or 1-800-U-ASK-SBA. There are local chapters and tons of information on the Web site.

Chapter 17

Accentuating the Positive

*W*hen you have AD/HD, you receive many negative messages (even in some of the pages of this book). You can easily develop a poor — and limited — view of yourself and your potential. This chapter can help balance your perspective, so you can avoid being tarred with negativity.

With all the difficulties that come with AD/HD, many positive aspects exist as well. For example, many people with AD/HD have boundless energy and deep stores of creativity. Some fearlessly follow risky ideas with faith and conviction (which can occasionally backfire but can often lead to great achievements).

In this chapter, we explore many of the areas in which people with AD/HD perform as well as — if not better than — people who don't have AD/HD. We start by examining the core symptoms of AD/HD and how they can positively influence your life. We then discuss the ways that these traits can benefit you. Finally, we help you identify the positives in your abilities and determine how to accentuate them in your life.

Seeing the Positive in Your Symptoms

Most of the symptoms that people with AD/HD experience can have a good side as well as a bad side. For example, consider these primary symptoms and their potential positives:

✔ **Hyperactivity:** Many people who are hyperactive have tons of energy that, when harnessed, can help them get a lot done. If an energetic person also has the tendency to hyperfocus, the combination of traits can be very advantageous in the workplace (although you must beware of becoming a workaholic; see Chapter 16). This energy can also manifest physically in the form of, for example, superior athletic abilities.

✔ **Impulsivity:** Impulsivity can be a problem when it results in doing something dangerous to yourself or other people. But when used effectively, this trait can be an asset. For example, what makes someone a successful entrepreneur? Often entrepreneurs are impulsive, which allows them to take chances on ideas that seem nuts to everyone else. They leap at opportunities while others are still thinking about them. Impulsivity has also been linked to creativity — specifically to the ability to make connections and pull ideas "out of a hat." (We explore creativity in the next section.)

✔ **Distractibility:** The positive side of distractibility is the ability to be aware of even the subtlest activity going on around you. For example, you may hear sounds that other people don't hear or notice things that other people don't notice. Tuning in to the environment in this way can be useful for certain types of jobs, such as firefighting, working in an emergency room, or running a daycare center. Some experts believe that distractibility contributes to creativity and intuition (which we cover in the next section).

✔ **Inattention:** Even though we talk about people having an attention *deficit,* most people with AD/HD don't have a deficit as much as they have a problem regulating their attention (see Chapter 2). One advantage of this trait is that you generally don't pay attention to things that aren't worth the effort. Many people with AD/HD are able to focus their attention when something interesting is going on. In fact, they focus so well at these times that everything else around them ceases to exist in their minds. (Just try to get the attention of a kid playing a video game!) This intense focus can be a major advantage when you are problem-solving or working on arduous (but interesting) tasks.

The positive aspects of the symptoms of AD/HD aren't limited to these primary symptoms. If you take some time to consider the secondary symptoms we discuss in Chapter 3 or the symptoms of the co-occurring conditions we describe in Chapter 6, you'll certainly discover potential positives in them as well.

Examining Areas of Aptitude

As the previous section illustrates, the symptoms of AD/HD can have a positive side for many people. The way the brain works in people with AD/HD can produce some abilities that are advantageous. Obviously, these abilities vary from person to person, but we cover some of the most prevalent in this section.

AD/HD: Advantage or disability?

A growing number of people — including health professionals — want to dismiss the troubling symptoms of AD/HD and paint the disorder as a gift for the person who has it. These people look at the symptoms and traits of AD/HD with respect, and they view people with AD/HD as simply being different. The "AD/HD-as-gift" group focuses on the things that people with AD/HD can do well, and it puts less — if any — attention on the struggles that these people have. When these people do consider the struggles of AD/HD, they often view those struggles within the context of society and place responsibility not on the individual but on the situation he is in.

On the other end of the spectrum, some professionals believe that AD/HD is a serious mental disorder with no positive traits. They have difficulty seeing anything but the negative behaviors and the challenges that the AD/HD person experiences. This viewpoint is based on the belief that the person with AD/HD doesn't fit the mold, and fitting the mold is crucial. These people often see all the struggles that a person with AD/HD goes through and realize how hard he tries to fit in.

Most people fall somewhere between these two extremes; they see AD/HD as both a liability and a blessing. They recognize that the struggles are real, but so are the positives. Perhaps with AD/HD, the need to work outside the box causes a greater dependency on creativity. If you break your right hand, you quickly become better at using your left hand; it is not a gift or a blessing but a compensatory strategy. Likewise, many people with AD/HD develop their strengths to compensate for their areas of weakness.

Capitalizing on creativity

Creativity is a common characteristic of people with AD/HD. The aspects of AD/HD that may contribute to creativity include the following:

- ✔ **Lots of thoughts coming and going:** Many people with AD/HD have very busy minds. Thoughts are constantly springing up, and some of them are bound to result in great ideas.

- ✔ **Uninhibited ideas:** One great gift that highly creative people have is the ability to examine any idea, no matter how absurd. Many creative motivators and teachers focus on this ability to let ideas flow without judgment, because they know that doing so is key to coming up with new ideas and solutions to tough problems. Many people with AD/HD don't need coaching because this skill comes naturally.

- ✔ **Making connections:** When ideas are flowing freely, it becomes easier to see connections that other people may miss (or dismiss). This skill is related to the AD/HD symptom of distractibility. When a person doesn't keep focusing on a logical train of thought, she can piece seemingly disparate ideas together. The result may be a picture that looks like a Picasso but has the brains of an Einstein!

Capturing chaos

Many people with AD/HD can tolerate — and even thrive in the midst of — chaos. For some people, chaos exists in their minds in the form of scattered or constant thoughts. For others, it exists in every aspect of life.

We talk a lot about organization in this book (see Chapters 14, 15, 16, and 18), but for some people a clean, organized environment is actually counterproductive. For example, consider how your coauthor Jeff writes books such as this: When I'm in the middle of a project, my desk is piled high with books and papers. These are my thoughts and ideas. If I clean this clutter, I also seem to wipe my mind clear of my thoughts. (Out of sight, out of mind.) This isn't a good situation for me because without these ideas, I can't complete my work. The clutter may look bad, but I know where everything is (well, almost). I make it a habit not to clear my desk until all the ideas on it are either included in, or discarded from, my project. Clearing my desk before this is done is like tossing my ideas out before I have a chance to explore them. For me, having this information at my fingertips helps me make connections and find creative solutions that I'm unable to do without this chaos surrounding me.

Being able to tolerate and even thrive in chaos is a talent that may allow a person to work in a situation where other people can't function at all, such as on the floor of the New York Stock Exchange, as a paramedic in the field, or as a disaster relief worker.

Because many people with AD/HD can handle chaos — and may even need it to be creative — having a perfectly clean, organized space is not always the best solution. If your clutter helps you think, don't be so quick to get rid of it. (But be honest with yourself here: Don't pretend the clutter is helpful when you're just too lazy to clean it up.)

Accessing energy

High-energy people — if they use their energy wisely — often get a lot done. Many people with AD/HD have difficulty directing their energy. But with practice, many find that they can channel this energy into satisfying, productive activities.

To use your energy wisely you need to find something that you're passionate about doing. Your activity of choice may be anything from running marathons (that'll wear you out!) to running your own business.

Recognizing your risk-taking nature

Risk-taking is a common trait of people with AD/HD and can be a tremendous asset if you harness it optimally. In fact, risk-taking has fueled innovation throughout history. By being able to throw caution to the wind and try an idea without hesitating — or at least without stopping yourself completely — you are able to accomplish things that other people are afraid to try. It can help you start a business, tackle tough projects, or scale a mountain — both literally and figuratively.

Unfortunately, this risk-taking nature of some people with AD/HD is a problem. It can cause injury; financial difficulties; and problems at home, school, work, or with the law. Someone who is impulsive has difficulty handling a mundane existence. If you have this trait, you must identify positive ways to channel your need for risk and stimulation. If you can't find a healthy way to express this desire, you'll likely find an unhealthy way to do it. The best thing you can do is to seek out a lifestyle that supports this need, whether that means you're a river guide, a firefighter, or an entrepreneur.

The risks you take don't need to be physical; they can be mental or emotional. So before you go climb Mt. Everest to get your thrills, maybe consider a less dangerous option. (Of course, if you really need to climb the mountain, go for it.) And remember that just because a risk isn't physical doesn't mean that it can't be dangerous.

Supporting your desire for independence

As we discuss elsewhere in the book (see Chapters 15 and 16, for example), many people with AD/HD have problems with authority. They don't like being told what to do and often believe that their ideas are the best ones. What better way to honor this tendency than by working independently?

This trait is the reason many people with AD/HD seek out careers and other activities that give them a large dose of independence. If you have this trait, you do best when you're not tied to a single location (an office cubicle, for example) and you have the freedom to come and go when you want without someone constantly looking over your shoulder. Perhaps your ideal situation is to own your own business, or perhaps being a freelancer or a salesperson is appealing. The challenge is to find a job that allows you the freedom to do your thing but also provides you with the security you need in order to support yourself and your family.

Being able to stand on your own without the support and approval of "the system" or other people has certain advantages. The world always needs innovators who are breaking new ground and exploring new territories. This is one area where many AD/HD people shine.

Exploring ambition

Many people with AD/HD are very ambitious. Couple this ambition with the other abilities we discuss in this chapter, and you can end up with a person who has tremendous potential. On the other hand, some AD/HD people have everything going for them *except* ambition. In this case, what's lacking is motivation, and we strongly encourage you to work on figuring out your personal values — the things that have the greatest importance to you.

Ambition is a topic worth exploring. When you want something, that means you don't yet have it. A gap exists between where you are and where you think you want to be. In order to cross that gap, you need some kind of propulsion. You need a plan to get around or over any obstacles between you and the thing you want, and you also need a super energy pack to boost you beyond where you are to where you want to be.

The problem some people with AD/HD have is that it's easy to get wrapped up in the goal without a realistic view of what it takes to get there. If you're impulsive, you may look before you leap. If you have unbridled enthusiasm, you may be hoping to accomplish something that isn't even humanly possible.

As well, for some people who have less than stellar social skills (we're being nice here), ambition can cause them to treat other people not-so-nicely while they chase their goals. If your tendency is not to consider the feelings of other people when you say or do something, you may have to work on your social skills (see Chapter 10). Or you may need to find a goal whose pursuit isn't dependent on working with other people.

Ambition can be a good thing as long as it's powered with extraordinary enthusiasm and tempered with realistic goals and a solid plan of action. If you have an idea for a breakthrough technology, for example, do your homework and get plenty of reinforcements before you drop everything in pursuit of this golden egg.

Involving intuition

Earlier in the chapter we discuss distractible people who observe things that other people don't. Many people with this ability are also able to intuit things about others or their surroundings.

The reality is that most of us are conscious of only a small percentage of the information that is available to us in the environment. If you have AD/HD, you don't always focus in a linear, logical manner, so you may be more suited than others to pick up on the millions of clues that the unconscious mind uses to perceive the world. That's what we call *intuition*. The ability really stems from not getting caught up in the ordinary perceptual protocols that are the currency of everyday life. If you don't have to see a spade as a spade, you may be more likely to see it as a heart with a handle.

With this intuition often comes a deep well of empathy and compassion for other people. That's because you can see through the differences of conventional appearance to understand the basic similarities of all our situations. When someone gets to that level, AD/HD shows itself to be an unusual gift, indeed. Combine this with the creative capacity, and you have a connection that you didn't even imagine could happen (unless you have AD/HD and were paying attention).

Examining adaptability

People with AD/HD are often highly adaptable. In many cases, in fact, their adaptability may have prevented their AD/HD from being detected at a young age. Among professional circles, there is a phenomenon called *the wall*. The wall is the point when a person with AD/HD can't rely on adaptability alone to get him by. For some people, the wall appears during middle or high school when the social and academic challenges force them to confront their AD/HD symptoms. For other people — especially the highly intelligent ones — the wall doesn't appear until college or even graduate school.

The challenge that these people face is learning how to transcend this ability. Being clever can cover up a host of insecurities and ineptitude, but when you hit the wall, suddenly you can't cope the way you used to. This gives rise to feelings of fear, frustration, and confusion. When you hit the wall, you have only one choice: Give up being who you are, or give up thinking that being clever is the only answer. If you're lucky, you realize that being who you are is the most important thing you can do.

Some people with AD/HD don't know how to make use of their talents. Instead, they get wrapped up in trying to be someone different. If this describes you, we encourage you to seek out the best treatments (check out Chapter 7) you can so that your AD/HD symptoms don't limit your abilities.

One of the most widely recognized forms of adaptability is intelligence. Intelligence is a tool, just like physical strength or the ability to carry a tune. Don't let society's value system convince you that intelligence is more important than it is. There's always someone smarter, stronger, taller, or more good looking than you, but there's no one exactly like you — anywhere.

Assessing athleticism

Couple high energy with the desire for stimulation, and you have a great mix for someone to get involved in athletics. Many people with AD/HD like the way they feel when they're playing sports, so they get involved and spend a lot of time pursuing athletics. Over time, they discover that they've gotten pretty good at them, too.

One of the best things about athletics for people with AD/HD is that the exercise can help reduce the impact of the AD/HD symptoms (see Chapter 14). Developing skills in sports can also increase self-esteem.

Finding and Nurturing the Areas Where You Excel

All these positive traits of AD/HD look good, don't they? By now you're probably wondering where you can get some of these attributes. Maybe you have boundless energy but have never been able to harness it in a positive way. Maybe your "crazy" ideas are your innate creativity trying to get noticed. Or maybe your inability to get along with others is just a sign of your desire to work by yourself.

The first step toward developing your positive AD/HD attributes is to learn to see them in yourself and others. Here are some ways to do this:

- ✔ **Look for the positive:** Take a good hard look at yourself and how you work. Look for the areas where you have some skills (or at least innate abilities). Look for the positive in yourself, and you'll likely find it.

- ✔ **Find a role model:** Somewhere between 3 and 6 percent of the U.S. population has AD/HD. With so many people in the same boat, you shouldn't have too much trouble finding someone who can act as a role model for you. (Many famous people have been thought to have AD/HD, including Thomas Edison, Benjamin Franklin, and Winston Churchill.)

- ✔ **Get help:** Sometimes an impartial observer, such as a therapist, can help you identify your best traits. We cover counseling and therapy in detail in Chapter 9.

After you identify a few of your abilities, you can work on developing them. Here are some ways to do this:

- ✔ **Get treatment:** Without some sort of biological, psychological, and social treatment for your symptoms, you may have a hard time developing your strengths. Take your AD/HD seriously enough to treat it properly, and you'll be more able to develop your skills.

- ✔ **Seek out opportunity:** With your areas of ability identified, start to find ways to incorporate them into your life. If you have a ton of energy, for example, look for situations and activities where you can burn this energy in a healthy, socially appropriate way.

- ✔ **Keep assessing:** As you uncover areas where you can excel and you work on developing your talents, you'll likely find other skills lurking under the surface. Keep on evaluating your abilities so you can see the areas that get uncovered.

If you struggle to nurture your positive attributes, you may lack self-esteem. One of the best ways that you can develop your skills is to work on enhancing your self-esteem (see Chapters 14, 15, and 16). Likewise, by finding areas where you excel and discovering the benefits of these abilities, your self-esteem will begin to grow. This positive cycle can help you to slowly reach your potential and allow you to discard the feeling of failure that haunts many people with AD/HD.

Part V
The Part of Tens

The 5th Wave   By Rich Tennant

"The funny thing is he's spent 9 hours organizing his computer desktop."

In this part . . .

*E*very *For Dummies* book has a Part of Tens — who are we to argue? If you're looking for quick and easily digestible information, this part is for you. We offer tips for getting organized (and staying there); improving your relationships with family members, friends, coworkers, and classmates; and — in case this book leaves you wanting even more — locating resources for further information about AD/HD.

Chapter 18

Ten (or So) Tips to Organize Your Life

Disorganization is one of the hallmark problems of AD/HD and affects every aspect of life. Someone with AD/HD struggles with scattered thoughts, poor time management, cluttered spaces, and unfinished projects, to name a few examples.

In this chapter, we explore ways that you can improve the organization of your thoughts, your time, your physical space, and the projects you undertake. At their core, many of these steps are similar, because the key is to develop a system to help minimize the scattered thinking that most people with AD/HD experience. In some instances, this system may employ high-tech toys, such as PDAs (personal digital assistants). Other situations are decidedly low-tech, such as sorting the mail as soon as you get it rather than waiting until you've got a few feet of paper stacked on your kitchen table.

Getting Your Thoughts Organized

People with AD/HD battle with scattered thinking, forgetfulness, an inability to think things through sequentially, and other symptoms that emerge from an unfocused mind. This section offers some ideas to help you win the battle.

Recording information

One of the best ways to start organizing your life and your thoughts is to use a recorder to make notes of things you want to remember. Get a small digital recorder or mini-cassette recorder, and dictate into it the things you need to remember. At the end of the day (or when you think you may have forgotten something), review what you've recorded and write it down. (See the next section for tips.)

The only real drawback to recorders is that you may have a hard time quickly locating the information you need. However, some of the newer digital recorders have the ability to categorize pieces of information, which makes finding a specific section much easier.

Writing down ideas and appointments

If you don't have a recorder or think that using one may be a hassle, you can always go the low-tech route and write the important things down. Even if you use a recorder, at some point you need to write down what you've recorded, or else you risk having to search through hours of messages listening for a specific piece of information you need.

Many people with AD/HD write notes on personal calendars, and others simply scrawl their ideas and appointments onto small notepads. You're better off keeping everything in one notebook rather than scribbling on a lot of loose papers. The main thing to remember is that your writing must be legible and organized if these notes are going to be useful.

Using a PDA

Personal digital assistants (PDAs) have matured enough that they no longer just hold addresses, phone numbers, and appointments. They also have enough memory that you can enter notes and reminders for yourself. Just be sure that if you use a PDA and put all your important information (and your faith) into it, you take every precaution not to lose it, or you may also lose your mind!

PDAs are great tools for people with AD/HD because information is easy to store and to retrieve (especially compared to a cassette recorder). Be sure to back up the information from your PDA onto your computer fairly frequently (setting a schedule to do this can help), because occasionally a PDA can lose its mind, just like we do.

PDAs can cost anywhere from under $50 to over $500, and literally hundreds of different options are available. This variety can make finding the right one daunting. Fortunately, a few great Web sites are available to help you weed through the options and find the best one for your needs and budget. These are:

- ✔ www.pdastreet.com
- ✔ www.pdabuyersguide.com
- ✔ www.pdalive.com

Organizing Your Time

Most people with AD/HD are not good time managers. Some may be chronically late, while others are chronically early. AD/HD seems to create a disconnect between the reality of how long it takes to do something and the perception of how long it will take. In the sections that follow, we offer some solutions for better organizing your time.

Employing technology

Technology alone cannot make sure that you show up on time (see the "Planning ahead" section later in this chapter). However, PDAs, computer contact databases and calendars, and pagers can certainly make remembering appointments and deadlines easier.

Depending on the features of a particular device, these pieces of technology can do the following (and much more):

- ✔ Sound an alarm you when you need to leave for an appointment
- ✔ Page you with reminders of important tasks
- ✔ Keep all your scheduling information in one place

With all this help, you only have to make sure that you don't lose the device, faithfully enter all important appointment times and deadlines into it, and back up your data regularly. (See, there's still plenty for you to do to keep busy.)

You may need some time to get the hang of using these high-tech aids, but after you get into the groove you can rely on them to keep you on track throughout your day.

Charting your schedule

Many people with AD/HD have a tough time retaining verbal information and keeping track of things in their minds. For this reason, having a visual layout of your schedule may be helpful.

Day planners and other calendars can help you keep track of appointments and things that need to be done, but you still need to be able to first lay out your day's events in the proper order. This task is easy for things like meetings or school schedules, but for activities that have no set start and end time, the challenge is much greater.

Here are some steps that can help:

1. **Write down all your timed events for the day on your day planner or calendar.** Be certain to leave ample time to get to and from each one.

2. **Identify periods of time available for untimed events, and assign an event to each time slot.** For example, if you have 30 minutes available after lunch before your next appointment starts, give yourself 20 minutes or so to work on one part of a project you need to do.

3. **Avoid the tendency to try to fit too much in a limited amount of open time.** Overscheduling your day can be frustrating and actually defeat the purpose of trying to get things done; you'll develop an aversion to doing tasks if you repeatedly fail at getting anything done.

Planning ahead

Many people with AD/HD have trouble showing up on time for appointments and meetings and gauging how long activities will take. To improve your time management skills, you need to work at realistically reviewing your schedule and determining whether you can fit everything into the time you have allotted.

If you find yourself often (or always) running out of time, let this serve as a red flag: You must adjust your thinking about how long activities will take and start adding in buffers to minimize your chances of lateness. Many adults with AD/HD do this, and the result is that they're chronically early for appointments. This is a much better situation than being chronically late; just make sure you bring some reading material or a portable project with you so you don't become antsy while you wait.

Here are a couple of ideas for gauging the amount of time required for certain activities and arriving to appointments on time:

- ✔ **Time your everyday activities.** If you know it takes 10 minutes to shower or 30 minutes to drive from home to work, you'll be able to look at the clock and decide if you have time for that activity before you have to move on to the next event in your day.

- ✔ **Plan your routes ahead of time.** When you need to travel to a new place, go to a travel Web site such as www.mapquest.com and print out a map for yourself. This map will not only show the best route to take but also tell you how long the drive will be.

This can be a tough lesson for some people with AD/HD: Just because you have five minutes before you have to leave for your next appointment, you probably don't have time to rearrange the patio furniture or wash the walls in the kids' bedrooms. Don't start a project unless you are confident you have time to complete it, or unless you're aware that you'll need to leave it unfinished and willing to complete it at a later time.

Here's another hint: If you always have trouble locating your car keys when you head out the door, start looking for them early enough to find them and still get where you're going on time. Even better, make it a habit to put things in the same place every time. (Then again, that would probably take all the fun out of your day!)

Completing Your Projects

Despite the best of intentions, many people with AD/HD can't seem to finish (or sometimes even start) projects such as reports for school or work. Often, the person with AD/HD isn't procrastinating because he doesn't want to do something or needs to feel the pressure of a deadline before getting into gear. Rather, the problem is an inability to make sense of a project and turn it into manageable pieces.

Breaking things down

Before you try to begin working on a project, take some time to break it down into its core elements. For example, say you have a book report to write. Assuming that you've already read the book, create an outline that lists the main ideas of what you want to cover in the report. Then think in terms of writing each piece of the report separately, so you have manageable chunks of work to do each day, rather than an entire report to start and finish in one sitting.

Or say you want to clean out the garage, which is on the verge of chaos. Before you start cleaning, take an inventory of the contents of the garage — in general categories such as sporting goods, automotive, junk, household, and so on. Next, make a sketch that indicates where each category of items should be stored. By doing so, you reduce the chances of feeling overwhelmed, and you improve your odds of starting — and completing — the project.

Making a plan

When you have the basic steps of a project laid out, you can start to develop a plan of attack. Look at your list of things to do, and prioritize the order of steps. For example, before you can organize the sporting equipment in your garage, you need to first remove everything and clean the space itself. Only then can you put things back into place. In the case of the book report, before you can write you need to do some research (by reading the book, for example).

Your plan should address all the steps in the breakdown you created for your project and have these steps in the order that makes the most sense to you. Consider writing down each of the steps on a separate index card and shuffling the cards around until they make sense.

Taking one step at a time

With your plan in hand, tackle the first step on the list before moving on to the second. Try not to over-think your plan — just follow it. If you find that your plan isn't working, step back and reassess your approach to the project. Feel free to make adjustments, but only if doing so is necessary to completing the project; don't spend so much time reworking your plan that you neglect to act on it.

As you get used to breaking your projects down into small steps, prioritizing these steps, and implementing them, you'll find yourself creating better breakdowns that will, in turn, make following through that much easier.

Don't expect miracles the first time you break a project down into small chunks and create a plan to complete each step. Developing plans that work takes experience through trial and error. As you get used to using this process, your project planning skills will improve, and eventually you may be able to tackle projects this way without having to think so deliberately about it.

Making Sense of Your Space

You can often get a glimpse into the chaotic minds of people with AD/HD by looking at how they live. Many people with AD/HD (and many without it) live in clutter. This clutter can make it hard for anyone to keep track of things. People with AD/HD often lose their car keys, homework, wallets, and purses. The best way to deal with this problem is to eliminate the clutter. The sections that follow offer two simple yet effective ideas for getting your space organized.

One problem that many people with AD/HD have is the "out of sight, out of mind" principle: If you put things away, you may forget where they are. You must be clever in this case so you can balance the need for workable space with the need to see your stuff. There are many ways to accomplish this balance. Here are some examples:

- Take pictures of your possessions and write on each picture the location of that item.

- Store items in clear plastic boxes so you can see where things are even when they're put away.

- Color code — check out the upcoming section "Creating a color-coding system."

Cutting clutter off at the source

The U.S. Post Office is responsible for a lot of the clutter in people's homes. Junk mail, catalogs, magazines, and newspapers add up quickly. Here are some ideas for reducing clutter at its source:

- **Remove your name from mailing lists.** You can do this in a couple of ways:

    - Call the individual companies that send you unwanted mail and ask to be removed from their lists.

    - Put your name on the "removal" list of the Mail Preference Service created by The Direct Marketing Association (an organization that most of your junk mail providers belong to). The easiest way to so this is by going to www.dmaconsumers.org/offmailinglist.html and completing the registration form. Submitting this form gets you taken off most lists, but you'll still likely get some mail from nonprofits organizations and local businesses.

- ✔ **Cancel subscriptions that you no longer read.** Most people have subscriptions to magazines, newsletters, and newspapers that they don't have time to read. Take a good, hard look at all the subscriptions you have and which ones you actually read. If you haven't looked at a certain magazine for the past several months, cancel the subscription.

- ✔ **Handle the mail only twice.** The first time you handle it, dump all the nonessentials (such as catalogs or solicitations), file the papers that need to be filed, read what needs to be read, and put the bills in a designated place. The second time you handle the mail is when you pay the bills.

The place you store your bills should be somewhere prominent, such as on the wall in your kitchen, so you'll see it everyday and be less likely to forget to pay a bill. On the outside of the bill's envelope, write in large numbers the date you need to mail the payment. Arrange the bills in order of their payment dates, with the earliest due date in front.

Putting things in their place

Commit to memory the old saying "a place for everything and everything in its place." If you create a place for all your things and make a habit of returning those things to their places when you're done using them, you've just taken care of one of the worst producers of clutter in your life.

Of course, this process is easier said than done; it requires that you actually find a place for everything. The best way to do this is to follow the steps we outline in the "Completing Your Projects" section earlier in this chapter. And after you've done a large-scale organization of your household, be diligent about finding spaces for new items you bring home.

Creating a color-coding system

Finding a place for all your stuff can be challenging, but finding it again after it's out of sight can be downright impossible. One of the best ways to handle this task is to develop a color-coding system that lets you know at a glance what's in a particular space.

To accomplish this, you assign colors to broad categories of things, such as blue for bills, red for projects you want to get to, green for letters you need to answer, and yellow for things that may be interesting if you find time for them. Another example is red for screwdrivers, blue for wrenches, green for nails, and so forth.

You can color code just about anything in your home; just use colored labels, pens, envelopes, or storage containers, and be sure you keep a list of the color key for each area of the house where you apply this system.

Deciding What's Really Important to You

A key step to getting organized is deciding what's important to you. Many people live unfulfilled lives because they think they can do a lot more than is humanly possible; they start hundreds of projects, and they can't possibly finish half of them. People with that tendency (which includes a lot of people with AD/HD) must realize that it's okay to let a good idea go sometimes, or to write it down on a list of things to do on that hypothetical rainy day.

If you can figure out what is really important to you and concentrate on that, you will likely get rid of a lot of confusion and clutter. The good news is that many people with AD/HD have a superior ability to be brutally frank. If you focus that ability on yourself, you can probably drum up the honesty it takes to decide what you really want.

Chapter 19

Ten (or So) Ways to Improve Your Family Relationships

AD/HD is hard on relationships. The symptoms of inattention, impulsivity, hyperactivity, distractibility, and forgetfulness, among others, often cause conflict and stress within a family. Because of these challenges we decided to dedicate an entire chapter to ways in which you can reduce the stress and conflict in your family and improve your relationships.

In this chapter, we offer suggestions for creating and keeping relationship harmony. We suggest ways to help reduce conflict, support personal growth, encourage individual responsibility, and make sure that everyone in the family gets what he or she needs.

Taking Responsibility

Some people try to use their diagnosis of AD/HD as a "get out of jail free" card and think they can act irresponsibly. After all, they can't control their behaviors because those behaviors are hardwired in the brain, right? Wrong. AD/HD is not an excuse; it's merely an explanation.

To put this issue in perspective, think about somebody who has no legs (a visible disability). Although you don't expect this person to run or to rise when a lady enters the room, you do expect him to continue treating himself and other people with respect.

Don't let yourself fall into the trap of thinking that you can do nothing about your symptoms or your behavior. Take responsibility not only for your actions but also for your AD/HD treatment. When you hurt someone's feelings, acknowledge it and apologize. If you forget to take your medication, develop a better system so that you remember the next time. Regardless of the cause of AD/HD, you're still responsible for managing your own behavior.

Likewise, if your loved one has AD/HD and keeps messing up, require her to take responsibility for her behavior while doing your best to understand her struggles. (In other words, have empathy.)

Focusing on the Positive

Many people are so focused on keeping themselves (or their child or spouse with AD/HD) in line that they focus almost exclusively on trying to stop and prevent undesirable behaviors. They fail to acknowledge — or even notice — the types of behaviors they want to encourage.

People respond better to praise than to criticism. One of the best ways to increase the frequency of desirable behavior is to acknowledge it. If you're the one with AD/HD, make a concerted effort to dwell on the positive things you do while putting less stress on the negative. If your loved one has AD/HD, rather than criticizing his negative behaviors, help him correct those behaviors without focusing on blame.

Releasing Anger and Resentment

One of the most common problems in families that have a member with AD/HD is the anger and resentment that can build up before AD/HD is discovered or while trying to cope with the challenges it creates.

Here are some suggestions for helping you release anger and resentment:

- ✔ **Don't take it personally.** When a loved one has AD/HD, it's easy to interpret her behavior as a personal affront to you.

- ✔ **Try to distinguish between the person and the behavior.** AD/HD is a medical condition, and the behaviors that result are only partly based on choice.

- ✔ **Find professional help.** Sometimes just being able to talk to someone else can help you recognize when and why you get angry and help you develop ways to diffuse that anger.

Getting Rid of Guilt

Regardless of whether you're the one with AD/HD or your child or spouse has it, chances are that you have frequent feelings of guilt.

As the parent of a child with AD/HD, you may feel guilty about not discovering the AD/HD sooner, about the parenting choices you've made, or about the feelings of anger you may have toward your child. As the spouse of a person with AD/HD, you may feel guilty about being so hard on your spouse or about not demanding that he seek help sooner. You may also feel guilt because you have feelings of anger and resentment toward your spouse for the way you've been treated. If you have AD/HD, you likely feel guilt about all the times you've made mistakes or let people down.

For many people, just knowing that there is a biological explanation for their (or their loved one's) difficulties is enough to release the guilt. But if your guilt doesn't go away quite so easily, don't beat yourself up any further. Chances are your guilt has been part of your life for years; you may need time and the help of a therapist to work through these feelings.

Don't be afraid to seek professional help for dealing with your feelings. (Well, you can be afraid if you want, but don't let it stop you!)

Talking It Out

One of the best ways to maintain family harmony is to talk about your feelings before they turn into anger and resentment. Keeping an open channel of dialogue can help everyone feel like their voices are heard. And by creating an environment where everyone feels safe to express their feelings, you prevent resentments from building up over time. Following are a few things you can do to foster healthy communication in your family:

- **Avoid blame.** Blaming or criticizing someone is a surefire way to put the other person on the defensive. You simply won't get your point across to someone who is feeling blamed.

- **Don't react emotionally.** After years of misunderstanding and being misunderstood, it's easy to jump to conclusions and feel as though you're being picked on. Take a breath and ask your partner or child to explain what he means before you jump to the wrong conclusion.

- **Get professional help.** If you find that you're not able to communicate without someone getting angry or hurt, find a therapist to help you.

Working Together

Everyone has strengths and weaknesses, and people with AD/HD are no exception. If a family member has AD/HD, instead of focusing on her weaknesses, focus on her strengths and help her cultivate them. Likewise, be willing to work with her to improve the weak areas.

For example, if you or your spouse has trouble being on time to appointments, work together to get organized ahead of time and develop a system so you or she can leave the house early enough to be on time. (In some instances, this may even mean tricking yourself or your spouse into leaving early by writing down your appointment time as being earlier than it really is or setting your clock ahead.)

If your child has difficulty getting homework done, work with him to stay on task, or break down the task into small pieces for him. That doesn't mean doing the homework for him; as we've heard many a parent say, "I already passed the fourth grade once."

Having Family Meetings

Regular family meetings are a way for everyone to get together and have their voices heard. The meetings should be highly organized and follow set guidelines. Here are some suggestions for running a family meeting:

- **Establish a set meeting time each week or every other week.** For example, you may choose to meet during dinner every Tuesday, or immediately after dinner every other Thursday. Having a set time allows you to develop some consistency and offers the best chance of everyone showing up.

- **Don't force participation.** If you have a teen who shuns authority, forcing him to attend will likely cause conflict and resentment. Make your meetings voluntary, but offer an incentive for being there — for example, an activity that's fun or good food during or after the meeting. People who want to attend get more from the meeting than people who don't.

- **Focus on the positive.** Avoid making the family meeting a time for complaining. Instead, focus on the positive things that have been going on since the last meeting. When you do address uncomfortable situations — such as undesirable behaviors — do so with tact and avoid blame.

- **Schedule family activities.** One of the main reasons for having a family meeting should be to talk about the fun activities you want to do together. Doing so improves the morale during the meeting and gives everyone something to look forward to, even during tough times.

✔ **Encourage togetherness.** The whole point of a family meeting is to bring the group closer together. Assuming you treat each other with love and kindness, having these meetings can build harmony and help you weather the tough times better.

Being Realistic

After you set up a treatment plan for your (or your loved one's) AD/HD, you're on the road to making positive changes in your life. (See Part III of this book for discussions of various treatment options.) The only problem is that you can easily have unrealistic expectations of the changes you'll see. No matter how good your AD/HD professional is, or how good the various treatment programs you employ, you can't expect overnight changes (although some people do experience such rapid progress).

Set goals for yourself and employ coping strategies so you can make steady progress to getting your symptoms under control. For some people, controlling symptoms takes very little time, but not everyone is so lucky. Show yourself (or your loved one) some compassion, and avoid getting frustrated if you don't see immediate progress.

Having Fun Together

Nothing breaks tension better than having fun and laughing. Schedule some time to do fun activities as a family. Go to a park, take a hike, go to the beach, or play a game. Try to pick an activity that everyone wants to do. Choose something that doesn't create more stress, such as going to a fancy restaurant or to a movie with a child who has a hard time sitting still.

The best family adventures involve being outside and active. As we say many times in this book, one of the best ways to reduce the symptoms of AD/HD is to be more physical. So whenever possible, choose family outings that get everybody moving.

Walking Away

If you feel stress building up and tempers starting to flare, take a timeout. Walk away from an argument or stressful situation for a few minutes to cool down. Avoid saying anything in anger that you may regret later.

Heeding this advice can be especially difficult if you're dealing with an impulsive-type person with AD/HD because he may say things that make you angry or hurt you. You may need to develop a thick skin and practice walking away before you react.

Taking a few minutes to cool off can save a relationship and keep your sanity intact. However, you may want to discuss this tactic with your family before you use it. Otherwise, loved ones may feel resentment or assume they aren't being heard if they see you simply walking away.

Taking Care of Yourself

If your child or spouse has AD/HD, dealing with the daily struggles of trying to keep your child on track or coping with your spouse's symptoms is draining. You need to make sure that you don't add to the problems by burning out. The best way to avoid getting burnt out is to take some time for yourself. Try working at least one of these stress relievers into your life:

- ✔ Taking a bath
- ✔ Reading a book in a quiet place, uninterrupted
- ✔ Meditating
- ✔ Taking a yoga class
- ✔ Going for a walk alone
- ✔ Working out at a gym
- ✔ Getting a massage

Really, you can relieve stress by doing anything that gives you some space and helps you tune in to your own feelings and desires. Giving yourself a break will help you feel refreshed and more prepared to handle the challenges that AD/HD creates.

Chapter 20

Ten Resources for Information and Support

- -

In This Chapter

▶ Discovering online AD/HD resources

▶ Finding resources in your area

▶ Exploring ways to get support

- -

As much as we tried to cover everything about AD/HD in this book, we couldn't possibly squeeze every bit of information into 360 pages. Even if we could somehow cover everything, new information about AD/HD would be discovered tomorrow. In light of this fact, we created this chapter to help you continue your AD/HD education by discovering other resources and sources of ongoing support.

In this chapter, we present several online resources — from discussion groups to information clearinghouses to sources for support groups. We also recommend ways of finding people in your area to learn from or commiserate with.

Internet Forums

Internet forums are a great way to communicate with other people without having to actually go out and meet them. For people who live in rural areas or don't have a ton of resources for AD/HD in their towns, these forums can be extremely useful.

Here are a few of the more active AD/HD forums on the Internet:

✔ **ADDers.org online support group:** www.adders.org

✔ **ADD Forums:** www.addforums.com/forums

✔ **Misunderstood Kids . . . Outside the Box:** http://pub4.bravenet.com/forum/show.php?usernum=311565634&cpv=1

- **Attention Deficit Disorder Help Center:** `www.add-adhd-help-center.com/add_adhd_discussion_frm.htm`
- **ADHD Support:** `http://adhdsupport.proboards23.com/`

Countless other forums are available on the Internet. You can find them by using your favorite search engine and typing in the keywords "ADD forums" or "AD/HD forums."

Web Sites

The Internet is a great place to find information on just about anything. Finding information is as simple as going to a search engine, typing in your keywords, and sifting through the results. The only problem with this approach is that you sometimes have to weed through a bunch of junk in order to find quality information. And if you're not sure what information is quality and what isn't, you can find yourself going down some dead-end roads.

To prevent you from wasting your time searching for credible sites, we've created a short list here:

- `www.add.org`: This site is the home of the Attention Deficit Disorders Association (ADDA). The ADDA is a membership organization that conducts an annual conference, publishes a quarterly newsletter, and offers general AD/HD information online and through audiotapes, videotapes, and teleclasses.

- `www.adhdnews.com`: This site has been around a while and offers lots of great information about AD/HD, including a message board where you can talk with other people with concerns similar to yours.

- `http://add.about.com/`: This site is part of the about.com network and offers lots of information and links on AD/HD.

- `www.reiinstitute.com`: This is coauthor Jeff Strong's Web site. You can find information about the services offered to people with AD/HD, as well as more general information about AD/HD. Because Web sites come and go frequently, we keep an updated list of AD/HD resources on our site to make your online search easier.

These sites are just a few many hundreds of Internet sites on AD/HD. If you want to research a specific area of AD/HD, you can narrow the list down very easily. For example, if you want to learn more about using homeopathics to help with the symptoms of AD/HD, do a search with the keywords "AD/HD homeopathic." You'll get a lot of hits, and you'll likely need to weed through the ads from homeopathic manufacturers first, but you'll undoubtedly find one or two good sites with reasonably unbiased information.

Support Groups

Support groups can be invaluable, and many different types of AD/HD support groups exist throughout the country. However, finding a local group can be a challenge. Here are some ways to go about it:

✔ Go to ChADD's Web site (www.chadd.org) and look for support groups listed there. ChADD sponsors support groups throughout the country.

✔ Ask your local AD/HD professional about local groups. (See the section on "Your AD/HD Professional," later in this chapter.)

✔ If your child is the one with AD/HD, talk to his or her teacher.

✔ Call your local college or university mental health program. (Check out the "Colleges and Universities" section later in this chapter for details on who to contact at a college or university.)

If all else fails, you can create your own support group by finding other people with AD/HD in your area. This can be done by talking to your AD/HD professional or your child's teachers, by putting an ad in your local paper, or by posting flyers in public places such as local markets.

As for finding a space to hold group meetings in, most churches will let you use their facilities for a group of this sort. Call your local church and ask if you can use one of its rooms for your meetings.

Your Child's School

Teachers, school counselors, and educational diagnosticians are generally well connected within the community. They often know about many of the AD/HD professionals and resources in your area and can be a great resource whether you or your child is the one with AD/HD.

Colleges and Universities

If your local college or university has a department for any of the professions listed below (and covered in detail in Chapter 4), it can generally steer you toward resources in your area. Call your local college or university and ask to be connected to one of the following departments:

✔ Psychology/counseling

✔ Psychiatry

✔ Neurology

 ✔ General medical education

 ✔ Special education

 ✔ Occupational therapy

 ✔ Speech/language pathology

Most colleges and universities offer at least one of these disciplines, and people in these departments are generally knowledgeable about who works with AD/HD in your area and whether support groups exist.

Your AD/HD Professional

For most people, the first place to look for information and resources on AD/HD is a healthcare professional. Depending on the professional you see, he may be connected to a larger group of professionals that he can refer you to while still overseeing your care.

We cover details about how to work with several professionals at once in Chapter 7.

Books

Chances are that when you found this book you also discovered a bunch of other books on AD/HD that caught your eye. If you want to read more books about this subject, we've found the following to be especially helpful:

 ✔ *Driven to Distraction: Recognizing and Coping with Attention Deficit Disorder from Childhood through Adulthood,* by Edward M. Hallowell, MD, and John J. Ratey, MD. This book was published by Touchstone, a division of Simon and Schuster, Inc., in 1994. *Driven to Distraction* meanders a bit, so it can be a somewhat tough read for people with AD/HD, but it relates many anecdotes and personal stories that can offer a view of AD/HD that may resonate with you.

 ✔ *Healing ADD: The Breakthrough Program That Allows You to See and Heal the 6 Types of ADD,* by Daniel G. Amen, MD. This book is published by Berkley Books and was released in 2001. With a title like *Healing ADD,* you'd probably expect this book to be all hype and no substance, but it truly is a good book. Dr. Amen is doing cutting-edge research at his clinic, and this book illustrates what he's discovered. Keep in mind, however, that his findings are just his — no one else has done this same research, so there is very little third-party support for what he's doing. This doesn't make his research less valid, but it means that you need to keep it in perspective.

✔ *Attention Deficit Disorder: A Different Perception*, by Thom Hartmann, Edward M. Hallowell, MD, and Michael Popkin. This book is published by Underwood Books and was revised in 1997. Thom Hartmann looks at people with AD/HD as "hunters in a farmer's world," and his perspective is heartening for people with AD/HD. He has written several books, and all focus on the positive attributes of people with AD/HD and offer great insight into this condition. Another of his books that we recommend is *Thom Hartmann's Complete Guide to ADHD: Help Your Family at Home, School and Work*, published by Underwood Books in 2000.

Dozens of AD/HD books are on the market, with more coming out every year. A good place to keep up-to-date on the best books (or at least the best-selling books) is www.amazon.com. Do a search using *ADD* or *ADHD* as the keyword, and feast your eyes on the results. One helpful thing about amazon.com is the customer reviews. These can save you time and money by letting you know ahead of time whether the book is any good or not.

The Library

Your local library, aside from offering some books on AD/HD, may have resources such as a copy of the DSM-IV (the American Psychiatric Association's diagnostic manual), specialized magazines or reports, or other AD/HD reference materials. Most libraries also have bulletin boards, where you may find information about an AD/HD support group.

Family and Friends

Because so many people have AD/HD (at least 3 percent of the U.S. population), it's likely that you already know someone who has been down the road you're traveling. Ask your family and friends if they have any AD/HD resources and what professionals they may recommend — chances are you'll find someone who can share some valuable information.

Group Therapy

Group therapy is not only a great place to talk with other people who are confronting the same issues as you but also a place where you can share resources with one another. Ask your AD/HD professional about group therapy in your area, or call someone listed under "counseling" or "psychologist" in your local Yellow Pages.

Appendix

Treatment Tracking Forms

As we discuss in Part III of this book, treating AD/HD effectively often involves juggling more than one treatment at a time, and adjustments need to be made on a regular basis. For this reason, you must have a way to keep track of your progress and any side effects from the treatments. (This is especially important if you include medication in your treatment strategy.)

This appendix contains some suggestions to help you keep on top of your treatment's effectiveness, as well as tracking forms to help you monitor your progress.

If you try more than one treatment at a time, you may have a hard time seeing exactly what effect each individual treatment is having. This is especially true if you employ more than one biological treatment at a time. In order to see what each approach is doing, you may want to limit how many you do at the same time. For example, if you undertake only one other biological treatment with medication, such as a repatterning therapy (see Chapter 12), distinguishing the results of the two approaches is fairly easy because the effects of medication often follow your ingestion schedule.

Some treatments, such as the repatterning or rebalancing therapies (see Chapters 12 and 13, respectively), include intake and exit assessments to determine the level of success you have on the program. In this case, your treatment professional helps keep track of your progress.

Keeping Daily Tabs on Your Treatment

The main treatments that you need to track from day to day are chemical-based approaches, such as medications and vitamin and herb supplements. The forms in this appendix can help you do so effectively.

When you fill in the information on these forms, keep these things in mind:

- **Write down all the specifics about the treatment.** This includes the time and the amount that you used, took, or gave.

- **Record your observations of the symptoms for the day.** Include any changes that you see throughout the day. This is especially important in the case of medication because the drug's effects change over time.

The first step to take is to complete the treatment effectiveness checklists on the next two pages. For each day of the week, both morning and evening, rate the positive and negative effects of your treatments on a scale of 1 to 10 (with 1 meaning poor results, 5 being acceptable, and 10 being excellent). Total your score for each time of day.

Next, complete the AD/HD Treatment Tracking Form. In each section, note your total scores from the checklists for that treatment's positive and negative effects.

Performing Periodic Assessments

The treatment effectiveness forms are things you want to complete every day. But you also want to take some time to assess your progress by doing the following:

- ✔ **Do a quick review of your status once a week.** Using the forms in this appendix, pick the same day every week to do a quick assessment of your plan. Make sure that you're following the proper protocol for each treatment and that you don't have any serious side effects that are making your life more difficult than it was.

- ✔ **Get an outsider's perspective.** Ask someone close to you to complete the forms in this appendix on your behalf once a week, if possible.

- ✔ **Once a month, perform more careful analysis of your progress.** Compare where you are to where you were a month ago (or two or three months ago) and to where you thought you'd be given the treatment plan you drafted for yourself. Be honest with yourself about the results of what you're doing to treat your symptoms, and make adjustments to your plan based on what you see.

If you're the one with AD/HD, you may find it difficult to accurately assess your progress (or lack thereof). In this case, you need the input of someone else to help you see how you're doing. This could be a family member or a professional. Make an appointment with your "touchstone" every month, and show up.

- ✔ **Adjust your plan as needed.** After you do your weekly review or monthly assessment, if you see things you don't like, don't be afraid to make adjustments to your plan. If a medication isn't working, meet with your doctor and discuss changing it. If the diet you're trying makes you feel worse, change it. Rarely is the first treatment strategy you use the strategy you continue to use indefinitely.

Positive Effects of Daily Treatments

Positive Effects	Mon am	Mon pm	Tues am	Tues pm	Wed am	Wed pm	Thurs am	Thurs pm	Fri am	Fri pm	Sat am	Sat pm	Sun am	Sun pm
Able to sit still, not feeling restless														
Able to focus and maintain attention on a task														
Accepted responsibility for actions														
Considered the needs and feelings of others														
Controlled impulses/considered consequences to actions before acting														
Able to handle frustrations														
Got along with others														
Followed through on an assignment or plan														
Remembered appointments/didn't lose personal items														
Emotions stable/moods under control														
Cooperative/respectful of authority														
TOTAL														

Negative Effects of Daily Treatments

Negative Effects	Mon am	Mon pm	Tues am	Tues pm	Wed am	Wed pm	Thurs am	Thurs pm	Fri am	Fri pm	Sat am	Sat pm	Sun am	Sun pm
Insomnia														
Agitation/irritability														
Nervousness/feeling "wired"														
Poor appetite/nausea														
Headache														
Grogginess														
TOTAL														

Don't just drop a treatment from your plan if things aren't happening as fast as you'd like. Change takes time. So before you stop — unless the side effects are too hard to live with — consult the professional you hired to help you with a treatment. If you decided on the treatment on your own based upon a recommendation or some research, talk to people or do more research into this treatment to see if you're doing something wrong, and look for ways to adjust the treatment.

AD/HD Treatment Tracking Form

Date: _____   Day of week: _____
Name: _____
Person completing form: _____

Medications taken:

Time of day: _____   Drug: _____
Dosage: _____   Positive effects score: _____
Negative effects score: _____

Time of day: _____   Drug: _____
Dosage: _____   Positive effects score: _____
Negative effects score: _____

Vitamin and herbal supplements taken:

Remember that the results of vitamin and herbal supplements are often subtle and can take a month or more to appear.

Time of day: _____   Supplement: _____
Dosage: _____   Positive effects score: _____
Negative effects score: _____

Time of day: _____   Supplement: _____
Dosage: _____   Positive effects score: _____
Negative effects score: _____

Other treatments used:

Name of treatment: _____
Time of day performed: _____   Positive effects score: _____
Negative effects score: _____

Name of treatment: _____
Time of day performed: _____   Positive effects score: _____
Negative effects score: _____

Index

• *E* •

Elavil, 115
Eldepril, 113
electroencephalogram (EEG), 72
elementary school issues, 232–233
eligibility for services
  insurance coverage, 62
  school services, 62–63
elimination diet, 154
embarrassment, dealing with, 203, 216
Emory, W. Hamlin (doctor), 117
emotional reaction to diagnosis, 75–76
emotions. *See also specific emotions*
  cognitive-behavioral therapy and,
    129–131
  coping with in workplace, 263
  expressing, 203–204, 303
  managing, 207–208
  regulation of, 23
empathy, exercising, 202, 285
employment setting
  ADA and, 261–262
  challenges of, 259–260
  disclosure in, 260–262
  professional manner in, 263
  relationships in, 264–267
  social treatment for, 98–99
  sticking it out at, 274
  value in, 274–275
enabling, 224
encouragement, offering, 221
endorphins, 226
energy, using wisely, 282
entrainment, 180
entrepreneurship, 43
environment
  allergens in, 169–172
  chemicals in, 172–173
  overview of, 168–169
  structured, creating for children,
    213–214, 244
epilepsy, 85
Eriksonian therapy, 129
ERP (event-related potential), 72–73
essay, composing, 234
evaluating healthcare provider, 59
evaluation process. *See also* diagnosis
  behavioral assessment, 71

differential diagnosis, 77–78
educational testing, 69–70
medical testing, 68–69
performance testing, 71
physiological testing, 72–74
preparing for, 13, 65–67
psychiatric/psychological assessment,
  67–68
skills testing, 70
event-related potential (ERP), 72–73
example, setting, 212, 214
executive functions, 22–24
exercising, 226–227, 286
expectations, setting. *See also* goals
  for child, 212–213
  in classroom, 244
  for employees, 267
  realistic, 305
  for school services, 238
  for self-employment, 276
experiential therapies, 94
explaining rules, 212
external control of behavior, 144

• F •

fabric, synthetic, 173
failure
  anticipation of, 37
  in school, 231
fairness, demanding, 210
faith in abilities, having, 221
family. *See* parenting; relationships,
  healthy
family meetings, 304–305
family therapy, 132
fatty acids, adding to diet, 153–154, 164
feed forward/feedback process, 140–141
Feingold diet, 159–162
fidgeting, 37
filter in heating system, 171
finicky eaters, 157
finishing things, problems with, 33
5-HTP supplement, 103, 167
fMRI (functional magnetic resonance
  imaging), 73

psychoeducational counseling, 96, 131–132
psychological treatments, options for, 95–97
psychologist, 13, 49, 51–52
psychotherapy, options for, 95–96
pycnogenol, 165–166

• Q •

QEEG (quantitative
    electroencephalogram), 26
Qi (life energy), 95, 190
questioning authority, 210
questionnaires, 67–68

• R •

rapid-cycling bipolar disorder, 81
Rapp, Doris, *Is This Your Child?: Discovering
    and Treating Unrecognized Allergies in
    Children and Adults*, 159
Ratey, John, *Driven to Distraction:
    Recognizing and Coping with Attention
    Deficit Disorder from Childhood through
    Adulthood,* 117, 310
reaction to diagnosis, 75–76
reading problems, 232
rebalancing therapies
  acupuncture, 189–192
  homeopathy, 192–194
  manipulation therapies, 194–196
  overview of, 95, 189
  sensory integration therapies, 149,
    196–198
rebound symptoms, as side effect of
    medication, 120
recess at school, 251
recorder, digital or mini-cassette, 292
referral, asking for, 137
reframing thought, 208
regret at diagnosis, 75
regulation of self, role of, 21–22
reinforcing positive behavior, 142, 143, 213
relationships, healthy
  with adult with disorder, 223–224
  anger, dealing with, 203, 302
  appreciation, expressing, 205

with child's teacher, 246–247
  communication, effective, 204
  conflict, dealing with, 205, 219, 305–306
  emotions, expressing, 203–204, 303
  empathy, exercising, 202, 285
  family meetings, 304–305
  guilt, dealing with, 203, 303
  healing past resentments, 206, 302
  overview of, 201
  positive, accentuating, 302
  realistic expectations and, 206
  responsibility, taking, 208–209, 263,
    301–302
  working together, 304
  in workplace, 264–267
relief at diagnosis, 75
Remeron, 115
repatterning therapies
  neurofeedback, 72, 176–179
  overview of, 94–95, 175–176
  Rhythmic Entrainment Intervention,
    179–182
  Tomatis Method and auditory integration
    training, 182–185
  vision therapy, 186–188
repetitive tasks, struggle with, 211
research
  anatomical, 25
  challenges of, 20–21
  chemical, 27–28
  functional, 26–27
  genetic, 24–25
  resources on, 24
research paper, writing, 234
researching treatment options, 101, 104–107
resentment, dealing with, 206, 302
resources. *See also* Web sites
  anti-candida diet, 159
  books, 310–311
  career, finding, 273
  educational services, 63
  family and friends, 311
  homeopathy, 194
  Internet forums, 307–308
  library, 311
  organizing, 225

BUSINESS, CAREERS & PERSONAL FINANCE

0-7645-5307-0   0-7645-5331-3 *†

Also available:

- Accounting For Dummies †
  0-7645-5314-3
- Business Plans Kit For Dummies †
  0-7645-5365-8
- Cover Letters For Dummies
  0-7645-5224-4
- Frugal Living For Dummies
  0-7645-5403-4
- Leadership For Dummies
  0-7645-5176-0
- Managing For Dummies
  0-7645-1771-6

- Marketing For Dummies
  0-7645-5600-2
- Personal Finance For Dummies *
  0-7645-2590-5
- Project Management For Dummies
  0-7645-5283-X
- Resumes For Dummies †
  0-7645-5471-9
- Selling For Dummies
  0-7645-5363-1
- Small Business Kit For Dummies *†
  0-7645-5093-4

HOME & BUSINESS COMPUTER BASICS

0-7645-4074-2   0-7645-3758-X

Also available:

- ACT! 6 For Dummies
  0-7645-2645-6
- iLife '04 All-in-One Desk Reference
  For Dummies
  0-7645-7347-0
- iPAQ For Dummies
  0-7645-6769-1
- Mac OS X Panther Timesaving
  Techniques For Dummies
  0-7645-5812-9
- Macs For Dummies
  0-7645-5656-8

- Microsoft Money 2004 For Dummies
  0-7645-4195-1
- Office 2003 All-in-One Desk Reference
  For Dummies
  0-7645-3883-7
- Outlook 2003 For Dummies
  0-7645-3759-8
- PCs For Dummies
  0-7645-4074-2
- TiVo For Dummies
  0-7645-6923-6
- Upgrading and Fixing PCs For Dummies
  0-7645-1665-5
- Windows XP Timesaving Techniques
  For Dummies
  0-7645-3748-2

FOOD, HOME, GARDEN, HOBBIES, MUSIC & PETS

0-7645-5295-3   0-7645-5232-5

Also available:

- Bass Guitar For Dummies
  0-7645-2487-9
- Diabetes Cookbook For Dummies
  0-7645-5230-9
- Gardening For Dummies *
  0-7645-5130-2
- Guitar For Dummies
  0-7645-5106-X
- Holiday Decorating For Dummies
  0-7645-2570-0
- Home Improvement All-in-One
  For Dummies
  0-7645-5680-0

- Knitting For Dummies
  0-7645-5395-X
- Piano For Dummies
  0-7645-5105-1
- Puppies For Dummies
  0-7645-5255-4
- Scrapbooking For Dummies
  0-7645-7208-3
- Senior Dogs For Dummies
  0-7645-5818-8
- Singing For Dummies
  0-7645-2475-5
- 30-Minute Meals For Dummies
  0-7645-2589-1

INTERNET & DIGITAL MEDIA

0-7645-1664-7   0-7645-6924-4

Also available:

- 2005 Online Shopping Directory
  For Dummies
  0-7645-7495-7
- CD & DVD Recording For Dummies
  0-7645-5956-7
- eBay For Dummies
  0-7645-5654-1
- Fighting Spam For Dummies
  0-7645-5965-6
- Genealogy Online For Dummies
  0-7645-5964-8
- Google For Dummies
  0-7645-4420-9

- Home Recording For Musicians
  For Dummies
  0-7645-1634-5
- The Internet For Dummies
  0-7645-4173-0
- iPod & iTunes For Dummies
  0-7645-7772-7
- Preventing Identity Theft For Dummies
  0-7645-7336-5
- Pro Tools All-in-One Desk Reference
  For Dummies
  0-7645-5714-9
- Roxio Easy Media Creator For Dummies
  0-7645-7131-1

* Separate Canadian edition also available

† Separate U.K. edition also available

Available wherever books are sold. For more information or to order direct: U.S. customers visit www.dummies.com or call 1-877-762-2974.
U.K. customers visit www.wileyeurope.com or call 0800 243407. Canadian customers visit www.wiley.ca or call 1-800-567-4797.

SPORTS, FITNESS, PARENTING, RELIGION & SPIRITUALITY

0-7645-5146-9

0-7645-5418-2

Also available:
- Adoption For Dummies
  0-7645-5488-3
- Basketball For Dummies
  0-7645-5248-1
- The Bible For Dummies
  0-7645-5296-1
- Buddhism For Dummies
  0-7645-5359-3
- Catholicism For Dummies
  0-7645-5391-7
- Hockey For Dummies
  0-7645-5228-7

- Judaism For Dummies
  0-7645-5299-6
- Martial Arts For Dummies
  0-7645-5358-5
- Pilates For Dummies
  0-7645-5397-6
- Religion For Dummies
  0-7645-5264-3
- Teaching Kids to Read For Dummies
  0-7645-4043-2
- Weight Training For Dummies
  0-7645-5168-X
- Yoga For Dummies
  0-7645-5117-5

TRAVEL

0-7645-5438-7

0-7645-5453-0

Also available:
- Alaska For Dummies
  0-7645-1761-9
- Arizona For Dummies
  0-7645-6938-4
- Cancún and the Yucatán For Dummies
  0-7645-2437-2
- Cruise Vacations For Dummies
  0-7645-6941-4
- Europe For Dummies
  0-7645-5456-5
- Ireland For Dummies
  0-7645-5455-7

- Las Vegas For Dummies
  0-7645-5448-4
- London For Dummies
  0-7645-4277-X
- New York City For Dummies
  0-7645-6945-7
- Paris For Dummies
  0-7645-5494-8
- RV Vacations For Dummies
  0-7645-5443-3
- Walt Disney World & Orlando For Dummies
  0-7645-6943-0

GRAPHICS, DESIGN & WEB DEVELOPMENT

0-7645-4345-8

0-7645-5589-8

Also available:
- Adobe Acrobat 6 PDF For Dummies
  0-7645-3760-1
- Building a Web Site For Dummies
  0-7645-7144-3
- Dreamweaver MX 2004 For Dummies
  0-7645-4342-3
- FrontPage 2003 For Dummies
  0-7645-3882-9
- HTML 4 For Dummies
  0-7645-1995-6
- Illustrator CS For Dummies
  0-7645-4084-X

- Macromedia Flash MX 2004 For Dummies
  0-7645-4358-X
- Photoshop 7 All-in-One Desk Reference For Dummies
  0-7645-1667-1
- Photoshop CS Timesaving Techniques For Dummies
  0-7645-6782-9
- PHP 5 For Dummies
  0-7645-4166-8
- PowerPoint 2003 For Dummies
  0-7645-3908-6
- QuarkXPress 6 For Dummies
  0-7645-2593-X

NETWORKING, SECURITY, PROGRAMMING & DATABASES

0-7645-6852-3

0-7645-5784-X

Also available:
- A+ Certification For Dummies
  0-7645-4187-0
- Access 2003 All-in-One Desk Reference For Dummies
  0-7645-3988-4
- Beginning Programming For Dummies
  0-7645-4997-9
- C For Dummies
  0-7645-7068-4
- Firewalls For Dummies
  0-7645-4048-3
- Home Networking For Dummies
  0-7645-42796

- Network Security For Dummies
  0-7645-1679-5
- Networking For Dummies
  0-7645-1677-9
- TCP/IP For Dummies
  0-7645-1760-0
- VBA For Dummies
  0-7645-3989-2
- Wireless All In-One Desk Reference For Dummies
  0-7645-7496-5
- Wireless Home Networking For Dummies
  0-7645-3910-8

HEALTH & SELF-HELP

0-7645-6820-5 *†   0-7645-2566-2

Also available:

- Alzheimer's For Dummies
  0-7645-3899-3
- Asthma For Dummies
  0-7645-4233-8
- Controlling Cholesterol For Dummies
  0-7645-5440-9
- Depression For Dummies
  0-7645-3900-0
- Dieting For Dummies
  0-7645-4149-8
- Fertility For Dummies
  0-7645-2549-2
- Fibromyalgia For Dummies
  0-7645-5441-7
- Improving Your Memory For Dummies
  0-7645-5435-2
- Pregnancy For Dummies †
  0-7645-4483-7
- Quitting Smoking For Dummies
  0-7645-2629-4
- Relationships For Dummies
  0-7645-5384-4
- Thyroid For Dummies
  0-7645-5385-2

EDUCATION, HISTORY, REFERENCE & TEST PREPARATION

0-7645-5194-9   0-7645-4186-2

Also available:

- Algebra For Dummies
  0-7645-5325-9
- British History For Dummies
  0-7645-7021-8
- Calculus For Dummies
  0-7645-2498-4
- English Grammar For Dummies
  0-7645-5322-4
- Forensics For Dummies
  0-7645-5580-4
- The GMAT for Dummies
  0-7645-5251-1
- Inglés Para Dummies
  0-7645-5427-1
- Italian For Dummies
  0-7645-5196-5
- Latin For Dummies
  0-7645-5431-X
- Lewis & Clark For Dummies
  0-7645-2545-X
- Research Papers For Dummies
  0-7645-5426-3
- The SAT I For Dummies
  0-7645-7193-1
- Science Fair Projects For Dummies
  0-7645-5460-3
- U.S. History For Dummies
  0-7645-5249-X

Get smart @ dummies.com®

- **Find a full list of Dummies titles**
- **Look into loads of FREE on-site articles**
- **Sign up for FREE eTips e-mailed to you weekly**
- **See what other products carry the Dummies name**
- **Shop directly from the Dummies bookstore**
- **Enter to win new prizes every month!**

* Separate Canadian edition also available

† Separate U.K. edition also available

Available wherever books are sold. For more information or to order direct: U.S. customers visit www.dummies.com or call 1-877-762-2974. U.K. customers visit www.wileyeurope.com or call 0800 243407. Canadian customers visit www.wiley.ca or call 1-800-567-4797.